In Pursuit of Influence

The Netherlands' European Policy during the Formative Years of the European Union, 1952-1973

P.I.E. Peter Lang

Bruxelles · Bern · Berlin · Frankfurt am Main · New York · Oxford · Wien

Anjo G. Harryvan

In Pursuit of Influence

The Netherlands' European Policy during the Formative Years of the European Union, 1952-1973

"European Policy"
No. 42

The author is grateful to the M.A.O.C. Gravin van Bylandt Stichting for its financial support of this study.

Éditions scientifiques internationales
Brussels, 2009
1 avenue Maurice, B-1050 Brussels, Belgium
info@peterlang.com; www.peterlang.com

ISSN 1376-0890
ISBN 978-90-5201-497-5
D/2009/5678/16

Library of Congress Cataloging-in-Publication Data
Harryvan, A. G. (Anjo G.), 1957-
In pursuit of influence : the Netherland's European policy during the formative years of the European Union, 1952-1973 / Anjo G. Harryvan.
p. cm. — (European policy ; no.33)
Includes index.
ISBN 978-90-5201-497-5
1. Netherlands—Foreign relations—Europe. 2. Europe—Foreign relations—Netherlands. 3. Netherlands—Foreign relations—1948-
4. Luns, Joseph M. A. H. (Joseph Marie Antoine Hubert), 1911-
5. European Economic Community countries—History. I. Title.
DJ149.E85H376 2009 327.4920409'045—dc22 2009003126

Bibliographic information published by "Die Deutsche Bibliothek"
"Die Deutsche Bibliothek" lists this publication in the "Deutsche Nationalbibliografie"; detailed bibliographic data is available on the Internet at <http://dnb.ddb.de>.

CIP also available from the British Library, GB

Contents

Acknowledgements

This book has been under way for a long time and I am grateful for the help given by many along the road. I am obliged to Bastiaan Aardema, Arda Krediet and Victor van Bentem for their dedicated research assistance and technical support. When Saakje van Dellen offered her help in transforming the typescript into a book she was answering a silent prayer. Saakje, dankjewel voor je hulp door de jaren heen en nu in het bijzonder. I owe a lot to the archivists of the Dutch and Belgian ministerial archives. Their support was indispensable for delivering the piece as a truly primary source based analysis. Mejuffrouw Bruseker, Mr. Robert Bos, Mr. de Hollander and Mr. Stegenga: thank you very much. Sierk Plantinga of the National Archives in The Hague deserves a special mention. Mr. Plantinga took the initiative for founding the Kersten group that enabled me to share and discuss my research results with colleagues from other universities in the Netherlands and Belgium. Tankje wol Sierk. Mrs. Eva Hillen deserves my warmest thanks for conscientiously compiling the index and formatting the text: She designed the elegant lay-out of this book. I am grateful to the University of Groningen, the Netherlands Organisation for Scientific Research and the M.A.O.C. Gravin van Bylandt Stichting for their organisational and financial support.

I owe a lot to my teachers, the professors Alan Milward, Albert Kersten, Pascaline Winand, Wilfried Loth and Bo Stråth. Thank you for your guidance and constructive criticism. My Nijmegen colleague and friend Jan Willem Brouwer provided feed-back and encouragement for which I am deeply grateful.

My friends indeed kept me going. If I make more sense now than in former years, a lot of that is to be attributed to Ate Klein, my socio-political sparring partner for some thirty years. Auke Pieter Jacobs showed me the way in terms of perseverance and making me laugh when I despaired. Joost Jonker was my safe haven, my big brother in troubled times.

I thank my wife Margaret and my daughter Maaike for being their delightful selves. My Mother for her love and values and the faith she brought me up with. Ye are the ones making it all worth while.

A special word of thanks for Jan van der Harst without whose collegial support and cooperation this book would not have seen the light of day. The latter four chapters of this study all started life as articles we wrote together. Thank you Jan for kindly allowing me to reproduce and expand upon our common research findings.

Doing the decent thing may require a lot of courage. On 13 December 2005, my brother-in-law Mr. Lorcan O'Connell donated a kidney to his sister Margaret, my wife. I dedicate this book to him. Thank you Lorcan for mustering that courage.

Let us then be up and doing
With a heart for any fate
Still achieving, still pursuing
Learn to labour and to wait.

From: A Psalm of Life, by Henry Wadsworth Longfellow.

List of Abbreviations

AASM	Associated African States and Madagascar
ARP	Anti-Revolutionaire Partij (Protestant Party)
BEB	Directoraat-Generaal voor de Buitenlands-Economische Betrekkingen (Directorate-General for External Economic Relations)
BLEU	Belgian-Luxembourgian Economic Union
CAP	Common Agricultural Policy
CECA	Communauté Européenne du Carbon et de l'Acier (European Coal and Steel Community)
CED	Communauté Européenne de Defense (European Defence Community)
CEEC	Conference on European Economic Cooperation
CET	Common External Tariff
CFSP	Common Foreign and Security Policy
CoCo	Coördinatiecommissie voor Europese Integratie en de Vrijhandelszone (Coordinating Committee for European Integration and the Free-Trade Area)
COREPER	Committee of Permanent Representatives
CPB	Centraal Plan Bureau (Netherlands Bureau for Economic Policy Analysis)
CSCE	Conference on Security and Cooperation in Europe
DGEM	Directoraat-Generaal voor het Economisch en Militair Hulpprogramma (Directorate-General for the Economic and Military Aid Programme)
DGES	Directoraat-generaal voor Europese Samenwerking (Directorate-General for European Cooperation)
EC	European Commission
ECSC	European Coal and Steel Community
EDC	European Defence Community
EDF	European Development Fund
EEC	European Economic Community
EEG	Europese Economische Gemeenschap (European Economic Community)
EFTA	European Free Trade Association

EGKS	Europese Gemeenschap voor Kolen en Staal (European Coal and Steel Community)
EIB	European Investment Bank
EMU	Economic and Monetary Union
EP	European Parliament
EPA	European Political Authority
EPC	European Political Community
EPC	European Political Cooperation
EPU	European Payments Union
ESB	Economisch-Statistische Berichten
EU	European Union
Euratom	European Atomic Community
EWG	Europäische Wirtschaftgemeinschaft (European Economic Community)
EZ	Economische Zaken (Ministry of Economic Affairs)
GASM	19 Associated African Countries plus Madagascar and Mauritius
GATT	General Agreement on Tariffs and Trade
HTK	Handelingen van de Tweede Kamer der Staten Generaal
IEA	International Energy Agency
IS	Internationale Spectator
JCMS	Journal of Common Market Studies
JHA	Justice and Home Affairs
KLM	Koninklijke Luchtvaart Maatschappij (Royal Dutch Airlines)
KSG	Kolen en Staal Gemeenschap (European Coal and Steel Community)
KVP	Katholieke Volkspartij (Catholic People's Party)
Min. AZ	Ministerie van Algemene Zaken (Prime Minister's Office)
Min. BZ	Ministerie van Buitenlandse Zaken (Ministry of Foreign Affairs)
Min. BZBrus	Archive of the Ministry of Foreign Affairs, Foreign Trade and Development Cooperation, Brussels
Min. EZ	Ministerie van Economische Zaken (Ministry of Economic Affairs)
Min. Fin.	Ministerie van Financiën (Ministry of Financial Affairs)
Min. Landb.	Ministerie van Landbouw (Ministry of Agriculture)
Min. Pres.	Minister President
NATO	North Atlantic Treaty Organisation

NEH	Nederlandsche Economische Hogeschool (Rotterdam School of Economics)
OECD	Organisation for Economic Cooperation and Development
OEEC	Organisation for European Economic Cooperation
OPEC	Organisation of Petroleum Exporting Countries
PRO	UK Public Record Office London
PTOM	Pays et territoires d'outre-mer (Overseas countries and dependencies)
PvdA	Partij van de Arbeid (Labour Party)
QMV	qualified majority voting
REA	Raad voor Economische Aangelegenheden (Economic Affairs Council)
REZ	Raad voor Europese Zaken (Council for European Affairs)
RGP	Rijksgeschiedkundige Publicatiën (Historical Publications on the Realm)
SUNFED	Special UN Fund for Economic Development
TK	Tweede Kamer (Lower house of the Netherlands' Parliament)
UK	United Kingdom
UN	United Nations
UNCTAD	United Nations Conference on Trade and Development
US	United States of America
USA	United States of America
WEU	Western European Union
WHO	Wereldhandelsorganisatie (World Trade Organisation)

INTRODUCTION

Small States' Politics, the Netherlands and Engineering Influence

Throughout history, small states have been the designated victims of international power struggles. Their limited capabilities made it hard to defend themselves against aggression from their more powerful neighbours. Century after century small Powers found themselves intimidated, blackmailed, invaded, financially drained and even annihilated by countries with the means to do so. Even if the small state managed to survive, its lack of coercive, inter-state power resources tended to minimalise its influence on other states and its impact on international relations in general.

The classic Greek historian Thucydides provides us with an example, fascinating in its lucidity, of how small state victimization was carried out and justified, in the case of the raid of mighty Athens against the small island state of Melos towards the end of the 5th century before Christ. The Athenians justified their attack as follows:

> For we both alike know that in the discussion of human affairs the question of justice only enters where there is equal power to enforce it, and that the powerful exact what they can, and the weak grant what they must. (...) And we will now endeavour to show you that we have come in the interests of our empire, and that in what we are about to say we are only seeking the preservation of your city. For we want to make you ours with the least trouble to ourselves, and it is in the interest of us both that you should not be destroyed.[1]

The Melians, answering that they would consider themselves weaklings and cowards not to fight for their freedom and suffer anything rather than becoming Athens' slaves, obtained the following reply: "Not so, if you calmly reflect: for you are not fighting against equals to whom you cannot yield without disgrace, but you are taking counsel whether or not you shall resist an overwhelming force. The question is not one of honour but of prudence".[2]

---

1 Thucydides, *Een blijvend bezit. De oorlog tussen de Peleponnesiërs en de Atheners. Vertaling Leo Lewin*, s.l., s.n., s.a., Vol. 5, No. 10.

2 *Ibidem*.

Therefore:

> If you are wise (...) you ought to see that there can be no disgrace in yielding to a great city which invites you to become her ally on reasonable terms, keeping your own land, and merely paying tribute; and that you will certainly gain no honour if, having to choose between two alternatives, sagacity and war, you obstinately prefer the worse. To maintain one's rights against equals, to be politic with superiors, and to be moderate towards inferiors is the path of safety.[3]

Because that is the way things go: "For of the Gods we believe, and of men we know, that by a law of their nature wherever they can rule they will. This law was not made by us and we are not the first who have acted upon it. We did but inherit it and shall bequeath it to all time, and we know that you and all mankind, if you were as strong as we are, would do as we do".[4]

Quintessentially: The strong do what they will, while the weak suffer what they must. The Athenian reference to nature and nature's laws as a justification for dominance and aggression of the Big to the detriment of the Small in interstate relations was to provide a dominant motive for action for many centuries of interstate relations, albeit generally cloaked by other, less cynical, historical, legal and missionary motives for application of violence in interstate relations. Both Machiavelli and the so-called realist school of international theory are indebted to its emphasis on power as an overriding argument in interstate conflicts.

The 1648 Treaty of Westphalia is generally regarded[5] as the first serious and lasting limitation to the unbridled use of power in interstate relations. In answer to the horrendous destruction the Thirty Years War had brought to Central Europe, the Treaty laid down the principles of what became known as the "modern state system": The kings, queens and other royalty of Europe mutually recognized each other's highest authority or, as it became known, "sovereignty" over their realms and citizens. Legitimate rule within a state could only stem from the sovereign ruler and his offspring, in line with the principle of dynastic succession. Internally, the sovereignty concept meant that other states no longer had a right to interfere in the internal affairs of another state. Externally, sovereignty provided rulers with autonomy and independence of action in their relations with other states. In theory, no Power had the right to tell another sovereign state what to do or not to do.

---

3 *Ibidem.*

4 *Ibidem.*

5 For a differing opinion, however, see A. Osiander, "Sovereignty, International Relations, and the Westphalian Myth", *International Organization*, 55 (2001), pp. 251-287.

In spite of notable exceptions – the division of Poland between Russia, Austria and Prussia in 1793-1795 appears as the most clamorous one – the Westphalian rules and the normative sovereignty concept which they embodied did indeed lend a degree of protection to Europe's smaller as well as its bigger states: the smaller states protection against the larger countries of Europe, the bigger against a raise to dominance by one hegemonic Power, notably France. Broken down under French hegemonism and expansionism, the Westphalian rules were restored in the aftermath of the Napoleonic wars, albeit in a somewhat modified fashion: Once dynastic authority in Europe again prevailed over the democratic concepts carried forward by the French revolution, the rulers reiterated the independence and right to security of their states, promised to respect each other's legitimate interests and undertook to settle their differences by diplomatic means. France's bid at dominance, however, having left its mark, the policy-makers of Great Britain, Prussia, Russia and Austria-Hungary (the Four) undertook to join together in a (counter) "balance" against a future expansionist state. No state was to aspire to dominance in Europe or even attempt to do so. France was admitted as a partner on equal footing with the four self-proclaimed guardian states, all of which were to police the new system. Thus, in devising what became known as the "Concert of Europe", the Five made an explicit distinction between themselves as the 'Great Powers' and the other states of Europe, basing themselves on a definition the Four had agreed upon previously, in March 1814, that a Power capable of contributing 60,000 troops in the fight against Napoleon should henceforward be considered a *Great* Power.

Although the Concert-system was supposedly for the benefit of all European states, a certain division of tasks was evident: whereas the Great Powers committed themselves to maintaining the interstate status quo, the position of the Smaller Powers was to be compared with what was expected of small children, i.e. "to be seen but not heard". A degree of protection could rightfully be expected, at the price, however, of being excluded from active, let alone significant, contribution to the interstate diplomatic debate.[6]

While lending a certain degree of uncertain stability to European interstate relations for almost a century, the Concert-system was unable to cope with the tensions resulting from the process of German unification. Consequently, in the Wilsonian post-Great War analysis, it was precisely the failure of Europe's Great Power diplomacy that had led to the

6 W.K.N. Schmelzer, "De mogelijke invloed van de kleinere staten in het huidige wereldbestel", *Internationale Spectator*, 26, 1972, 793-802 (795-796). This article summarizes the text of a ministerial speech by Schmelzer on 22.2.72 in Leuven, Belgium.

bloodshed and atrocities of the "Great War". In the same vein, the League of Nations can be regarded as a Kantian inspired alternative for Great Power dominance, i.e. as an attempt to safeguard the Westphalian principles by *institutionalizing* and *democratizing* their application and safeguarding. The nominal equality of sovereign states was re-established and, as Wilson worded in his "fourteen points", the League was to provide for "mutual guarantees of political independence and territorial integrity *to great and small states alike*" (emphasis mine, AGH). Moreover, out of the legacy of the Russian and Austrian-Hungarian empires, the Versailles Treaty restored and created a considerable number of small states, thus adding to the potential role of Small Powers in international affairs.

Nevertheless, in the subsequent years, the League's protection proved insufficient to exempt small or weak states from aggression by more powerful ones: Japan conquered large parts of China, Italy occupied Albania and present-day Ethiopia, and Nazi-Germany overran Czechoslovakia and Poland, the latter event leading to the outbreak of the Second World War. Subsequently, another overhaul of the Westphalian system materialised in the post-Second World War United Nations world system, aimed at both globalizing and institutionalizing the Westphalian *cum* Wilsonian notions of interstate behaviour as well as the return of a special responsibility for world peace for the Great Powers, which found expression in their permanent membership of the Security Council and their right to veto in that forum. Nevertheless, the UN system has been beneficial, by and large, for the Small State. Arguably, no small state's sovereignty has been extinguished by force in the post-Second World War era.[7] The UN's defining principle of "sovereign equality" provides small states with a moral, legal and political line of defence against their larger counterparts.[8] Moreover, the UN's "one state, one vote" rule for the General Assembly, combined with a sharp rise in Small Powers' numbers due to post-war decolonisation in the 1950s and 1960s as well as the split up of the Soviet empire in the 1990s, entailed a Small Powers' majority in that forum which underpinned their potential role in world affairs, if and when they managed to speak with one voice. Which so far has been a rather rare event. For small or weak states today, a larger chance of survival is not necessarily matched by a larger say in world affairs. In the greater scheme of things, therefore, the role of Small Powers in international relations was and is

---

7 B. Russett and J. Oneal, *Triangulating Peace. Democracy, Interdependence and International Organizations*, New York: Norton, 2001, p. 21. One could cite the Chinese occupation of Tibet as well as the occupation of East-Timor by Indonesia as exceptions to this general observation.

8 "The Organisation is based on the principle of the sovereign equality of all its Members", *Charter of the United Nations*, article 2.1.

one typically characterized by both vulnerability as well as a lack of international influence, or even international impotence. As Vital worded it: "The smaller the human and material resources of a state the greater are the difficulties it must surmount if it is to maintain any valid political option at all and, in consequence, the smaller the state the less viable it is as a genuinely independent member of the international community".[9]

Nevertheless, not *always* do small states constitute weak and uninfluential actors: some noteworthy exceptions to the general rule can be identified. Although certainly not the only one, the status of the Republic of the United Provinces during the latter half of the 17th century is among the most intriguing of these exceptions. A cluster of seven separate provinces, restricted in population and territorial extent, which shortly after breaking away from the Habsburg Empire "(...) swiftly became a Great Power inside and outside Europe for almost a century".[10] Its strength in inter-state relations was founded on economic wealth, providing it with the financial resources needed to raise substantial armies, turning it into a formidable military Power, as well as the most effective naval Power until well into the 18th century. In spite of being a geographically small state, the Netherlands constituted the wealthiest country in Europe, controlling a large part of international trade, industry and finance, with enough military clout not only to wage a war of independence and cast off the rule of the Spanish-Austrian Habsburg dynasty (1572-1648), but also to raid the Sound when free trade with the Baltic States was in danger (1660), to resist a combined Anglo-French invasion (1672), to lead the coalition against French expansionism and to wage the first successful invasion of England since 1066 (Chatham, 1667). Arguably, the Netherlands constituted the first hegemonic Power of the modern state system.[11] Its seat of government, The Hague, was in the words of the Swedish King, Gustavus Adolphus, "The theatre of all actions in Europe".[12]

Historical anomalies attract historical interest. Huizinga, among others, was fascinated by the Republic's oddball status: "How is it possible, one asks oneself, that such a small and rather distant area as the Netherlands in the 17th century were, reached such predominance as a state, as

---

9 D. Vital, *The Inequality of States. A Study of the Small Power in International Relations*, Oxford: Glarendon Press, 1967, p. 3.

10 P. Kennedy, *The Rise and Fall of the Great Powers Economic Change and Military Conflict from 1500 to 2000*, London: Unwin Hyman, 1988, pp. 85-89 (p. 85).

11 R. Gilpin, *The Political Economy of International Relations*, Princeton: Princeton University Press, 1987, pp. 73-74.

12 J.J.C. Voorhoeve, *Peace, Profits and Principles. A Study of Dutch Foreign Policy*, Leiden: Martinus Nijhoff, 1985, p. 3.

a trading power and as a source of civilisation, as the Republic did actually attain?". Huizinga explains the "Dutch miracle" in terms of the civil and economic liberties prevailing in the Netherlands, allowing a mercantile elite to successfully fight the war of independence and subsequently lead the world economically, politically as well as culturally.[13]

Huizinga's explanation is one of a self-admitted inadequacy. He finishes his analysis by referring to an elevated level of virtues to be ascribed to the Dutch nation: "Wij Nederlanders weten, dat van het beste wat onzen Staat en ons volk in de zeventiende eeuw groot heeft gemaakt, de kracht, de wil tot daden, het besef voor recht en redelijkheid, de barmhartigheid, de vroomheid en het Godsvertrouwen, ook nu en voor de komende tijden nog niets verloren is".[14]

As Kossmann comments, Huizinga presents the Dutch Republic as a unique case. "It is clear that the unique can not be explained. It is therefore to be admired and described as a gift from God".[15] Uniqueness can indeed be regarded as a barrier to historical explanation, albeit that, as Kindleberger demonstrates, each nation, at least in its youthful stage, is – as each individual person – inclined to regard itself as unique. Young countries, Kindleberger argues, feel unique and look ahead. In later stages they loose confidence in their exceptionalism and are inclined to resort to nostalgia for one or more golden ages.[16] This argument appears to speak out in favour of historical analysis on a *comparative* base.

The alternative is to break away from the individuality of the Dutch Republic's case and moot the question in a more general way as a theory of international relations problem: Small states tend to be Small Powers, but exceptions to this rule are possible. Apparently, there is no exact proportional relation between the geographic or demographic size of a

---

13 J. Huizinga, *Nederland's Beschaving in de 17de Eeuw*, Haarlem: Tjeenk Willink, 1956, 2nd ed., pp. 1-41 (p. 3).

14 "We Dutchmen know, that now and in the time to come nothing has been lost of what in the seventeenth century has made great our State and our people, to wit our force and will to act, our sense of justice and reasonability, our mercy and piety and trust in God". Huizinga, *Nederland's beschaving*, p. 161.

15 E.H. Kossmann, "Some Meditations on Dutch Eighteenth-Century Decline", in: F. Krantz and P.M. Hohenberg, eds. *Failed Transitions to Modern Industrial Society: Renaissance Italy and Seventeenth-Century Holland*, Montreal: Interuniversity Centre For European Studies 1974, pp. 49-54 (p. 49); quoted in: C. P. Kindleberger, *World Economic Primacy 1500-1990*, New York: Oxford University Press, 1996, p. 211. A comparable comment on Dutch uniqueness by Schama: "The most extraordinary invention of a country that was to become famous for its ingenuity was its own culture (…) The Dutch created a fresh identity". S. Schama, *The Embarrassment of Riches: An Interpretation of the Dutch Culture of the Golden Age*, New York: Knopf, 1987, p. 67. *Ibidem*.

16 Kindleberger, *World Economic Primacy*, pp. 211-212.

state and its power and influence in international relations.[17] How are the Dutch Republic and other exceptions to the rule to be understood? Or, worded slightly more generally: How and under which conditions can geographically and/or demographically small states bridge the power and influence gap with larger states?

Small States' Politics (SSP), a subdiscipline of International Relations theory, provides us with concepts for understanding the position of small states in international relations. Its general line of argument can be summarized as contradicting the textbook wisdom that small countries are the minor actors in IR.

Firstly, SSP highlights the *relative* nature of the dimensions of size and strength among states. As Mosser argues, the debate whether or not to call states "small" or "weak" leads to contentious, counterproductive and endless angels-on-heads-of-pins discussions. In this respect SSP argues that small states are either smaller or weaker than their counterparts, but not necessarily both. Nigeria, for example, is a large state in terms of area but a Small Power in terms of power and influence. Switzerland, Japan, and the Netherlands are small states in terms of area but are more powerful politically and economically than their small size would lead one to surmise.[18]

Secondly, SSP argues, the *primacy* of the Great Powers in International Relations is equally a relative one. The confrontation between small power and great power becomes a naked confrontation *only* in crisis situations. In other situations it would be more appropriate to speak of relationships characterized by tests of wills and skills, not unlike the quality of cunning which Machiavelli recommends to the Prince.[19] Strong states do not always act according to their capabilities; small states may rise to occasions. Size, in the words of Katzenstein, should be dealt with as a variable rather than as a constant.[20]

Hence, thirdly, there is *room for manoeuvre* for small states to overcome power differentials. In this, context and issues at stake are the dominant factors which, carried to their extremes, as Hirsch has it, make

---

17 Hence, following Voorhoeve, we will speak of small states if the size of the country in terms of territory and/or population is the subject and of Small Powers when power is the object of comparison. By capitalizing the first letter of "power" when we refer to a state we distinguish power as an asset from Power as an actor. Voorhoeve, *Peace, Profits and Principles*, p. 4.

18 M. Mosser, "The IO as enabler: Institutional Realism as an Explanation for Influence in International Organizations" (unpublished manuscript 2002), p. 2.

19 M. Hirsch, "Influence without Power: Small States in European Politics", *The World Today*, March 1976, pp. 112-118.

20 B. Thorhallsson, *The Role of Small States in the European Union*, Aldershot: Ashgate 2000, p. 1.

it "perfectly possible for a state to be both small and big at the same time".[21] More cautiously, Voorhoeve concludes, that usually a small state is not a major influence in the world system, but that its policies can be of importance "if it is determined, if it pursues its goals with an able diplomacy, is located in a strategic area, and if other circumstances are propitious".[22]

The most important means for the small state to overcome its weakness in contemporary international politics, SSP argues fourthly, is *international organization.* International organization not only helps small states and Smaller Powers generally to mitigate some of the effects of international anarchy, it also provides them with a means to punch above their weight. Apparently, in spite of Realism's assumption of anarchy and its attendant consequences, international organization provides small states *cum* Smaller Powers with more power and influence than they "ought" to have. The precise functioning of this mechanism is far from clear. Rosenau describes "the conundrum of smaller state power in international organizations" as a "genuine puzzle". Countries weak and strong support internationally structured formal institutions, known as international organizations, with a view to reducing risks and uncertainty in their mutual relations. In the resulting process, however, international organisations empower smaller states to garner more influence than they "should" otherwise possess. Presumably, international organizations facilitate Small Powers in exerting "soft power", the ability, as Joseph Nye defines it, "to get what you want through attraction rather than coercion".[23]

The European Union (EU) may well be considered the ultimate case in point in Small Power influence. Firstly, the EU provides its member-states with a guarantee that international and European law rather than interstate power relations will prevail. For Europe's small states, the Union means that for the first time in the history of the continent, it is run by law rather than by force. European citizens are gradually waking up to this paradigmatic revolution in international relations and becoming aware of Europe being a unique experiment in international relations.

Secondly, in a SSP context, the Union provides Smaller Powers with a power base.

---

21 Hirsch, "Influence", p. 113.

22 Voorhoeve, *Peace, Profits and Principles*, p. 9.

23 J. N. Rosenau, *The Scientific Study of Foreign Policy*, London: Frances Pinter, 1980, pp. 29-30; J. Nye, *Soft Power, the Means to Success in World Politics*, New York: Public Affairs, 2004, p. X; Soft power is also described as the ability "to get others to want what you want", "America and the Arabs", *The Economist*, 23.3.2002, p. 11.

Without questioning the primacy of the Great Powers[24] we agree with *The Economist* "that the present EU system is [...] hugely stacked in favour of small countries". In the EU's first pillar, where qualified majority voting is the rule, voting is so heavily weighted in favour of the smaller member-states "that it borders on the anti-democratic".[25] In the second and third pillar, dealing with respectively the Common Foreign and Security Policy (CFSP) and intergovernmental cooperation on Justice and Home Affairs (JHA), respect for the sovereign equality of all member-states allows them to make their presence felt and their approval mandatory if and when consensus is the rule. The large member-states experience the institutional set-up of the Union as increasingly problematic. Since 1957, a series of successive enlargements with predominantly small accessants has resulted in a situation in which the six large member-states, to wit Germany, France, Britain, Spain, Poland and the UK, representing three quarters of the EU population barely command half the total number of voting points in the Council of Ministers. A system, Duverger sighs, with the hallmark of the Marx brothers. An image of six giants under permanent supervision by nineteen dwarfs evokes such feelings in some of the large member-states, particularly in France.[26]

Small State power in the European Union is an instance of a more general manifestation. Smaller states use international organizations to exert influence and shape the world according to their preferences. Mosser theorizes that smaller states engage in "binding behaviour" by purposefully creating and then manipulating the rules of nascent international organizations to best fit their purposes. He calls this "engineering influence".[27] The engineering influence hypothesis provides us with a

---

24 Moravcsik, it will be remembered, equalled the outcome of EU decision making with the Lowest Common Denominator of the policy preferences of France, Britain and Germany. A. Moravcsik, "Negotiating the Single European Act: national interests and conventional statecraft in the European Community", *International Organization* 45, winter 1991, pp. 19-56.

25 "Tyranny of the Tiny?", *The Economist* 25.1.2003, p. 31.

26 M. Duverger, "Surmonter l'obstruction des petits États", Le Monde, 3.3.1994; T. Ferenczi, "Europe: la révolte des petites nations", *Le Monde*, 10.5.2003; J.-C. Boyer, "Grands et petits États: un clivage artificiel?", *Le Monde Diplomatique*, April 2004, pp. 12-13.

27 Mosser deliberately uses the term "engineering" to connote a conscious and purposeful strategy of smaller-state institution-building that is not conveyed by expressions as "exerting" or "exercising". M.W. Mosser, "Engineering Influence: The Subtle Power of Small States in the CSCE/OSCE", in: E. Reiter and H. Gärtner (eds.), *Small States and Alliances*, Heidelberg: Physica-Verlag, 2001, pp. 53-71. M. Mosser, "The IO as enabler: Institutional Realism as an Explanation for Influence in International Organizations" (unpublished manuscript 2002), p. 6.

perspective to analyse small states' policies and their role in the making of the European Community.

This study analyses the Netherlands' pursuit of engineering influence during the formative years of the European Economic Community. Its central question is whether, under which conditions and by which means the Netherlands have exerted engineering influence on the economic and institutional architecture of the EEC – as forerunner of the present-day European Union – on eight identifying issues during the EEC's formative years. The expression "formative years" refers to the period of the "Original Six", the integrational development of the European Communities from the inception of the European Coal and Steel Community in 1952 to the first enlargement of the European Economic Community in 1973. Our method is the historical one, i.e. analysis of the primary source material in the Dutch national and ministerial archives. The vast and rapidly growing body of historical literature on the European integration process during the 1950s and 1960s provided us with scholarly guidance throughout the process.[28] This historical study consists of three parts. In the first part "Conceiving the Common Market", we concentrate on three identifying issues during the 1950s, the first formative decade of the *construction européenne*. Our first chapter analyses the launching of the Beyen Plan as a Smaller Power's exercise in exerting influence in international relations. In his response to the proposals for a European Political Community, Dutch Foreign Minister Jan Willem Beyen, set Dutch European policy on an entirely new footing (1952-1954). The second chapter plumbs the depths of Beyen's ambitions and the Netherlands' role in the *relance européenne*, the European integration revitalization project during the mid 1950s (1954-1955). From the second half of the 1950s onwards, as will be demonstrated throughout our analysis, Beyen and his successors pursued a policy of *functional supranationalism*, characterized by the transfer of national policy competences to a European economic community endowed with a strong executive.

The so-called Benelux-effect is the central topic of the third chapter: the Benelux experiment provided the Netherlands and its Benelux partners with first hand information on the realities of regional economic integration. Also, Benelux foreign policy cooperation enhanced the Netherlands' diplomatic position in Europe. To which extent did the Netherlands manage to put these two Benelux dimensions to good use on the negotiation tables which brought about the EEC Treaty of Rome (1955-1957)?

[28] The volumes published by the "groupe de liaison des professeurs d'histoire contemporaine auprès des communautés européennes" proved particularly helpful.

The second part of our study deals with three defining issues during the second decade of the European integration process, i.e. during the 1960s. This part is called "Defending the Community". This title may sound slightly confusing, in that in the course of the 1960s the Netherlands *did* successfully realise the country's most important post-Second World War European policy goal. The EEC's Customs Union did indeed become a reality by July 1968. Thus, The Hague obtained the Greater Benelux it had campaigned for since the 1952 launching of the Beyen Plan. Nevertheless, during most of the 1960s, we find the Netherlands also in a much more *defensive* role, fighting to preserve the communitarian nature of the European integration experiment. Chapter four, dealing with the so-called Fouchet negotiations on a European Political Union, analyses the Netherlands' use of engineering influence to torpedo French president De Gaulle's plans to de-supranationalise the European integration experiment (1959-1962). In the fifth chapter, we analyse the Dutch handling of the empty chair crisis of the mid-1960s and the extent in which the Hague government managed to defend and further its European policy goals under the conditions entailed by the crisis (1965-1966). Chapter six focuses on the Hague summit conference of December 1969, a meeting of heads of state and government, which is generally regarded as the diplomatic breakthrough which ended the De Gaulle induced stagnation of the 1960s. This chapter analyses Dutch European policy and resulting engineering influence with regard to the Hague summit and its instrumental importance for re-launching European integration (1968-1970).

The third part of this study deals with two consequences of the Rome Treaty on the European Economic Community (1957) of which we can safely conclude that the Netherlands got more than they bargained for. From the late 1950s onwards, the Common Market developed an external political dimension that at least partly opposed Dutch geo-political interests and constituted a potential threat to Atlantic unity in particular. Hence the third part, "Externalizing Europe", which focuses on two diachronic EEC externalities: Firstly foreign policy cooperation in the European Political Cooperation (EPC) framework and secondly EEC's association policy with developing countries. Chapter seven addresses the question to which extent and how the European Community, in lieu of a threat to Dutch Atlanticism, grew into an actively pursued policy forum for engineering influence in the area of high politics from the early 1970s onwards (1957-1973). Chapter eight deals with the question to what extent successive Dutch governments were willing to endorse overseas EC involvement, particularly in Africa and, to what degree, did they attempt to influence multilateral negotiations and policy outcomes on this matter (1956-1969).

The Netherlands' policies on Europe have to be understood against the background of the country's political system and the structure and traditions of The Hague's governmental apparatus. The ins and outs of Dutch decision-making on Europe find clarification in a final Note on "The Making of the Netherlands' European Policy during the 1950s and 1960s".

Since we concentrate on eight identifying issues some other aspects of the Netherlands European policy during the period under scrutiny, particularly regarding the Euratom negotiations (1955-1957) and Benelux' development during the 1960s, receive less attention than they would receive in a fully-fledged history of the Netherlands' European policy for the period concerned.

It could be argued – and has been argued – that Small States' Politics is unsuitable as an approach to analyse Dutch foreign policy, since the Netherlands does not qualify as a Small Power. Admittedly, in the period under discussion the stature of the Netherlands in international relations was a topic of debate, in the country itself as a well as in international Academia.

Stikker, serving the Netherlands as Foreign Minister (1948-1952) at the start of the period under scrutiny, was of the opinion that the loss of empire in general and the formal recognition of Indonesian independence in December 1949 in particular, turned the Netherlands into a Small Power.[29] Stikker's successor, Luns, (1952-1971) on the other hand, thought the notion of the Netherlands as a small country repulsive: "The Netherlands is a very important country"[30] References by Dutch nationals to their country as a small country he deprecated as *zelfkleinering* (self-belittlement)[31] In his view, the country's history and political and economic importance, rather than its territorial size, determined the scope of the Netherlands in world politics. As testified by his proposals for a European Security Conference mooted during a state visit to Yugoslavia in the Spring of 1968:

"Countries of our size can play an influential role, both bilaterally and multilaterally, in exploring ways and means to gradually arrive at solutions for the problems in Europe because the great powers often do

---

[29] D.U. Stikker, *Memoires. Herinneringen uit de lange jaren waarin ik betrokken was bij de voortdurende wereldcrisis*, Rotterdam and 's Gravenhage: Nijgh & Van Ditmar, 3rd edition, 1966, p. 213.

[30] While addressing the *Tweede Kamer* (Lower House of Parliament) on 9 December 1970, as quoted in: P.R. Baehr, "The Foreign Policy of the Netherlands", in: R.P. Barston (ed.), *The Other Powers, Studies in the Foreign Relations of Small States*, London: George Allen and Unwin, 1973, pp. 61-91 (p. 71).

[31] J.L. Heldring, "Zelfkleinering en zelfoverschatting", *NRC Handelsblad* 25-2-1997.

not dispose of the same room for manoeuvre".[32] In his memoirs Luns depicts himself as an exponent of the "Dutch vision", a vision, successful, above all in Europe. Referring to the first extension of the European Communities during the early 1970s, he states:

> The Dutch vision, of which I was the exponent, resulted in both the Six and the English acknowledging the Netherlands as the leading force towards the developments successfully rounded off in the spring of 1971. Which goes to show that in specific constellations in international politics a middle-sized Power can play a large role.[33]

Luns' successor, Schmelzer, (1971-1973) addressed the same theme on a slightly more modest tone. Using the concept of "Smaller States", apparently including the Netherlands, he argued that their role in world politics might be larger than ever before. The parts played by Cuba and Albania in world politics, as well as the role of Canada in the UN and the Luxembourg presidencies in the European Communities, constituted a case in point. The role of Smaller Powers in international relations, Schmelzer argued, was dependent on objective factors, above all the international context, as well as subjective ones, most importantly their quality of vision and political determination. He stressed the importance of quality of vision, as a power factor bearing no direct relation to political or military power. Increased global interdependence, enhanced international communication and the stalemate between the superpowers enabled Smaller Powers to make the difference in international politics. Thus, Schmelzer referred to the role of the Benelux countries in European integration as a source of ideas. "They had a vision", he argues, by acknowledging European interdependence and putting their trust in establishing European institutions.[34]

In much the same vein, Beyen, the Netherlands' Foreign Affairs minister (1952-1956), responsible for much of the country's diplomatic successes at the European negotiation tables during the 1950s, ignores the Big Power – Small Power debate and stresses, in line with the abovementioned insights of Small States' Politics, the importance of international organization as an enabling structure for the Netherlands: "As a member of an ever more organized international society, the

---

[32] "Minister Luns in Joegoslavië", *Keesings Historisch Archief*, 29, March 1968, as quoted in B. de Graaff, "Nederland in de wereld van de twintigste eeuw", *Internationale Spectator*, 57, 2003, pp. 360-366 (p. 362).

[33] M. van der Plas, Luns: *"Ik herinner mij..."*. *Vrijmoedige herinneringen van Mr. J.M.A.H. Luns zoals verteld aan Michel van der Plas*, Leiden: Sijthoff, 1972, p. 171.

[34] W.K.N. Schmelzer, "De mogelijke invloed van de kleinere staten in het huidige wereldbestel", *Internationale Spectator*, 26, 1972, 793-802. This article summarizes the text of a ministerial speech by Schmelzer on 22.2.1972 in Leuven, Belgium.

Netherlands can play a significant role through knowledge, [diplomatic] expertise, and a continuous striving for the maintenance of the international legal order".[35]

In Academia, opinions on the stature of the Netherlands in international relations equally diverge. In his seminal work *Peace, Profits and Principles. A Study of Dutch Foreign Policy* (1985), Voorhoeve depicted the Netherlands as a "small, yet influential" Power.[36]

Two decades later he arrived at a different conclusion. Observing the degree in which the Netherlands' power resources compensated for its demographic and territorial smallness, he qualified it as "a pocket-sized Middle Power".[37] Goldstein characterizes the country as a regional activist exercising power beyond its size.[38] George and Bache portray the country as a middle-sized one, attempting to carve out an independent sphere of action by joining international frameworks like the European Communities.[39] Heldring, the doyen of Dutch foreign policy commentators, repeatedly stressed the importance of empire. As the third colonial Power in the world, the Netherlands' influence in international relations exceeded a Small Power status. The loss of the Dutch East Indies (1949), Netherlands' New Guinea (1962) and Surinam (1975) substantially reduced The Hague's leverage in world affairs. The Netherlands' position in Europe in the 1950s and 1960s, however, concludes Heldring, constitutes an exception to this rule.[40]

---

35 J.J.C. Voorhoeve, *Peace, Profits and Principles. A Study of Dutch Foreign Policy*, Leiden: Martinus Nijhoff, 1985, p. 3.

36 Voorhoeve, *Peace, Profits and Principles*, p. 11.

37 J.J.C. Voorhoeve, "Nederland en de wereld", in: J.A.M. Baak, L.J. Bal & J.J.C. Voorhoeve (eds.), *Nederlands buitenlands beleid*, Heerlen: Open Universiteit, 1994, Vol. 1, pp. 15-40 (p. 36). The expression "Middelgrote mogendheid in zakformaat" (pocket-sized Middle Power) correctly denotes the country's position in world affairs, stated Foreign Affairs Minister Bot in September 2005, referring to the Netherlands ranking on the Newsweek power index (10th position) and its position in international-economic relations (14th largest economy in the world). Bernard Bot, "Bestaande kaders, nieuwe wegen? Nederland en de Europese mid-life crisis. Toespraak door dr. Bernard Bot, Minister van Buitenlandse Zaken van het Koninkrijk der Nederlanden, ter gelegenheid van de viering van 60 jaar Nederlands Genootschap Internationale Zaken", Den Haag, 27.9.2005, p. 4.

38 J. Goldstein, *International Relations*, New York: Pearson/Longman, brief 2nd edition, 2005, p. 63.

39 S. George and I. Bache, *Politics in the European Union*, Oxford: OUP, 2001, p. 200.

40 J.L. Heldring, "Zelfkleinering en zelfoverschatting" *NRC Handelsblad*, 25.2.1997, J.L. Heldring, "Een uitzonderlijk man", *NRC Handelsblad*, 2.3.1999, J.L. Heldring, "Toch een uitzonderlijk man", *NRC Handelsblad*, 22.4.2004. Brouwer relativizes the impact of decolonization on the Netherlands' role in the world. Jan Willem Brouwer, "Afgedaald 'tot de rang van Denemarken'? Nederlands internationale positie na de dekolonisatie", in: D.A. Hellema, C. Wiebes and B. Zeeman (eds.), *Derde Jaarboek*

As Hanf en Soetendorp argue, until the early 1990s Dutch policymakers were quite confident of their relative influence within the EC decision-making process.[41] Trausch recounts the discussion at a dinner party thrown by the Dutch EC Presidency during the second half of 1991. Prime Minister Lubbers told his guests that a popular topic of debate in the Dutch political class was the question whether the Netherlands was the smallest of the large Powers, or the largest of the smaller Powers in Europe.[42] Dutch confidence, however, received a blow at "Black Monday", later in 1991 when it became suddenly and rather embarrassingly clear that a large majority of the member states refused to agree with the Dutch presidency's draft on political union. According to Trausch, the Netherlands' presidency "convaincue que les Pays-Bas étaient un grand pays", was punished for its lack of modesty. In their attempt "de donner au projet un cachet néerlandais dans un sens assez fédéral" the Dutch made a fatal error and were forced to withdraw their draft Treaty at the last moment. The Netherlands' self-image, Trausch concludes, was not in line with its standing with the truly Great Powers of Europe: "Les Pays-Bas ont beau avoir 17 million d'habitants, pour les grands (la France, la Grande-Bretagne et l'Allemagne) ils sont classés petit pays et traités comme tel".[43]

For all intents and purposes the impact of "Black Monday" on the Netherlands' view of its position in Europe appears to have remained limited in time. When British Prime Minister Blair organized a summit meeting with French president Chirac and German Chancellor Schröder in November 2001, their Italian and Spanish counterparts protested and obtained invitations to attend the meeting. Dutch Prime Minister Kok did not wait for an invitation. He went to London to attend the meeting.

Such anecdotal evidence of the Netherlands' self-image may indeed bear some, but not necessarily much, relationship to the actual stature of the country in international relations. Since Vital published his classic *The Inequality of States. A Study of the Small Power in International Relations* in 1967, numerous attempts have been made to classify states according to their coercive power as well as influence. The outcomes are generally ambiguous, *a fortiori* so when dealing with Small Powers or Smaller Powers within the framework of the European Union. Smaller

---

voor de geschiedenis van de Nederlandse buitenlandse politiek in de twintigste eeuw, Den Haag: SDU, 1996, pp. 91-107.

41 B. Soetendorp and K. Hanf, "The Netherlands: Growing Doubts of a Loyal Member", in: K. Hanf and B. Soetendorp (eds.), *Adapting to European Integration. Small States and the European Union*, Harlow: Longman, 1998, pp. 36-51 (p. 50).

42 G. Trausch, "Quelques remarques sur la place et le rôle des petits pays en Europe", in G. Trausch (ed.), *Le rôle et la place des petits pays en Europa au XXe siècle*, Baden-Baden: Nomos, 2005, pp. 27-42.

43 Trausch, "Quelques remarques", p. 31.

Powers in Europe, even if they do not possess coercive power faculties, may well have influence and thus, according to Russell's definition of power as "the production of intended effects", access to a certain degree of power. As Baillie words it, in the Union's institutional framework, a small state is not necessarily a weak state.[44] Large Powers are not always aware of this, which can lead to short-sightedness as far as the Small Power's autonomy is concerned. The mere fact that a Small Power does not want to align itself to the point of view of a Large Power is often interpreted by the latter as a sign that it must be the satellite of another Great Power. "Si vous voulez être bien vu à Paris, il faut aimer la France et n'aimer qu'elle", Belgian Foreign Minister Spaak wrote to his Luxembourgian counterpart Bech, as early as 1936.[45]

This state of affairs provides both Small Powers as well as countries of an intermediate standing with a convincing incentive for pursuing engineering influence.

Groningen and Amsterdam, November 2007

44 S. Baillie, "The Seat of the European Institutions. An Example of small-state influence in the EU", in: G. Trausch (ed.), *Small Countries in Europe. Their Role and Place in the XXth Century*, Baden-Baden: Nomos, 2005, pp. 465-479 (p. 467).

45 J.W. Brouwer, "La myopie du 'grand' face au 'petit'. L'exemple de la France devant les pays du Benelux, 1944-1950", in: G. Trausch (ed.), *Le rôle et la place des petits pays en Europe au XXe siècle*, Baden-Baden: Nomos, 2005, pp. 505-521 (p. 521).

Part I

Conceiving the Common Market

CHAPTER 1

The Beyen Plan as the Dutch Response to the EPC Proposals

Introduction: On Dutch European Policy and Benelux, 1945-1952

The post-war reconstruction of the Dutch economy was seriously hampered by prohibitive protectionism in Western Europe and concomitant bilateralisation of international trade and monetary relations. The economic curtaining off of the important German hinterland, the continued disruption of economic relations with the East Indies as a result of Indonesia's war of independence and the need for domestic industrialisation in the metropolitan Netherlands themselves, emphasized and increased the traditional dependence on foreign markets as well as the need for new markets. Awareness of the country's difficult position was the major driving force behind Dutch support for economic cooperation and liberalization in Europe. Repeatedly, the Hague government as well the *Tweede Kamer*, the lower house of the Dutch Parliament, articulated that Dutch European policy should aim at 'economic disarmament' in Western-Europe by means of economic cooperation, liberalisation and possibly integration and that close Benelux cooperation was the apt instrument to further this end. Both economic liberalisation and Benelux were to remain at the heart of Dutch post-war foreign policy.

From its inception in 1944, economic and monetary cooperation between the Belgian-Luxemburg Economic Union and the Netherlands was a complicated and at times, difficult intergovernmental exercise.[1] In 1950, a Preliminary Economic Union saw the light of day; the projected Economic Union itself was still under construction by the late 1950s when it was caught up by the integrative development of the wider European framework of the Rome Treaties. Nevertheless, slow and protracted Benelux decision-making methods never dissuaded the three governments from claiming a special position in multilateral European

1 On the origins of the Benelux cf. A.E. Kersten, "België en Nederland in London 1940-1944. Werken aan de na-oorlogse betrekkingen", in: *Colloquium over de geschiedenis van de Belgisch-Nederlandse betrekkingen tussen 1815 en 1945. Acta*, Gent, s.n., 1982, pp. 495-520.

discussions, referring to their exclusive real life experience in regional economic cooperation and integration. Likewise, since the end of the Second World War the Benelux countries successfully presented themselves as a political co-operative 'unity', thus enhancing their collective leverage. At the Paris Conference on European Economic Cooperation (July-September 1947), which drafted the European Recovery Program, the Benelux-countries participated with a common delegation and presented a Benelux Memorandum containing a Benelux plan of action. This operation found its mark. The same recipe was applied in order to be admitted to the Western discussions on the future of Germany in London in February 1948. The Brussels Pact negotiations constituted another example. As proposed by the Benelux governments, the Pact was to contain articles on economic, social and cultural cooperation, so that the image of an exclusively military agreement was avoided. Despite these successes political Benelux cooperation was temporarily discontinued. In the negotiations on the North Atlantic Pact in 1949 as well as in the Fritalux/Finebel talks with France and Italy in 1950 the three governments refrained from coordinating their policies.

Policy coordination among the Benelux-countries was equally lacking in the discussions on the Schuman and Pleven Plans in 1950 and 1951, even though the defence of identical opinions on crucial issues conveyed the impression of the contrary to the other participants. Regularly informal contacts between senior officials were insufficient to effectuate a return to previously successfully applied coordination methods. Personal differences between Dutch Foreign Minister Stikker and his Belgian counterpart Van Zeeland prevented the Benelux from joining forces. Even so, the Netherlands continued to examine "jusqu'à quel degré des prises de positions communes sont possibles, ceci sera un automatisme pendant toutes les années 50". From 1953 onwards, when Jan Willem Beyen had taken over as Foreign Minister, Benelux reemerged as a foreign policy co-operation framework. Kersten points out, however, that only during the discussions on the Eden proposals for Western European Union in autumn 1954 a common stance would again be realized.[2]

As regards foreign economic relations, the Benelux governments held common views on the general patterns of international economic relations and cooperation, as their common memorandum to the Conference on European Economic Cooperation (July 1947) demonstrated. It

---

2 A. E. Kersten, *Maken drie kleinen één grote? De politieke invloed van de Benelux 1945-55*, Bussum: Van Holkema & Warendorf, 1982, pp. 5-12; S. Elgersma, "Les Pays-Bas face à la France entre 1950 et 1957", in: *Historians of Contemporary Europe*, Vol. 9, No. 1-2, June 1994, pp. 35-60 (p. 52). We shall argue in this chapter that Kersten's date is rather late. Benelux foreign policy co-operation revived during the EPC negotiations and the latter half of the EDC negotiations.

urged for liberalization of intra-European trade on a multilateral basis in combination with enhanced monetary convertibility. The document also voiced the common Benelux view, that the participation of Germany was a precondition to the economic reconstruction of Western Europe. The memorandum had been drafted in The Hague and strongly reflected two basic elements of Dutch policy towards economic cooperation in Western Europe: (a) the necessary multilateralisation of trade and monetary relations and (b) the inadequacy of eliminating quantitative restrictions in intra-European trade if and when this was compensated for by equally protectionist prohibitive tariffs.[3]

The Dutch government initially hoped that along these lines progress could be made within the Marshall Plan setting, i.e. in the Organisation for European Economic Co-operation (OEEC). Promoting multilateralism within this policy framework, however, proved discouraging. Although a number of agreements on abolishing quantitative restriction in intra-European trade were agreed upon, their impact was limited due to prohibitive high tariffs and other barriers to trade. Attempts at further-reaching arrangements than were feasible in the OEEC by means of a more limited regional grouping of countries, in the so called Fritalux, foundered on the Dutch demand of German participation which was unacceptable for France.[4] Nevertheless, the Fritalux negotiations were of value for the Netherlands' delegation headed by Dirk Spierenburg, in that they provided insight in the economic and policy problems a regional economic grouping of this size entailed. In this sense, although never seeing the light of day itself, Fritalux can well be considered a forerunner for Beyen's greater Benelux conception at the heart of this chapter.[5]

For the time being, however, the Hague government tried once more the OEEC framework to achieve its European economic aims with the Plan for Action tabled by Foreign Minister Stikker in June 1950. Economic cooperation, Stikker pointed out, should lead the way to an increase of the general standard of living, to an equilibrium of Western Europe's balance of payments with the rest of the world and eventually to a stable level of employment. Specialization of production and an improved division of labour were the instruments for realising these aims. The creation of a European "common market" by way of a step by

---

3 Archief van het Ministerie van Buitenlandse Zaken te Den Haag (*Archive of the Ministry of Foreign Affairs in The Hague*) (henceforth: Min. BZ), DGEM, dossier 1209: Benelux memorandum July 1947.

4 R.T. Griffiths and F. Lynch, "L'échec de la 'Petite Europe': les négociations Fritalux/Finebel, 1949-1950", *Revue Historique*, Vol. 274, 1986, pp. 172-189.

5 W.H. Salzmann, *Herstel, wederopbouw en Europese samenwerking. D.P. Spierenburg en de buitenlandse economische betrekkingen van Nederland 1945-1952*, 's Gravenhage: SDU, 2000, pp. 203-209.

step removal of all impediments leading to a free circulation of products, labour and capital between the sixteen OEEC member-states, was called for to realise such benefits. Since it was obvious that a general liberalisation process on this scale would entail serious risks to the national economies involved, emanating difficulties should no longer be dealt with by national protective devices. Collective responsibility and financial solidarity were called for. The Stikker Plan envisaged two phases for the establishment of the proposed common market. First a reduction of 25% of quantitative restrictions in intra-European trade was to be established. During the projected second phase the remaining 75% of quantitative restrictions as well as the abolition of other barriers to trade were to be eliminated, step by step, in one industrial sector of industry after another. The Plan highlighted and emphasized OEEC-wide liberalisation of the basic industries – primarily of coal and steel – followed by agriculture and those manufacturing industries whose further specialization would constitute a vital contribution to an internationally competitive European economy. The reconstruction and modernization of the European key industries was to be financed by means of a European Integration Fund.[6]

The shelving of the Stikker Plan by the OEEC during the early 1950s did not diminish the conviction of The Hague's governing elite that overall economic liberalization was elementary for the sake of European and more specifically the Netherlands' economic survival and future prosperity. Nevertheless, the Hague remained ambivalent on the question whether to head for overall (or "horizontal") economic disarmament and cooperation in Western Europe or, alternatively, to promote a succession of less ambitious sectoral (or "vertical") market integration projects, until, in Autumn 1952, Stikker's successor Beyen squarely opted for the first.

Beyen launched what in retrospective can well be regarded as the most important and – eventually – most successful campaign in post-war Dutch diplomacy, a campaign for overall regional economic integration between the six ECSC countries on a supranational footing. The European Economic Community (EEC) treaty of 1957, the completion of the EEC Customs Union by July 1968 and the "Europe 1992" campaign for completing the EEC internal market were the stepping stones to the realization of Beyen's ideal. Hence we may well regard the launching of the Beyen Plan as the starting point for Dutch attempts at effecting engineering influence on the framing of today's European

6 A summary of the Stikker Plan has been published in: Ministerie van Buitenlandse Zaken, *Jaarboek van het Ministerie van Buitenlandse Zaken 1949-50*, 's Gravenhage 1950, pp. 36-38.

Union. This chapter analyses the launching and pursuing of the Beyen Plan as a Smaller Power's exercise in international relations.

I. Jan Willem Beyen Sets Off: the Luxembourg Resolution

Nothing on Jan Willem Beyen's official track record predicted his transformation into an ardent supporter of continental regional integration on a supranational footing. Rather the contrary, as a mundane witty and rather cynical international banker without party affiliations, he appeared completely free of federalist inclinations. Which helped him considerably in winning the confidence of Prime Minister Drees, who was afraid of and averse to a 'Vatican led Europe' as well as European political and military experiments with possible detrimental effects on NATO unity. After some gentle prodding by the royal family, with which Beyen entertained a long-standing friendship, Drees selected Beyen as Stikker's successor at the Foreign Ministry.[7] As the new Foreign Minister Beyen was responsible for multilateral European cooperation and integration issues. Joseph Luns, who had been the Catholic People's Party's (KVP) candidate for the job, was appointed as minister without portfolio, responsible for extra-European affairs.

Apparently a safe bet, the new Foreign Minister would nevertheless bring about a major transformation of the Netherlands' European policy. To Drees' dismay he traded in Stikker's reticent stance on European integration for a pro-active offensive campaign in which European integration among the Six, in lieu of a potential threat to the national interests or a necessary evil at best, henceforth represented welcome politico-legal leverage for the creation of a liberal trade regime in Western Europe.

The change was considered as rather abrupt. Forty years later, Beyen's close advisor Van der Beugel, who later was to become Foreign Secretary for European Affairs, remembered Beyen's entry and subsequent conversion vividly and as a miracle:

> He was an incredibly captivating man, although I thought him of a rather frivolous mind. He was a frivolous man. And that was expressed most of all in that he never took anything really seriously. He was so intelligent and of quick thinking that he fathomed any issue in no time. He himself was never captivated, never committed. That is why it is a miracle how that changed on the European issue. That within three months after joining the Depart-

---

7 W.H. Weenink, *Bankier van de wereld. Bouwer van Europa. Johan Willem Beyen, 1897-1976*, Amsterdam: Prometheus, 2005, pp. 285-294.

> ment he was emotionally grasped and intellectually almost obsessed by the European issue. It is the only thing Beyen has ever been committed to.[8]

It would show, rapidly. On 10 September 1952 the Foreign Ministers of the six ECSC countries met in Luxembourg and reached agreement on a proposal by the Italian government, backed by the French, to speed up the negotiations on a new European Community. This European Political Community was to serve as a political superstructure for both the Coal and Steel Community and the Defence Community. Article 38 of the EDC treaty, namely, had charged the general assembly of the future EDC with the drafting of a new treaty for such a European Political Community (EPC). The government in Rome now came forward with an alternative proposal to not wait until the EDC treaty would be ratified and the organisation's general assembly established. In lieu of the Article 38 procedure the Foreign Ministers agreed to commission the drafting of the EPC treaty to an "*ad hoc* Assembly", consisting of members of the ECSC parliament and other representatives of member states, among whom members of the national parliaments. When Germany's Chancellor Adenauer, while chairing the meeting, requested each member-state to delegate a representative to a committee that would work out the composition and mandate of the proposed Assembly an unusual occurrence took place. Edmond Wellenstein, at the time a young civil servant in the Foreign Ministry vividly remembers the general surprise when Beyen stated that he himself, rather than a high-ranking civil servant, would represent the Netherlands on the committee. The new Dutch minister's move, although "highly unorthodox" was not to be attributed to inexperience but to his desire to broaden the scope of the Assembly's mandate. As the sole government minister on the drafting committee Beyen secured the chair and had no problems in achieving his policy aim. Thus the ECSC resolution of Luxemburg of 10 September 1952 states that the political unification of Europe could only be successful "par des réalisations concrètes créant d'abord une solidarité de fait" and "par l'établissement de bases communes de développement économique et à une fusion des intérêts essentiels des États-Membres".[9]

---

8 A.G. Harryvan, J. van der Harst en S. van Voorst (eds.), *Voor Nederland en Europa. Politici en ambtenaren over het Nederlandse Europabeleid en de Europese integratie, 1945-1975*, Amsterdam: Boom, 2001, pp. 31-61 (pp. 41-42).

9 Ministerie van Buitenlandse Zaken, *Jaarboek van het Ministerie van Buitenlandse Zaken 1954-55*, 's Gravenhage, 1955, p. 234; Jean Monnet Oral History Project "Vraaggesprekken met Nederlandse beleidsmakers inzake Europese integratie", "Addendum bij het gesprek van drs. R.P.B.A. Dingemans en drs. J. Schram met Dr. E. P. Wellenstein", Den Haag/Groningen, 2001, p. 4. Weenink, *Beyen*, p. 322.

The phrase "l'établissement de bases communes de développement économique" was to become a catchphrase of Dutch diplomacy for the years to come. Known as the "Resolutie van Luxemburg" it served Beyen and his collaborators as a politico-legal base for their initiatives for horizontal economic integration in Europe.

With the benefit of hindsight Beyen's "conversion" to European integration is not as miraculous as it appeared at the time. Weenink demonstrates that in the course of the 1930s Beyen obtained the conviction that the survival of Europe required a certain degree of unification. In this he was motivated by practical rather than ideological considerations. Since the general welfare had developed into a governmental responsibility the governments of Europe were obliged to co-operate since there were no national solutions for the problems they had to cope with: prohibitive barriers to trade, unemployment, monetary obstacles and war, to name the most important. Such compelling co-operation, Beyen argued, would imply loss of national sovereignty. Hence, Beyen's views on Europe and the necessity of European cooperation were practically rather than ideologically inspired, as the outcome of his analysis as a banker and economist implied and his personal experiences during the 1930s. At the outbreak of the Second World War Beyen was president of the Bank for International Settlements in Basle. He left Switzerland and came to London. As financial and economic advisor of the Dutch government in exile he was involved in the Benelux negotiations with Belgium as a first practical exercise in regional economic group formation. During the London years he was impressed and influenced by David Mitrany, professor at the University of Princeton in the United States and advisor to Beyen's other employer, the Anglo-Dutch corporation Unilever, for which he worked as a financial director. Mitrany founded the "functionalist" approach to international co-operation, advocating the sharing of international interests by transfer of national policy competences to supranational "functional organisations" run by a-political technocrats. The resulting learning process would facilitate gradual further integration at consecutively higher levels. Mitrany's philosophy appealed to Beyen in that it treated national economic and social interests preferentially over political and military interests of state. This was fully in line with Beyen's conviction that economic decision-making should be at the heart of post-war politics. As Mitrany argued prosperity and general well being of the people was to precede over sovereignty. International economics and trade called for effective international organisation.[10]

Beyen did not share Mitrany's preference for a global functional organisation per economic sector. During the interwar period, experience

---

[10] Weenink, *Beyen*, pp. 318-319.

had taught him that global arrangements tended to fail. There was no reason to assume that they would fare better after the Second World War. Regional integration was also to be preferred since it was easier to realise. Likewise he dismissed sectoral integration as too limited as it would lead to a fragmented economy. Beyen's belief in supranational organisation did not make him a federalist. On the contrary, he deemed attempts at creating a European Federation utopian. A network of effective international organisations would eventually result in political co-operation, but in that order and not the other way around.[11]

At the end of the war Beyen left for Washington where he served as a director of the Worldbank until his return to the Netherlands in the Summer of 1952. His views on Europe were unknown to the public at large and to Prime Minister Drees when he selected Beyen as Foreign Minister in the third Drees government (1952-1956). To his displeasure Drees' supposedly safe bet turned out a cuckoo's fledgling in his cow-bird's nest. Apart from looking for kindred spirits in the *Ministerraad* in attempts at teaming up against Beyen and his plans there was not much that he could do about it: in the Netherlands' coalition governments the prime-minister, although responsible for the upkeep of the coalition and the quality of cabinet decision-making, is not a leader of government in the British or German way. The Minister of Foreign Affairs and the Cabinet as a whole determine foreign policy. (See "A note on the Making of Dutch European Policy during the 1950s and 1960s" at the end of this book.)

II. The Beyen Plan: Pressing for European Economic Integration

The Italian-French initiative to speed up the negotiations for a European Political Authority confronted the Dutch with a new political situation. In this new constellation the wording of the economic clause of the Luxembourg Resolution had been Beyen's first step in his attempt to safeguard the national interests in the European integration framework.

In November 1952 Beyen told the Cabinet that further action was called for. In view of the poor show of interest shown in 'the economic aspects of European integration' by the other West-European governments, the Dutch would have to awaken that interest, he pointed out to his colleagues by giving concrete form to the Dutch ideas with regard to economic integration and by bringing them into the open as elaborated concepts by means of a diplomatic campaign.

Moreover, both at home and abroad, the Hague government was accused of clinging to demands for economic integration for solely tactical

---

11 *Ibidem*.

motives and, of using these demands, as a means to torpedo political integration without having to speak out against it in the open. A set of proposals, clearly stating what the Netherlands positively wanted, was therefore indispensable. Lastly, such an initiative would support the position of the Dutch members of the Assembly *ad hoc* in their efforts to push for economic integration while drafting the EPC-treaty concept.[12]

In a report entitled "The Foundations of the Dutch Stance on European Integration" he presented an outline for these concepts: He pleaded for economic integration of Europe as absolutely essential for the future of the continent. Democratic Europe, threatened by communism and fascism both from within and outside, would only survive if the totalitarian virus was eliminated by means of a gradual but continuous improvement in the standards of living of its population. The necessary enlargement and improvement of European production would not be possible as long as the region remained split up into small markets, each protected against the other by trade barriers. In this sense European economic integration was considered by Beyen a condition for the salvation of European civilisation.

Such integration, however, would only be feasible if there was enough *corporate sense* among the participating countries to allow for the sacrifices which such a process of integration would entail. This corporate sense certainly played a key role in Beyen's philosophy. It was not so much formal relations between partners as this sense of unity which was the decisive factor in conditioning the degree and effectiveness of co-operation between countries, he reasoned. The formal ties between the countries co-operating in Benelux e.g., for example, were rather loose, compared with the formal framework of the Dutch-Indonesian Union. Still Benelux had been much more successful in bringing about real co-operation than the latter: corporate sense had been the decisive factor.

In order to bring about this corporate sense on a European scale, the "fusion des intérêts" referred to in the Luxembourg Resolution, would have to play an important role. Integration was, in Beyen's view, much more than the introduction of a particular political structure on a supranational basis; he considered it a continually evolving process with economic, political and military aspects which were considerably interrelated. "Political" integration without simultaneous "economic" integration, that is, a political structure for Europe which would only pertain to the co-ordination of military affairs and regulations for the coal and steel sector, would fail to produce this vital sense of unity.

12 Nationaal Archief, The Hague (Henceforth: NA), MR (397), Notulen (Minutes) Ministerraad 17.11.1952 and 24.11.1952.

A first practical consequence of this view would be that the French stance, which saw further integration as necessarily limited to the political aspects of the coal, steel and defence sectors, would be unacceptable, just as it was unacceptable in view of the Dutch national interests, since such a limitation would imply a transfer of sovereignty without gains in the field of economic integration. A second conclusion for the Dutch would be that political integration outside the framework of ECSC and EDC would only make sense if it led towards economic integration and would otherwise be equally undesirable. This point of view, however, would in turn be unacceptable to the French and Italians. There was a problem here, as Beyen did not fail to notice; and he pointed out that the international differences of opinion were such that no agreement at all would be reached if the Dutch limited themselves to the negative stance that political integration without economic integration was unacceptable. A compromise would be possible along the following lines: limited political integration within the ECSC and EDC frameworks would be acceptable for the Dutch if coupled with some degree of progress in the field of *general* economic integration. The Dutch proposals and diplomatic campaign therefore would have to deal with both (a) how far the Hague government would go in accepting political integration and, (b) what it positively wanted and claimed as far as economic integration was concerned.

With regard to (a), Beyen suggested the acceptance of the attribution of new areas of authority as well as – "in principle" – the attribution of certain legislative powers to the future EPC Assembly (as compared with the powers of the ECSC and EDC assemblies). Also he suggested the partial abandonment of the unanimity rule for decisions of the Council of Ministers. Direct elections for the Assembly, however, had to be rejected, not only because this would introduce a "destructive communist element" to this body, but also because such a directly elected parliament "would run ahead of the existing corporate sense and, therefore, instead of furthering the growth of the latter would on the contrary reduce it". The new institution which was to emanate from this should be based on the principles of supranationality. It could be set up in such a way that in the course of time it could take charge of the powers which gradually would be assigned to it by intergovernmental treaty. Auto-extension by self-legislation outside the control of the governments was clearly not what Beyen had in mind. In this way the new institution could, in due time, be provided with the responsibility for integrating traffic, public health, education etc. It should, however, be guaranteed that the new Community would make an immediate start with the groundwork for the economic integration of Western Europe.

With regard to (b), the aim of economic integration should be to raise the standards of living in Europe. In order to allow for the necessary rise in production and productivity, the integration effort should be centred on the diminution and, where possible, the abolition of trade restrictions. The eventual goal should be a general *customs union* between the participating countries and to this end should be embodied in a treaty. The realisation of this aim would have to take place gradually and the effort should be directed first of all against those barriers which hampered competition and towards a more rational division of labour, standardisation and economies of scale. For eliminating these protectionist barriers the supranational organisation to be created would have the task of both drawing up rules for their reduction as well as formulating measures to provide for the economic and social disturbances which this process of liberalisation would bring about. Economic integration on this basis called for a certain degree of social and monetary coordination. A common monetary unit and a supranational central bank, however, would for some time remain impossible. Likewise, and just as before, convertibility was to be pursued within the bigger framework of the EPU. All this should in no way lead to the formation of a West European block politically and economically isolated from the rest of the world. The relations with both the USA and the United Kingdom (*cum* Sterling Area) were to be considered essential, those with the Scandinavian countries important. It should be noted that the distinction between sector and general integration, which would play a key role in Dutch politics during the 1950s, was now formulated, as a dilemma, for the first time. By now Beyen clearly supported the "general" approach, although sectoral solutions for e.g. agriculture remained acceptable to him for the time being.[13]

Beyen asked Cabinet to approve the setting up of an interdepartmental Committee under his chairmanship, which would work out these ideas and give concrete form to them with a view to their presentation on an international level. Cabinet agreed. The new organisation, officially called the "Interdepartmental Advisory Committee for European Integration", became generally known as the "Beyen Committee", even though Beyen hardly ever attended its meetings.[14] It was indeed the concepts summarised above elaborated and modified by the Beyen Committee between December 1952 and May 1953 (and propagated by means of an extensive diplomatic campaign), which were going to constitute the so-called Beyen Plan. This Beyen Plan would remain the official Dutch policy line for a great many years until its political reali-

---

[13] Archief van het Ministerie van Financiën te Den Haag (*Archive of the Ministry of Finance, The Hague* (henceforth: Min. Fin.)), Generale Thesaurie (henceforth: Gen. Thes.) BBV, 1262-8, "Nota inzake de grondslagen voor het Nederlandse standpunt met betrekking tot het vraagstuk der Europese integratie", 14.11.1952.

[14] NA, MR (397), Notulen Ministerraad 17.11.1952.

sation in 1957. In the light of its historic importance, a more thorough analysis of its coming into existence seems justified and will follow here.

The first task Beyen and his collaborators set themselves was the elaboration of the economic integration proposals to be presented to the other Western European governments. In December 1952, their studies resulted in a memorandum, addressed to the ECSC partners. This new document largely followed the argument of Beyen's note for Cabinet. It stressed the importance of economic integration in general terms and referred to the principle laid down in both the ECSC Treaty and the Luxembourg Resolution: "Le principe que l'Europe ne se construira que par des réalisations concrètes créant d'abord une solidarité de fait, et par l'établissement de bases communes de développement économique".[15]

On the basis of this principle the concept of an EPC which would merely function as a political superstructure for EDC and ECSC was dismissed: the new organisation should be furnished with real tasks and real powers in a new area of integration. The conclusion was drawn that the governments without awaiting further developments should proceed to action concerning the "fusion des intérêts essentiels" as mentioned in the Luxembourg Resolution. It would be particularly difficult for the Dutch government, the memorandum warned, to support the future establishment of a European Political Community, if at that time no tangible results had been reached in the field of economic integration. In the opinion of the Hague government such results should mean a Western European agreement on at least the following five issues.

- The gradual establishment of a "Communauté Tarifaire" in a limited number of years, leading to the abolition of all internal tariffs and the introduction of a common tariff for trade with third countries. The first issue to be collectively agreed upon was the abolition of prohibitive tariffs.
- Common responsibility for temporary disturbances in the national economies caused by the integration process.
- A number of safety clauses (permitting escape facilities for individual countries in specific situations); under condition that the application of these clauses would be decided upon by the Community, i.e. not by those individual countries requiring them.

15 "Memorandum door de Nederlandse Regering op 11 December 1952 toegezonden aan de Ministers van Buitenlandse Zaken van de andere landen, die deel uitmaken van de Europese Gemeenschap voor Kolen en Staal, betreffende de taak en de bevoegdheden van een Europese Gemeenschap op economisch gebied", in: Ministerie van Buitenlandse Zaken, *Jaarboek van het Ministerie van Buitenlandse Zaken 1952/ 1953*, s.l., 1953, 234-236.

- Co-operation with non-participating countries. The Dutch government adhered to its policy line that the economic integration of Europe would eventually have to comprise as many countries as possible. The proposed system was meant to favour the long term development towards that aim.
- The early establishment of supranational organisations by the participating countries for those sectors where detailed preliminary study had already taken place, particularly Western European agriculture.[16]

It can be concluded that in comparison to Beyen's "Note" for Cabinet from November the December Memorandum introduced a number of novelties: First of all, the long-term aim of a Western European customs union was no longer mentioned. The proposals were now focused on a short-term attack on in the Dutch view, the most important aspect of the economic integration issue: the tariff problem. A tariff community was going to be the price the other countries would have to pay in exchange for Dutch support for the EPC. (This did not mean, however, that the non-tariff barriers to trade, transport and invisibles would remain unregulated. The memorandum specified that the latter would have to be "taken into account" during the negotiations.) Clearly, this focus on tariffs was to serve as a complement to the OEEC liberalisation campaigns, which had successfully eliminated quantitative restrictions in West European intra-trade, leaving governments with tariffs as their main policy instrument for protecting the national economy. Secondly, whereas in the November paper it was considered a task of the new supranational institution to draw up rules for the elimination of trade barriers, the new document insisted on a prior general agreement on the details of the foreseen tariff community between the participating countries. Thirdly, the general economic integration issue was now linked to some kind of agreement on the problem of European agriculture and the establishment of a separate supranational organisation for this sector.

III. Rethinking the Beyen Plan

A second more elaborate draft of this set of ideas was sent to the Ministers of Foreign Affairs in February 1953 and presented by Beyen at a conference of the ECSC countries later that month.[17] In his letter, Beyen

---

16 *Idem.*

17 Ministerie van Algemene Zaken te Den Haag, (*Ministry of General Affairs*, henceforth: Min. AZ), Kabinet Min. Pres. 351.88(4)75:32, "Ontwerp van een Memorandum bestemd voor de regeringen", 28.1.1953, with accompanying letter Beyen to Drees 30.1.1953; "Brief van de Minister van Buitenlandse Zaken, Mr. J.W. Beyen, op 14 Februari 1953 toegezonden aan de Ministers van Buitenlandse Zaken van de

stressed once more the necessity to combine political with economic integration, as well as the need to aim wholly at economic integration on a general level, instead of the step by step or sector approach which would neither do justice to the disparities in and between the national economies, nor produce the necessary sense of European solidarity. Moreover, the repercussions of sectoral integration were not limited to the sectors concerned but also involved the entire national and international economy. Even under the best imaginable conditions, Beyen argued, sectoral integration would lead to nothing but some form of cartelisation at the expense of other sectors. He drew the conclusion that Western Europe should head for *general* economic integration. Therefore, the EPC Treaty would have to state in general terms the aim of establishing a Western European *Common Market*, Beyen wrote. This new stance reflected the more "modern" views of the Department of Economic Affairs and, in particular, of BEB[18] director Linthorst Homan, according to whom a "simple" customs union without free factor movements would in the longer run not be viable. The dispositions for the first step towards this aim, the tariff community, would have to be specified in the treaty in detail, i.e. both the target year and the timetable for achieving it: "La réalisation progressive, moyennant des délais préalablement fixés, d'une Union Tarifaire, devrait figurer dans ce Traité".[19]

It was clear that the Dutch government did not wish to entrust the actual realisation of this tariff community to the new supranational institution all by itself. In fact, in relation to moves towards economic integration, the major functions for the proposed EPC executive were limited. It would be given the competence to judge requests for the application of safety clauses by member countries plagued by "troubles fondamentaux". It would also have the function of drafting "proposi-

---

andere landen, die deel uitmaken van de Europese Gemeenschap voor Kolen en Staal, betreffende de taak en de bevoegdheden van de Europese Gemeenschap op economisch gebied", in: Ministerie van Buitenlandse Zaken, *Jaarboek van het Ministerie van Buitenlandse Zaken, 1952/1953*, s.l., 1953, pp. 237-241; Min. Fin., Gen. Thes., BBV, 1262-10, Verslag van de Ministers Conferentie van de zes Schuman landen te Rome op 24 en 25 Februari 1953, 28.2.1953, with accompanying letter Beyen to Prime Minister 28.2.19; see also Annex 4 of this report.

18 The roles of the various departments in The Hague's policy making are discussed in a note at the end of this book on the making of the Netherlands' European policy during the 1950s and 1960s.

19 "Brief van de Minister van Buitenlandse Zaken, Mr. J.W. Beyen, op 14 februari 1953 toegezonden aan de Minister van Buitenlandse Zaken van de andere landen, die deel uitmaken van de Europese Gemeenschap voor Kolen en Staal, betreffende de taak en de bevoegdheden van de Europese Gemeenschap op economisch gebied", in: Ministerie van Buitenlandse Zaken, *Jaarboek van het Ministerie van Buitenlandse Zaken 1952/1953*, s. l., 1953, pp. 237-241; Quotation in: Annex 4 of Verslag van de Ministers Conferentie van de zes Schuman landen te Rome op 24 en 25 Februari 1953.

tions" aimed at remedying underlying structural difficulties. These propositions would comprise schemes both for the reorganisation of the sector(s) concerned and for the modernisation of production methods. The schemes could be financed in part by the Community, which would have at its disposal a special Fund for that purpose. These powers for the Community were, in spite of their limited nature, nevertheless considered cornerstones of the Beyen approach: Because of the automatic nature of the system aimed at by the Dutch, the possibility of escape from such automatic treaty obligations by Community use of a safety clause, (for member countries in serious economic or social difficulties) was of crucial importance. The supranationally administered Fund was of equal importance. It reflected the common responsibility on all member countries of the consequences of integration. In this respect, the earlier drafts for general economic integration submitted to the OEEC, such as the Pella Plan, showed a fundamental weakness, in that they left the responsibility for coping with the effects of the integration process at the discretion of the individual governments. Supranationality, the transfer of part of national sovereignty, was a necessary precondition to the Fund's functioning:

> Or, ce n'est qu'en instituant une autorité supranationale, personnifiant la responsabilité commune, que les conséquences de l'intégration économique pourront être supportées, conséquences qui dans le seul cadre national rendaient toute mesure envisagée illusoire. Il y a donc nécessité d'un transfert d'une partie de la souveraineté des pays à une autorité supranationale avec des pouvoirs et des responsabilités sur le terrain économique.

As Beyen worded it.[20] For agriculture and other sectors, where the impact and repercussions of integration would be considerable, the system of safety clauses threatened to halt all progress. Therefore, special measures had to be taken for these sectors, such as the establishment of a specialised authority and the creation of a common fund.

The first reactions to the Dutch proposals from the ECSC-partners were of a mixed nature. During the conference in Rome, in February 1953, all Foreign Ministers proclaimed their agreement with the *underlying* principles of the Beyen approach. Moreover, Van Zeeland from Belgium and De Gasperi from Italy gave full support to their Dutch colleague on the particulars of his scheme – the idea of linking the EPC to a tariff community included. They argued that a European Community without simultaneous and concrete steps towards economic integration would be unacceptable. "We're not on our own anymore", a buoyant Beyen reported to the Cabinet. Agreement was not unanimous, however. Chancellor Adenauer and French Foreign Minister Bidault

20 *Idem.*

argued against writing down in the EPC Treaty itself the foundations of economic integration in general and a tariff community in particular since this would, in their view, both delay and endanger the coming into force of the European Defence Community. Even Benelux partner Luxembourg's Foreign Minister Joseph Bech publicly doubted the wisdom of linking EPC to the concept of a Western European customs union. Chancellor Adenauer underlined the necessity of a speedy realisation of Western Europe's new defence framework, referring to the Soviet military build up on the one hand and American isolationist tendencies, which might be provoked by European inactivity, on the other.[21]

Meanwhile, in November 1952, the *ad hoc* Assembly in Strasbourg had made a start with the drafting of a concept treaty for the future Political Community. According to the Luxembourg Resolution, the Assembly's proceedings would have to take place under the "guidance" of the Foreign Ministers of the countries concerned. In practice, however, the Dutch efforts to substantiate this supervision principle were unsuccessful. The sole result of the intergovernmental talks on this subject was a rather incomplete and superficial list of questions the Assembly would have to take into account while drafting the EPC treaty. Real involvement of the governments turned out to be impossible not least because of the fear within the Belgian government that it may have to commit to the outcome of the Strasbourg negotiations.[22] The consequent freedom of movement had an unfavourable impact on the proceedings of the Assembly, unfavourable at least from the point of view of the Hague government. This was because the parliamentarians, who were now guided only by the rather vague wordings of the Luxembourg resolution, constructed a draft treaty which at several points ran counter to the standpoint of the Dutch government.

Right from the beginning of the talks the majority appeared to be concerned more with organisational and institutional aspects of the future Community, than with the problem of the tasks and powers to be attributed to it. This tendency was reinforced by the widespread accep-

---

21 NA, MR (398), Notulen Ministerraad 2.3.1953; Min. Fin., Gen. Thes., "Verslag van de Ministers Conferentie van de zes Schuman landen te Rome op 25 en 25 Februari 1953", 28.2.1953, with accompanying letter Beyen to Prime Minister 28.2.1953. For Luxembourg's stance on the Beyen Plan see also 3.3.

22 Min. AZ, Kabinet Min. Pres. 351.88(4):075:32, "Verslag van de bespreking van experts der zes K.S.G.-landen te Bonn op 4 october 1952", 7.10.1952, with acccompanying letter Beyen to Prime Minister 7.10.1952; and: "Europese Politieke Gemeenschap", with accompanying letter Beyen to Prime Minister 5.2.1953; Min. Fin., Gen. Thes., BBV, 1262-8, "Procès-verbal de la réunion des délégués chargés d'élaborer le questionnaire à soumettre à l'Assemblée en exécution de la décision du Conseil du 10 septembre 1952", 4.10.1952.

tance among the parliamentarians of the French concept that these EPC powers had at first to be limited to the field of competence of the ECSC and the EDC. According to this point of view the Community was to be drafted as a political superstructure incorporating the "specialised" Coal and Steel and Defence communities while at the same time establishing effective democratic control over the executive. Extension of the EPC powers to *new* fields was regarded as a future affair. Consequently, a lot of attention was paid to the drafting of the structure of the parliamentary body. A two-chamber system was designed, consisting of a People's Chamber directly elected by the citizens of the member states and a Senate elected by the national parliaments. A European Executive would supervise and gradually take over the powers of the EDC Commission and the ECSC High Authority. A Council of national ministers would play the role of watchdog, safeguarding the national interests. A European Court completed this scheme.[23]

The Dutch members of the Assembly, who were in close contact with the Hague government and who fully supported Beyen's "no political integration without economic integration" stance, campaigned in vain for the attribution of real economic powers to the Executive. Their efforts were unsuccessful, firstly because of French resistance to any attempt to give concrete form to such powers concerning economic integration and, secondly, because of a more general feeling that such powers would endanger the ratification of both the EDC and EPC treaties by the French parliament.[24]

When on March 10, 1953, the vote on the final draft was taken the Dutch members of the *ad hoc* Assembly supported the proposed "Concept Treaty for the European Community". They did this, however, with the express reservation that their vote should not bind them in regard to the attitude to be adopted in due course in the Dutch national parliament. The official handing over of the draft EPC Treaty by representatives of the *ad hoc* Assembly to the Foreign Ministers of the Schuman countries in Strasbourg on March 9, 1953, gave rise to a debate in the Netherlands on the merits and demerits of the proposed "Statute". As far as the Cabinet was concerned, however, there were few merits evident in the

---

[23] Min. BZ, GSI, 910.13 Eur. Int. deel I, "Kort verslag van de zittingen der subcommissies der 'commission constitutionnelle' der Assemblée ad hoc, (15-25 November 1952)", undated; AZ., Kabinet Min. Pres., 351.88(4)075:32, "Samenvatting van de conclusies van de Tweede Zitting van de Assemblee Ad Hoc", 16.1.1953; and: Verslag van de Derde Zitting van de Assemblee Ad Hoc, 16.3.53; and: "Samenvatting Ontwerp-Statuut EPG", 18.2.1953, with accompanying letter 19.2.1953; and: "Europese Politieke Gemeenschap", undated., with accompanying letter Beyen to Prime Minister 5.2.1953.

[24] See previous footnote and: J. Linthorst Homan, *Wat zijt ghij voor een vent*, Assen: Van Gorcum, 1974, p. 195.

proposals. Beyen more or less defended the draft as 'a good working paper'; although, with the exception of Mansholt – the only real "European" (i.e. federalist) in the Cabinet – the general reaction was negative and even cynical. Beyen himself stressed the need to continue pressing for economic integration, although he admitted that the whole situation was rather unclear, especially with the noticeable change in the French attitude since the Rome conference. In contrast with their former stance, the French now did not seem very keen on political integration. (Diplomatic sources suggested that precisely the growing pressure for economic integration by the Benelux countries and Italy had made the Paris government less enthusiastic about the whole idea.) Prime Minister Drees agreed with Beyen on the need to continue elaborating proposals for economic integration. Drees was convinced and argued repeatedly, however, that the other ECSC countries did not really want economic unification, and would refuse it. Consequently, he warned against the establishment of a complex institutional construction which would be 'without any real value for the Netherlands'. A customs union was to be considered an absolute condition for Dutch participation in the EPC. He doubted, however, whether the EDC Treaty would ever be ratified by the French *Assemblée Nationale*. In that case, a Political Community, serving only as a superstructure for the ECSC, would be undesirable. It could be expected then, he added prophetically, that the EDC would fall through and that its downfall would also mean the end of the EPC-project.[25]

Because of these uncertainties concerning the EDC ratification, the Foreign Ministers had arranged during the meeting in Strasbourg to convene again in May. In the event of sufficient progress they could then decide on the intergovernmental conference which would draw up the final version of the Political Community's Statute, as prescribed by the EDC Treaty. In the meantime, the individual governments would study the draft of the *ad hoc* Assembly.[26] In the Netherlands the Beyen Committee was charged with this task and, in its economic subcommittee, a critical discussion of both the Assembly's "Project" and the Dutch proposals took place. The result of these talks was the reformulation of Dutch proposals in a new memorandum for the ECSC-partners.[27]

---

25 NA, MR (398), Notulen Ministerraad 16.3.1953, 20.4.1953, 29.4.1953; Min. AZ., Kabinet Min. Pres., 351.88(4)075:32, Frankrijk en de Europese integratie, 11.2.1953.

26 Min. AZ., Kabinet Min. Pres., 351.88(4)075:32, "Procès-verbal de la réunion des six ministres des affaires étrangères à Strasbourg, le 9 mars 1953", 16.3.1953; Min. Fin., Gen. Thes., BBV, 1262-10, "Verslag Conferentie v.d. Zes Ministers van Buitenlandse Zaken op 9 Maart 1953 te Straatsburg", 12.3.1953.

27 Min. AZ, Kabinet Min. Pres., 351.88(4)075:32, "Concept voor Nederlands memorandum inzake de Europese Gemeenschap" undated, accompanying letter 4.5.1953; NA, MR (489), Mémorandum du Gouvernement des Pays-Bas concernant la Com-

The first novelty of this new document was that the tariff community, as the short-term aim, was *de facto* traded in for a general customs union. Although the tariff community was still maintained as a first aim, it was now completely linked to the abolition of quantitative restrictions on trade between the member countries, co-ordination of their foreign trade policies with regard to third countries and the creation of a common external tariff. The timetable to be written into the Treaty would have to deal with the abolition within a certain period of time for *both* tariffs and quota.

This change from the former tariff community approach towards something which would come down to a customs union reflected the criticism of the tariff community concept expressed by the Beyen Committee itself. Such a Community, though technically possible, would not suffice as a means to the Dutch end, the Committee argued, if the member countries retained their freedom of action concerning other barriers to trade. First and foremost, the establishment of a Community should not lead to a rise in non-tariff barriers, it reasoned and it was decided to take quantitative restrictions into account as well.[28] The Dutch experience with the OEEC liberalisation program, which had often led to the substitution of quota by protectionist tariffs, certainly acted as an important motivating force here.

Also, the new approach fitted in with criticism from Benelux-partner Belgium. Brussels had given full support to Beyen's pro economic integration policy in general and the tariff community goal in particular. It had stressed, however, that the preoccupation with tariffs should not push equally essential problems like those concerning quota and payments into the background:

> Il ne conviendrait cependant pas que l'énoncé explicite d'une première étape – communauté tarifaire – puisse porter à croire que d'autres réalisations – dont le caractère présente une égale urgence – seront laissées à l'arrière-plan. Il s'agit notamment de l'abolition progressive des restrictions quantitatives aux échanges et des mesures à prendre pour améliorer le régime des paiements entre pays membres.

Lastly, as the Beyen Committee had pointed out, the Customs Union was – contrary to the tariff community concept – mentioned and specified in both the Havana Charter and GATT. Linking up with these two agreements would be advantageous in that it allowed the Dutch to

munauté européenne, 5.5.1953; accompanying letter Beyen to Foreign Ministers 5.5.1953.

28 Min. AZ, Kabinet Min. Pres., 351.88 (4)075: 32, "Rapport van de Economische Sub-Commissie", 22.4.1953 with accompanying note Min. van Buitenlandse Zaken entitled "Ontwerp-verdrag, houdende het Statuut ener Europese Gemeenschap", 24.4.1953.

demonstrate their non-discriminatory intentions both to their partners and to the rest of the world. The conclusion was drawn by the Committee that the tariff community should be laid down in the Treaty as an "interim agreement leading to the formation of a customs union". Moreover in the Treaty mention should be made of a common market as the "ultimate" goal.

Like its predecessors, the memorandum expressed the view that a target date at which all internal tariffs and quantitative restrictions were to be abolished should be incorporated into the Treaty. Beyen retained this clause, probably in view of the criticism the EPC draft Treaty proposals had received from his colleagues in the Cabinet, against the advice of the Economic subcommittee.

Nevertheless, both the memorandum and the subcommittee's Report now stressed the need for policy co-ordination much more than had been the case in the earlier documents. For real economic integration, the subcommittee pointed out, the elimination of tariffs and non-tariff barriers to trade would not suffice. Given the different conditions for production in the various countries, this aim would hardly be feasible if economic and social etc. policies were not – to a certain degree – going to be co-ordinated or harmonised. Agriculture served here as an example. The Memorandum similarly emphasised the need for co-ordination, yet it warned that this was not meant in the sense of uniformity. The aim would have to be "parallelism" in production costs. How this co-ordination was to be brought about and who was going to be responsible for it was less clear.

Also, the memorandum, following the report of the Beyen Committee, distanced itself from the earlier concept of special sectoral arrangements and specialised High Authorities as for Western European agriculture and perhaps for transport. The Committee had studied the merits and demerits of functional integration and the question of whether a partial sectoral approach within the general framework of integration would be desirable. Its answers to these questions were negative. The memorandum made it explicitly clear that, as far as the Dutch were concerned, functional integration came down to cartel-building detrimental to both consumers and other, economic and societal sectors. Therefore, agriculture should be treated in the same general way as other sectors. However distinction between different groups of products and the use of various timetables for the elimination of quotas and tariffs ought to remain possible.

Finally, both the memorandum and the Report underlined that the Customs Union should be geared to economic expansion and the modernisation of European production and therefore should be open and non-protectionist. Given the Dutch stance in earlier years, this should occasion no surprise. Moreover, this approach reflected the outcome of the Beyen Committee's analysis of the consequences a customs union would entail for the Netherlands. The most important disadvantages for the Netherlands would be an upward movement in production costs and prices because of the linkage with more "expensive" economies as well as the higher tariffs the country would be faced with in its commercial contacts with third countries. Both factors would, to a certain degree, damage the Dutch competitive position on the world market.

In particular the possibility of high external tariffs caused some anxiety in Dutch government circles. An internal note by the Ministry of Finance for example had warned against overestimating the importance of the "Schuman Area" for Dutch trade. Given its dependence on transit trade, such a tariff wall might have serious consequences for the Dutch economy, the note continued and would most certainly not contribute to the diversification of national exports.[29]

The contents of the new memorandum were specified in a number of draft economic articles for the future EPC Treaty. As Beyen pointed out to the Cabinet, these articles were meant for informal use only, as an indication of the legal structure the Dutch had in mind. According to these draft articles, the European executive would have to submit a schedule for the elimination of tariffs and quotas to the Council of Ministers and, subsequently, to the European Parliament, within one year after the coming into force of the EPC-Treaty. Both organs would accept or reject this timetable by majority decision. The entire liberalisation operation should maximally last "X", that is, a not yet specified, but fixed number of years. (Beyen himself envisaged at this stage that such a transition period would last up to a minimal 5 and maximal 10 years.)

Undoubtedly, the proposed system made the actual realisation of the customs union much more plausible than had been the case with the economic articles of the draft EPC Treaty of the *ad hoc* Assembly. Nevertheless, as Prime Minister Drees pointed out, it still did not contain a watertight guarantee that such a customs union would in fact materialise. Therefore, it was to be feared, he commented, that it would be impossible to realise the tariff and quotas elimination programme. The point was that because of the opposition to economic integration in the various countries, a majority for *any* integration scheme in the European Parliament seemed implausible. Essential, therefore, was a clause, which would automatically lead to the extinction of all internal Western European tariffs and quantitative restrictions, had the customs union come into being after a period of for instance 5 or 10 years subsequent to the signing of the Treaty. Also, in view of this opposition to

[29] Min. Fin., Gen. Thes., BBV, 1262/8, "Betreft: de verschillende plannen tot verlaging der tarieven", 20.3.1953.

economic integration, the Dutch would need to have certainty on their economic issues in general before acquiescing to the resolution of the institutional problems.

Beyen agreed that the guarantees suggested by Drees were, indeed, vital. He added that precisely that question of which guarantees for economic integration were to be considered sufficient by the Dutch government was going to be the key problem in the future negotiations.[30]

IV. Intergovernmental Deliberations on EPC

As had been arranged in Strasbourg the Foreign Ministers met in Paris on May 12 and 13, 1953, to discuss the *ad hoc* Assembly's draft treaty and the procedure for further action on the EPC-project. The most spectacular as well as most threatening contribution for the Dutch to this conference was the West German one. In line with his earlier attempts to speed up the decision making process on the EDC and the EPC, Chancellor Adenauer made clear that he aimed at a fast and simple procedure which would quickly lead to results. He deemed further study of the matter by national experts as unnecessary. Taking the *ad hoc* Assembly's concept as the starting point, the ministers should limit themselves to the cutting of the institutional knots left over by the Assemblee and charge the ECSC Council of Ministers Secretariat with drawing up, on the basis of these ministerial decisions, the legal text for the articles to be amended or inserted in the Treaty. In order to avoid further complications and retardation, he argued, the treaty and the EPC itself should be kept plain and simple. The Community should be set up as a superstructure for EDC and ECSC, integrating them by taking over the competencies of these two organisations while at the same time allowing for a fair measure of democratic control by a European Parliament. For the time being no new powers should be attributed to the new body; an enabling clause which would make it possible for the Community to accept future powers (to be attributed in due time by agreements between the member states) would suffice for the moment. In fact, Adenauer's approach resembled only too well the "institutionalist" or "minimalist" line of thought as had been expressed by many a French delegate in the *ad hoc* Assembly's sessions.

---

30 NA, MR (398) Notulen Ministerraad 11.5.1953 Min. BZ I, 913.10 Europese integratie Deel 2 "Projet de dispositions économiques du Traité portant Statut de la Communauté Européenne"; Marcel Ermers & John Kragt, "Tussen tradities en traktaten. Minister Beyen en de Europese integratie 1952-1956" (unpublished MA thesis, History Department of the University of Nijmegen, August 1988) provides a wealth of detailed information on various aspects of Dutch decision-making during the subsequent EPC and EEC negotiations.

Belgium's Foreign Minister, Van Zeeland, led the Benelux attack against the Chancellor's proposals. On the basis of both the Luxembourg Resolution and the *ad hoc* Assembly's concept treaty he stressed the link between the EPC and extension of European supranational powers to the economic field. The new political institutions could not do without a sound economic base, he told his colleagues. Especially for the smaller Western European nations, a common market was indispensable, since they were threatened with economic suffocation because of a lack of export markets. Moreover, Beyen added, an EPC which would only serve as a superstructure for the specialised communities had never been acceptable to the Dutch government. In line with the stance taken by the Cabinet, he emphasised the necessity of deciding on the new economic powers to be attributed to the Community, before going into detailed discussions regarding its institutional arrangements.

Foreign Minister Bidault of France indirectly supported the Benelux case, stating that he could not possibly submit to the French parliament an only slightly altered draft Treaty. Given the far-reaching consequences an on-going study on behalf of the national governments was indispensable. Interestingly enough, he also challenged the Chancellor's minimalist approach by demonstrating that more than half of the articles of the *ad hoc* Assembly's draft did not bear any relation to either ECSC or EDC; in other words: the EPC-project obviously should go further than the prevailing situation. Since the French government, however, had not yet taken a stance on the matter, he did not want to commit himself to concrete statements about the nature of the new powers to be attributed. Bidault's support for an on-going study can be understood as delaying tactics reflecting the change of mood in France on EDC since early 1953.[31]

Italy's De Gasperi basically defended his country's federalist approach. The Western European countries could and should not discuss their future *ex novo* anymore, since there was already the *ad hoc* Assembly's draft EPC treaty, which "soit à la base de nos discussions". Although he too expressed the opinion that concrete results should be obtained as soon as possible, this did not mean that he supported Adenauer's minimalist view with regard to the competencies of the future Community.

---

31 NA, MR (398) Notulen Ministerraad 26.5.1953 Min. BZ, II, 913.100, inv. No. 26: "Verslag van de conferentie van Parijs, 12-13 mei 1953"; with accompanying letter Beyen; Wilfried Loth, "L'Allemagne et les petits États dans la construction européene", in: Michel Dumoulin, Geneviève Duchenne & Arthe van Laer (eds.), *La Belgique, les petits États et la construction européenne*, Brussels: P.I.E.-Peter Lang, 2003, pp. 247-258 (pp. 249-250).

Consequently, the German Chancellor became isolated and his proposals were rejected. Eventually the ministers agreed that a new – now intergovernmental conference for drawing up an EPC Treaty was to take place in Rome from June 12 onwards. Its results would be discussed by the Foreign Ministers at a conference in The Hague on July 12. No clear agreement was reached on the exact status of the concept of the *ad hoc* Assembly. Bidault, presiding over the meeting, concluded that the draft should serve as a basis for discussion; nevertheless it was up to the individual governments to decide if and to which degree they felt committed to this concept treaty.[32]

In his report to the Cabinet, Beyen showed himself greatly relieved that the institutionalist threat had been staved off. Approvingly he made mention of Adenauer's surly remark that Benelux foreign policy cooperation had won the day. He was aware, however, of the possibility that this victory would turn out to be only a short-lived one. It remained to be seen, for instance, on which stance the French government would finally decide. Moreover, he reasoned, Western Germany and Italy clearly wanted to see results at short notice, not in the least because of strong electoral pressures. One had to reckon with the possibility, he concluded, that at the future intergovernmental conference more attempts would be made to push for a limited Political Community. Hence it was advisable that the Cabinet, as soon as possible, form a notion of the objections which would be raised against the Dutch proposals at the forthcoming conference. Now that The Hague had made known its line of thought in detail, it should both try and overcome its remaining internal differences of opinion, as well as explore the reactions to its approach in the five partner capitals.[33]

Hence, in order to bridge their internal differences the Hague policy makers met in a series of cabinet meetings and interdepartmental committees. Once more Prime Minister Drees aired his disbelief of the prospect of realising a satisfactory degree of economic integration within the EPC framework. At the other extreme, Minister for Agriculture Mansholt pleaded in favour of a less economic-oriented and more institutionalist approach, i.e. the creation of a European political structure along the lines of the French and Italian conceptions. These deliberations did not produce tangible results. Beyen, with the support of Economics Minister Zijlstra skilfully steering a middle course between Scylla and Charybdis, could not prevent the Dutch delegation leaving for Rome with an extremely strict set of instructions allowing for very

---

32 NA, MR (398) Notulen Ministerraad 26.5.1953 Min. BZ, II, 913.100, inv. No. 26: "Verslag van de conferentie van Parijs, 12-13 mei 1953"; with accompanying letter Beyen.

33 *Idem.*

little room for manoeuvre during the negotiations.[34] Secondly, with a view to sounding reactions and clarifying the Dutch point of view abroad, a team of two senior civil servants was sent on a tour of the Western European capitals. During the end of May and early June 1953, Linthorst Homan, director of the Foreign Economic Relations Department (BEB) of the Ministry of Economic Affairs and Van der Beugel heading the Economic and Military Cooperation Department of the Foreign Ministry visited Brussels, Luxemburg, Paris, Bonn and Rome, discussing the three memoranda constituting the Beyen Plan and the perspectives for the Rome negotiations in general. Their reports to The Hague demonstrated that, in spite of general appreciation of the Beyen Plan as a basis for discussion (as yet, no other country had come forward with clear-cut proposals), internal division within the other governments was as least as substantial as in the Netherlands. Favourable arrangements towards embodying economic arrangements in line with Beyen's suggestions, they learned, could not be taken for granted. In Brussels, Benelux-partner Belgium eventually agreed to the general line of the Dutch approach. Allegedly, American pressure overcame Foreign Minister Van Zeeland's Drees-like anti-EPC sentiments. Van Zeeland's support for economic integration therefore, was not completely trusted, nor were his pleas for policy harmonisation appreciated by the Dutch. Some argued that Van Zeeland's new policy line was aimed at torpedoing the EPC-talks by complicating them and at luring the Dutch into stands that could be used against them in the current negotiations on the establishment of an economic union between the Benelux countries. The Dutch delegates felt themselves more at ease with their interlocutor from the Ministry of Economic Affairs, J. Snoy et d'Oppuers. Over the years this department had advocated economic co-operation and integration, in spite of the dominance of the Foreign Ministry on the matter.[35] In Luxemburg the government showed itself preoccupied with its nation's agricultural interests and, apart from that, seemed inclined to copy the Belgian stances during the forthcoming negotiations.[36] In Rome, Linthorst Homan and Van der Beugel were confronted with reticent Italian attitudes. More than ever Italian reasoning seemed institutional-

---

34 NA, MR (398), Notulen ministerraad 29.4.1953, 10.5.1953, 8.6.1953, 29.6.1953; Min. BZ, I, GS, 913.10 "Europese Integratie deel II", Beyen/Luns to Drees, 12.6.1953 with accompanying instruction for Dutch delegation; and: "Nederlands voorstel voor economische verdragsartikelen (3 Juli 1953)" (with accompanying letter Beden to Draait, 4.7.1953.).

35 Min. BZ, I, GS, 913.10, "Europese Integratie deel II", Codetelegram Beyen/Luns to Washington, 9.6.1953; Min. BZ I, 913.100, No. 66 Beelaerts van Blokland to Van der Beugel, 16.5.1953; Min. BZ, 913.100, 27, Linthorst Homan/Van der Beugel to Klim, Min. BZ, 22.5.1953.

36 Min. BZ, I, 913.100, No. 27, Codetelegram Van der Beugel/Linthorst Homan to Min. BZ, 23.5.1953.

ist-oriented and stuck with the idea that the creation of a political community could solve both Europe's and Italy's problems. The message was clear. More than sympathy for the Dutch economic proposals as a blueprint for possible future action was not to be expected.[37] More encouraging were Dutch experiences in Bonn. The minimalist stance adopted by Adenauer earlier in the year which had been a cause of alarm in the Netherlands, was now under serious challenge by pro-economic integration initiatives from Secretary of State Hallstein and the Ministry of Economic Affairs. The latter's Academic Advisory Council came forward with a note which characterized political unification without economic integration as "unimaginable" and in which the establishment of a customs union – to be developed into a common market – as well as a considerable degree of policy harmonisation, were advocated. This note and, more importantly, the fact that it obtained the official blessing of the Federal Government, was welcomed by the Dutch as winds of change in the right direction. Adenauer, who had the final say in the matter, however, had not yet made up his mind, according to diplomatic sources. Whether the German Chancellor would, wholeheartedly or not, support a pro economic integration policy seemed dubious, Beyen realised. If he did, on the other hand, there was the risk of the German delegation in Rome coming up with highly ambitious economic demands which would appear unacceptable for the Paris government.[38] Unfortunately, for the time being the question of what would be acceptable for France was to remain an academic one, since at the end of May the French government led by René Mayer had tendered its resignation. During the trip to Paris, it became clear that few certainties could be found about future French European policy. The French administration was divided. The stance taken by the French foreign office remained negative. Loss of sovereignty, social consequences, the Union Française, Europe's shortage of raw materials, cross border labour movements and "le danger de la concurrence" were among the arguments brought to the fore. The Paris Interministerial Committee on European economic co-operation issues, however, waged a devastating campaign

---

37 Min. BZ, I, G.S., 913.10 "Europese Integratie deel II", Codetelegram Boon to Min. BZ, 6.6.1953; and: codetelegram Beyen/Luns to Washington, 9.6.1953; Min. BZ I, 913.100, 28, Codetelegram Van der Beugel:, Linthorst Homan, Eschauzier to Min. BZ, 12.6.1953. On this trip Linthorst Homan and Van der Beugel were accompanied by the Director-General Political Affairs, H.F. Eschauzier.

38 Min. BZ, I, G.S., 913.10 "Europese Integratie deel II", codetelegram Beyen/Luns to Washington, 9.6.1953; and codetelegram Lamping to Min. BZ, 2.6.1953; and codetelegram Lamping to Min. BZ 6.6.1953; Min. BZ, 1, 913.100, No. 27 codetelegram Linthorst Homan/ Van der Beugel to Min. BZ, 29.5.1953 Min. BZ, DGEM 516/73, "Der Wissenschaftliche Beirat beim Bundes- wirtschaftsministerium hat sich auf seinen 24. Tagung von 24. April bis 1 Mai 1953 mit der Frage der Wirtschaftlichen Integration Europas befasst und dazu wie folgt Stellung genommen", 1.5.1953.

in favour of economic integration against the opposition of the Quai d'Orsay.[39]

The demissionary state of the Mayer government also led to a postponement of the scheduled Rome conference. It was not until September 1953, that the experts of the six "Schuman Countries" would finally meet, in order to discuss in detail the various national proposals, as well as (according to some: on the basis of) the draft proposal of the *ad hoc* Assembly.

Meanwhile, the ministers of Foreign Affairs met informally in Paris on June 22, 1953. Since nothing substantial could be decided upon, this meeting served mainly as a modest attempt to show the German and Italian electorates as well as the Washington government that the European integration process was alive and still on course.[40] Another ministers' conference at Baden-Baden (August 7 and 8, 1953) did not produce tangible results either, apart from the fact that the wording of its communiqué, stressing the idea that the EPC would be "a community of sovereign states", dashed the hopes of many of those who believed in a truly federalist Europe. For Beyen, who considered European integration as a means to an economic end rather than an aim in its own right, this outspoken anti-federalist novelty was perfectly acceptable.

Hardly any attention was paid to economic integration during these meetings, which enabled the Dutch to devote their attention to fine-tuning their proposals for the forthcoming experts' conference.

Tellingly, after their Baden Baden conference, the Foreign Ministers hardly discussed EPC among themselves. As an object of intergovernmental talks, EPC was relegated to the levels of deputies and civil-servants. In these discussions, events took a turn not unfavourable for the Netherlands, in that Adenauer, bucked up by his 1953 electoral victory, wanted European integration to steam ahead, enabling the German delegation to take the Hallstein line in favour of economic integration within the EPC framework, consistent with the Academic Advisory Council paper. Belgium, by and large, supported The Hague customs union proposals. Luxembourg said it was willing to go along with the latter, on condition that the country's protective exception clauses and overall protected status within the Belgian-Luxembourgian Economic Union (BLEU) would find continuation in the EPC. Provided

---

39 Elgersma, *Les Pays-Bas*, pp. 54-55.

40 Min. BZ, 1, 913.100, No. 39, "Procès-verbal de la réunion des six ministres des affaires étrangères, Baden-Baden les 7 et 8 Août 1953". Min. BZ, DGEM, dossier 514, inv. no 17, "Betreft: Economische punten op de ministersconferentie te Baden-Baden". Min. Fin., Gen. Thes., BBV, 1262 No. 10, "Verslag van de vergadering van de zes ministers van de KSGlanden, gehouden te Baden-Baden op 7 en 8 Augustus 1953".

economic integration was dealt with succinctly in the Treaty, Italy too agreed, leaving France as the only participating country objecting to an economic dimension of EPC as such. The other Five also declared themselves in favour of the customs union concept. Isolating France was Beyen's strategy and he was willing to make substantial concessions on, amongst others, institutional issues, in order to maintain a common front against French unwillingness on the main issue. Germany's role in this was vital. When the Five succeeded in keeping up a common stance, American pressure on France would eventually, once the EDC was ratified, force Paris to agree with the customs union.[41]

In spite of such progress, by late 1953, it was evident that a *political* breakthrough on EPC was deemed impossible for the time being, i.e. as long as the French parliament did not ratify the EDC treaty. In the meantime, Beyen stuck to the Dutch point of departure that a European Community without an economic dimension was unacceptable. Strong American pressure notwithstanding, he was unwilling to make concessions in any shape or form on this matter.[42] His policy was aimed at shifting American pressure on to France while tactfully maintaining a cohesive relationship with the other five partners.[43]

During the Hague conference on November 26, 1953, it was decided at Beyen's suggestion to charge a working party of experts with the hitherto unsolved political and economic problems, leaving the members time to come up with proposals till March 15, 1954.[44] Beyen hoped that American pressure to make concessions to France (with a view to the ratification of the EDC-treaty by the French parliament, see 1.5) would, by then, have vanished.[45] Moreover, the Netherlands, then chairing the ECSC, would nominate the chairman of each of the working parties.

Throughout the first half of 1954 a common front of the Five on the economic dimension of EPC was indeed successfully upheld. However, Beyen's assessment that France would eventually give in and accept the economic features of EPC proved wrong.[46] Instead of Paris accepting the Beyen Plan component of EPC for the sake of the Defence Community, the year 1954 would bring an altogether different outcome.

---

41 Ermers and Kragt, *Tussen tradities*, pp. 75-96.

42 P. Borguignon, "De l'entrée en vigeur du traité de Paris à celle de traités de Rome", *Studia Diplomatica*, 34, 1981, p. 323.

43 *Ibidem*.

44 Max Jansen en and Johan K. De Vree. *The Ordeal of Unity. The Politics of European Integration, 1945-1985*, Bilthoven: Prime Press, 1985, p. 131.

45 NA, MR (398), Notulen Ministerraad 30-9-1953.

46 R.T. Griffiths and A.S. Milward, *The Beyen Plan and the European Political Community*, E.U.I.-Working Paper No. 85/199, Florence: EUI, 1986, pp. 20-27.

V. Endgame: the Backlash of the European Defence Community

When, in October 1950, French defence minister Pleven launched his proposal for a European Army, reactions from the Netherlands had originally been negative. The Hague was in favour of a German contribution to the defence of the West, hence of German rearmament within the framework of the Atlantic Community, i.e. by NATO-membership of the Federal Republic. Pleven's scheme, however, advocated a European Defence Community (EDC) incorporating German forces, thus eschewing the sensitive issue of a restoration of the *Wehrmacht*, or, at least, the creation of a new national army in Germany[47]. The French, in Warner's elegant phrasing, "hoped to spin a cocoon of supranational restraints around West Germany from which it could never escape".[48]

The Hague deemed its national security interests better served within NATO than by means of a European Army. The Dutch foreign policy elite looked askance upon integration experiments in the area of high politics, the latter regarded as potential threats to NATO unity and coherence. Stikker felt that the proposed European Army and the adjoining political institutions would entail the construction of a fully-fledged federal state. He felt strongly against The Netherlands being part to such a state. As he worded it in his memoirs:

> (…) I was held back from taking an active role in European federalism, as the majority of the Dutch people in an upsurge of idealism wanted at that time, precisely because I saw no indication of how these grand ideas would fit into the pattern of world policy so long as the United States, on whose monopoly of nuclear weapons we all relied, and Great Britain and the Commonwealth had not clarified their thinking on these complex and formidable problems.[49]

In the Summer of 1951 a change in American policy forced Stikker, as he had predicted in November 1950, to change course. For a number of reasons, among other things the prospect to "Bring American boys home", the United States now became an active supporter of the Pleven Plan. As a result, the Netherlands changed its status at the Paris EDC conference from observer to active participant and set to work to dress

---

47 Johan K. De Vree and Max Jansen, *The Ordeal of Unity. Integration and Disintegration in Modern Europe*, Amsterdam: Blackwall Publishing, 2nd edition, 1998, pp. 121-122.

48 G. Warner, "The United States and the Rearmament of West Germany, 1950-54", *International Affairs* 61 (1984-1985) 2, pp. 110-111 as quoted in: Jan van der Harst, *The Atlantic Priority. Dutch Defence Policy at the Time of the European Defence Community*, Florence: European Press Academic Publishing, 2003, p. 139.

49 Dirk U. Stikker, *Men of Responsibility. As seen through the Memoirs of a Participant in Years of World Crisis*, New York: Harper and Row, 1965, p. 177.

down the supranational, military and budgetary scope of the Defence Community, as well as claiming a substantial institutional role for its smaller member-states.

The role of *enfant terrible* at the negotiations was taken over by the Belgian delegation, whose "critical, almost uncompromising attitude" allowed the Netherlands to play a constructive intermediary role between Belgium and the other participants. Thus Benelux foreign policy co-operation underwent a revival of sorts.[50]

Under substantial American and British pressure on the Benelux countries, Germany and France – in which the threat of diminishing American military assistance played a powerful role – the Six overcame their differences. The EDC Treaty of Paris was signed on 27 May 1952. It showed that there was considerable leeway given to the Benelux objections against Pleven's original proposals. The single European Minister of Defence, advocated by Pleven, was substituted for a Council of Ministers which would decide on all budgetary and other important matters pertaining to this new institution by means of unanimity. In the eyes of the Dutch government, the EDC was now acceptable, but as a necessary evil only. Stikker's successor, Beyen, showed moderate support for the Defence Community Treaty purely due to its being inextricably linked to the EPC and hence to his customs union campaign.[51] Although Drees had reckoned with EDC ratification problems in Germany, because of the discriminatory elements against that country in the Treaty, it was the French Parliament which became increasingly critical of the political and military integration project even though the latter had been launched by French governments. *Anti-CEDisme* (Anti EDCism) became a force to be reckoned with in French politics. From May 1952 till August 1954, consecutive French governments postponed submitting the EDC treaty for ratification, meanwhile – with some degree of success insisting on additional 'protocols' containing further concessions from the Five to France.

With a view to exerting pressure on Paris, American Secretary of State Foster Dulles, demanded the remaining five countries to speed up their national ratification procedures. Again, the threat of an "agonising reappraisal" of American policy on Europe in the event of EDC failure, proved effective. Beyen managed to convince his reluctant colleagues in the Cabinet to submit the Treaty for parliamentary approval. On 23 July 1953, the *Tweede Kamer* ratified the Treaty with a large majority of

---

50 Van der Harst, *The Atlantic Priority*, pp. 142-157 (p. 156).

51 Elgersma, *Les Pays-Bas*, p. 39. Van der Harst, *The Atlantic Priority*, p. 170.

75 votes to 11. Again, as Elgersma words it, "le parlement néerlandais est plus favourable aux projects supranationaux que le gouvernement".[52]

It was to no avail. In assuming that the Treaty, once it was ratified by the other five member-states, would of necessity be ratified by France, Foster Dulles had underestimated the strength of the combined forces of nationalism (Gaullism, more specifically) and communism in French national politics. In August 1954, *Anti-Cedists* of the Left and Right managed a majority of 319 parliamentarians over 264, whose combined votes secured a definitive stop on the EDC ratification procedure.

In The Hague, the news of French obstruction was received with equanimity (as a vessel for German rearmament the Treaty had been second choice, anyway), with one notable exception: Beyen. The eventual refusal of the French parliament to ratify the EDC treaty dealt a death blow not only to EDC but likewise to the European Political Community and, with it, to the Beyen Plan for a West European customs union.[53]

Thus, amid a drastic change in the international context caused by the downfall of the European Defence Community, Beyen's campaign for a liberal economic trade regime among the Six came to a grinding halt.

Like Foster Dulles and unlike Prime Minister Drees, Beyen had steadfastly held to the belief in EDC ratification by the French Parliament. Even as late as June 1954, he still thought that if the French were finally confronted with the fundamental choice between either ratifying the Treaty or accepting German membership of NATO, they would eventually see the light.[54]

VI. Discussion

Beyen's policy saved the Netherlands from having to reject the EPC. Initially, his plans for horizontal economic integration within the EPC framework got little positive response, either at home or abroad. And in the end EDC turned out to be too large an obstacle. Arguably, Beyen remained sanguine for too long on the chances of the EDC treaty finding ratification, as well as fostering unrealistic expectations of the effect of American pressure on France. The causal chain also worked the other way. As Loth argues: "L'insistance néerlandaise en faveur de la Communauté économique conduisit à l'échec des négociations sur la Communauté politique, lequel entraînait l'échec final de la Communauté de

52 Van der Harst, *The Atlantic Priority*, pp. 175-183; Elgersma, *Les Pays-Bas*, p. 39.

53 F.W.E. Fursdon, *The European Defence Community. A History*, London: MacMillan, 1980, pp. 296-297.

54 Van der Harst, *The Atlantic Priority*, p. 183.

défense".[55] Like Foster Dulles, Beyen had banked on convincing Germany and isolating France. Although both aims did eventually materialise, his policy failed. Whereas Foster Dulles had underestimated the strength of *anti-CEDisme* in French national politics, Beyen, deeming that France had become "intellectually isolated", had invested too much trust in French EDC ratification.[56]

On the other hand, Beyen managed to get the Netherlands' economic *desiderata* back on the European integration negotiating table and to arrive at a substantial degree of agreement on the desirability of European economic integration between five of the six member-states of the Communities, thus laying the intellectual and diplomatic foundation for the future discussion and eventual implementation of his ideas in the European Economic Community.

Contrary to his predecessor Stikker, Beyen did not deprecate supranational integration or the establishment of a continental block. During his term of office he turned out to be an enthusiastic supporter of European economic integration on a supranational footing. His experiences as an international banker appear to have played a part here. For all that, during the Stikker and Beyen years (1948-1956), Dutch policy displayed a great deal of continuity in that both pursued step-by-step liberalization of intra-European trade as the first aim of the Netherlands European policy. Institutionally, even Stikker eventually had had to reconcile himself to the prospect of a European federation of sorts, a rather uninviting prospect to him, but at the same time recognised as the inevitable outcome of the course undertaken when founding Benelux, i.e. liberalisation by means of regional integration for the benefit of the Dutch economy. For Beyen, however, supranationalism was no threat but a challenge and an opportunity for realising fundamental long-term aims of Dutch foreign policy.

This does not necessarily imply or entail a federalist conviction. Duchêne, commenting on the Netherlands' reticent stance during the EDC negotiations, observed "the Benelux countries were not at all their later federalist selves".[57] Duchêne is right, up to a point. From the early 1950s both Parliament and public opinion expressed substantial federalist sympathies and support for European unification. Among the government, the Foreign Ministry and foreign policy making elite as whole, however, federalist convictions were a scarce commodity. Griffiths links what he describes as "the overwhelmingly pro-European reputation" of the Netherlands in the 1950s to its Parliament and parliamentarians and

55 Loth, "L'Allemagne", p. 250. Van der Harst, *The Atlantic Priority, passim*.

56 Van der Harst, *The Atlantic Priority*, p. 182.

57 R.T. Griffiths, *The Netherlands and the integration of Europe, 1945-1957*, Amsterdam: NEHA, 1990, p. XI.

wonders how "in a supposedly democratic system" the latter seemed incapable of exercising any significant pro-federalist influence on the government's European policy. For the Stikker years (1948-1952) this is undeniably true. The intergovernmental approach was dominant.[58] The Hague's insistence on incorporating a Council of Ministers in the ECSC framework has been mentioned. Reluctance by the Drees government to serious delegation of power to the EDC was in the same vein. In a supranational structure, Stikker and his ministry argued, the Larger Powers would unavoidably dominate the smaller ones. As Van der Harst observed, this approach contrasted sharply with the fact that in later years supranationalism was looked upon as a major instrument for *protecting* the interests of smaller states.[59] The initiator of this change was Beyen.

For Beyen, supranational institutions and supranational decision-making were a means to an end, to further and protect the Netherlands' interest. From the second half of the 1950s onwards the Beyen approach – which we could call "functional supranationalism" – became a leading principle of the Netherlands' policy on Europe. Apart from the institutional method, Beyen changed the scope of the Dutch liberalization campaign from the broad OEEC framework, including Britain and the Scandinavian countries to the more limited grouping of the six ECSC countries, precisely for the reason that in this "little Europe" by means of supranationalism, results could be achieved where OEEC had failed.

During the period under consideration Benelux policy co-operation played a variable role. After its initial successes, Benelux as a foreign policy coalition became limp during the Fritalux, Schuman Plan and European Army negotiations. Mutual personal dislike between Stikker and his Belgian colleague Van Zeeland appears to be the cause. After Beyen came to the fore in August 1952 Benelux talks were revived and wherever possible the two countries supported each other during the EPC and the latter half of the Defence Community negotiations.

---

58 Stikker himself, however, mentions the pro-integration majority as one of the two major reasons for not staying on as Foreign Minister in 1952 (the other being disagreement with his parliamentary party on Dutch New Guinea policy): "I felt that the creation of a separate group of six, before we really knew what directions its foreign or defence policies might take, was too risky an enterprise. I feared that the establishment of a restricted bloc of six, which might even become autarkic, would, instead of leading to wider Western European unity, split Western Europa into blocs, I likewise feared the dangers that it posed to the vital need for unity within the Atlantic Alliance. Here again, however, the majority of the New Dutch Parliament felt otherwise". Dirk U. Stikker, *Men of Responsibility. As seen through the Memoirs of a Participant in Years of World Crisis*, New York: Harper and Row, 1965, p. 250.

59 Van der Harst, *The Atlantic Priority*, pp. 148-149.

Both Stikker and Beyen can be said to have pursued a policy aimed at engineering influence in the making of the Communities. Stikker's reactive and predominantly defensive approach towards European integration and supranationalism within the framework of the Six found replacement by Beyen in initiating a pro-active and intellectually challenging campaign for a liberal and supranational trade regime among the Six.

CHAPTER II

The Netherlands, Benelux, and the *Relance européenne*

Introduction

The refusal of the French National Assembly, on August 31, 1954, to ratify the treaty for the European Defence Community (EDC), forced the Dutch Government to reconsider its policy towards Western European integration. The collapse of the EDC project effectively put an end to all plans for a European Political Community, and, with these, torpedoed the Dutch Government's main lever for promoting economic integration by means of a customs union between the six participating countries of the European Coal and Steel Community. In brief, the "No political integration without economic integration" approach of the Dutch Government had been robbed of its meaning. This chapter deals with a period in the post-war history of European integration which is generally referred to as the "Relance européenne", the European Re-launch. During the nine months between the shipwrecking of the European Defence Community Treaty by the French Parliament in August 1954 and the start of new intergovernmental negotiations which were the result of the Messina Conference in June 1955, various plans for the future of European integration were presented. Arguably, the most important of these schemes was the joint proposal of the governments of Belgium, Luxembourg and the Netherlands. The so-called Beyen-Spaak initiative resulted in a common Benelux-memorandum, which laid the foundation of the Resolution of Messina, which, in turn, started the negotiations on what was to become the European Economic Community.

The aim of this chapter is to present a detailed analysis of the Beyen-Spaak initiative, as much as possible on the basis of primary source material, with a view to gauging the pursuance of engineering influence by the Netherlands and its concomitant use of Smaller Power policy instruments.

I. Saving Western Europe's Defence from the EDC Wreck

During the weeks following the decision of the French Parliament, Foreign Minister Beyen and his colleagues in the Dutch Government came to the conclusion that, for the time being, no real progress in the field of Western European integration could be made. This pessimistic view of the future of the aims of his own policy was largely coloured by Beyen's perception of French foreign policy as formulated by the Mendès-France Government. The Dutch Foreign Minister had had serious misgivings about the direction and underlying intentions of the policy of the French Government towards Western European Integration well before the debacle of the EDC Treaty. The rejection of the EDC Treaty by the French Parliament confirmed Dutch suspicions of French intentions, or lack of intentions, in Western Europe. Beyen perceived this decision as an important and unpromising victory of nationalism over supranationalism in the foreign policies of Western European states, rather than as a protest against the rearmament of Western Germany[1]. The decision served as a vote of confidence for Mendès-France and his return to what was considered a pre-ECSC, nationalistic policy. Beyen showed himself deeply disappointed and concluded: "The history of the EDC has shown that for the present we should not place a lot of hope on further supranational organisation of Western Europe (whatever the scale and in whatever framework), considering that Mendès-France will probably continue playing the most important political part in France for a long time".[2] In the Queen's speech on 21 September the government reconfirmed its adhesion to supranational political and economic integration[3] and hence to the policy which Beyen had consistently pursued since September 1952. During the following months the government did not air an elaborated concept of its European policy goals and ambitions.[4]

The failure of the EDC project, however, raised immediate, concrete problems. Western European Governments had still to resolve the fundamental question of the rearmament of Western Germany, and, therefore, the West German contribution to the whole Western defence effort. This problem was dealt with, in the course of a series of conferences held in London and Paris during September and October 1954, on the basis of a set of proposals presented by Sir Anthony Eden, the

1 NA, 400, Notulen Ministerraad 13.9.1954.

2 Min. BZ, I, GS, 913.10, inv. No. 663 (Europese integratie deel III): Codetelegram Beyen/Luns 190, 8.11.1954.

3 *Handelingen der Staten-Generaal 1954-55* (henceforth: Handelingen 1954-55), Eerste Kamer (Upper House), 2.

4 *Handelingen 1954-55, Tweede Kamer* (henceforth: TK), bijlage 3700, No. 15, 7-8.

British Foreign Secretary. The Paris Agreements were the outcome of these talks. In accordance with Eden's proposals an agreement was reached that on the one hand allowed Germany and Italy to become members of NATO, but on the other hand imposed certain restrictions on German rearmament within the framework of the Brussels Treaty.[5]

The Eden Solution was a solution founded on an intergovernmental basis. The Brussels Treaty Organisation, now transformed into the Western European Union (WEU) lacked the supranational features of the proposed EDC, which, in fact, was precisely why it was acceptable to the UK Government. The UK's commitment to maintaining its military presence on the Continent on the other hand was, together with the restrictions on German rearmament, of the utmost importance in piloting the Eden solution through the French Parliament.[6]

For the Dutch Government, the Eden Plan was acceptable as a solution for the Western European defence problem. It was regarded a technical solution with a certain practical value. Its relevance for European economic integration, however, was considered null and void. British participation in WEU was, of course, looked upon favourably. Nevertheless, British participation excluded the possibility of considering WEU as a nucleus of future Western-European integration on a supranational basis.[7] Beyen wrote:

> The WEU is an alliance which has come into being not owing to logic as such but because of a lamentable but undeniable reality, to settle the question of Germany's rearmament. There is no fundamental difference from other forms of intergovernmental cooperation like NATO, OEEC, etc. It is not exaggerated to state that the furthering of European supranational cooperation taking the WEU as a starting-point is bound to remain a castle in the air only leading to disappointing experiences because of (a) the United Kingdom being a member and (b) the attitude of the French Government.[8]

On this point Beyen was at odds with many of the ardent pro-European (i.e. federalist oriented) parliamentarians in the Netherlands, who generally stressed a need to prevent the stagnation of the movement towards Western European integration and to maintain the new-found momentum provided by the solution of the European defence problem by initiating further moves in the political and economic fields. Also

5 'La Conférence de Londres et Paris en septembre et octobre 1954', in: *Chronique de Politique Étrangère* viii (1955), 15-26; R. Massigli, *Une comédie des erreurs 1943-1956, souvenirs et réflexions sur une étape de la construction européenne* (Henceforth: Comédie des erreurs), Paris: Plon, s.a. [c. 1978], pp. 457-498.

6 A.J. Zurcher, *The Struggle to Unite Europe 1940-1958*, New York: New York University Press, 1958, pp. 129-130.

7 Min. BZ, II, 913.100, No. 19, Memorandum Eschauzier to Beyen, 15.11.1954.

8 *Ibidem*.

(according to Beyen: therefore) they were inclined to regard the WEU as "a kind of" EDC, now including the UK as well as the continental Six, and therefore, as a suitable starting point for "further" or "real" European integration within the framework of the WEU. This attitude was looked upon by Beyen with scorn. In his opinion it was futile, if not dangerous, to blur the borderline between cooperation and integration, that is between intergovernmental and supranational organisation. Apart from the practical limitations set by French and British policies as they were, cooperation and integration should be kept apart for the benefit of the realm.[9]

II. Patience and Defensive Reticence

This line of thought was enlarged upon in Beyen's cabinet paper of 19 November, 1954 on "The Policy of the Dutch Government concerning European Cooperation".[10] The document comprised a long litany of woes against French foreign policy. It made the point that as far as European integration was concerned nothing constructive could be done while French European policy remained as it was. Moreover, because of the nationalist tendencies in France, such a change was not likely to occur in the near future. The Dutch government, therefore, should pursue a *defensive* policy. This policy should be aimed first of all at defending the existing supranational institution, i.e. the European Coal and Steel Community, against possible French attacks. The ECSC, Beyen expected, would be subjected to attempts to suppress its supranational identity, e.g. by extending the powers of the Council of Ministers at the cost of those of the High Authority. Beyen wrote:

> The defence of the ECSC against impending undermining by the French is of the utmost importance both to our country and to the Benelux, firstly because we have to defend the principles of cooperation which have been accepted for this important economic sector and secondly because the Community offers facilities to protect our direct economic interests against protectionist tendencies.[11]

The interests of the Coal and Steel Community would be best served, Beyen continued, by concentrating on the realisation of objectives embodied in the original ECSC-Treaty. The point was that attempts to extend the powers of the Community to related economic sectors like transport could, in the present political situation, easily be counter-

---

9 Min. BZ, I, GS, 913.10, inv. No. 663 Codetelegram Beyen/Luns – Ambassade Washington, 8.11.1954; NA, MR (400), Notulen Ministerraad 20.9.1954.

10 Min. BZ, I, GS, 913.10, No. 19: "Het beleid van de Nederlandse regering ten opzichte van de Europese samenwerking", 19.11.1954.

11 Min. BZ, II, 913.100, No. 19, "Het beleid van de Nederlandse regering ten opzichte van de Europese samenwerking", 19.11.1954.

productive. Given the French attitude, any renewal of the political discussions on the Treaty might actually lead to a curtailment of these powers. In the circumstances, government initiatives aiming at such an extension (called for by the Strasbourg Assembly, with the support of Monnet and the High Authority) would be most undesirable and should be guarded against.

Secondly, this policy should defend the perspective for future European integration against attempts at what Beyen called *fake integration:* traditional constructions based on inter-governmental cooperation without political powers of their own and therefore without a political responsibility of their own to be carried independently from the national governments of the member countries. Cooperation and integration, Beyen argued, should be kept apart, not so much for the sake of tidiness in political theory as because of the danger that France, "by a dialectic of its own, already skilfully applied by Mendès-France", would see its chance to render void the notion of supranationality and transform it into a political slogan serving the various needs of French foreign policy. The French proposals for a common Armaments Production Pool within the newly established Western European Union framework may serve as an example. These proposals presented as "first steps on the way towards a supranational solution" were looked upon in the Dutch Cabinet as a scheme which was primarily designed to serve the French national interest in general and the French armaments industry in particular, without offering any clear commitment for a development towards supranationality. Under these circumstances, Beyen reasoned, the pressure of the ardent "pro-European" (i.e. federalist) parliamentarians in the Netherlands, who wanted him to maintain the new-found momentum provided by the Eden solution of the European defence problem by initiating further moves in the political and economic fields, was naive and even dangerous.[12]

Thirdly, Beyen argued, the concept of "Integration on the basis of supranationality" had to be defended against the threat of *resurging bilateralism*. He referred to the plans recently presented by the French and German governments on October 26, 1954 concerning closer cooperation between these two countries, plans which foreshadowed a long-term Franco-German trade agreement advantageous both to German industry and to French agriculture. Clearly these plans constituted a potential threat to the Dutch and Belgian positions in intra-European trade. Moreover, he pointed out, there was cause for alarm in that these initiatives demonstrated once more the French tendency to deal with problems of a multilateral nature in a bilateral way: a tendency shown

[12] 22. Min. BZ, I; GS, 913.10, folder 663: Codetelegram Beyen/Luns – Ambassade Washington, 8.11.1954. NA, MR (400), Notulen Ministerraad 20.9.1954.

during the WEU negotiations and afterwards when the proposals for a European Armaments Pool were presented.

This approach, Beyen continued, constituted a threat to the smaller countries and to their interests. Under the circumstances close Benelux cooperation, especially in the field of foreign policy, was more than ever necessary. During the discussions in Cabinet Beyen put a lot of emphasis on this last point. Underlining, as far as supranationality and integration went, the extremely limited room for manoeuvre, he stressed the importance of defending multilateral cooperation as such, suggesting talks with Spaak on the question whether it would be feasible to undertake joint Benelux action to tackle this problem of resurging bilateralism. As a possible course of action Beyen mentioned the idea recently launched by Baron Snoy et d'Oppuers, the Secretary General of the Belgian Ministry of Economic Affairs, that the Benelux countries might take the initiative to start discussions in the OEEC on the formation of a Free Trade Area.[13]

This last remark in particular demonstrates that, during the last months of 1954 the Dutch Minister entertained no hopes whatsoever of a speedy economic integration of Western Europe along the lines of the Beyen Plan.

When discussed in Cabinet, Beyen's policy met with little criticism. Pessimistic and defensive as it was – and acknowledged as such – it gained acceptance. In December the Foreign Minister told Parliament, which had exerted some pressure in favour of a new governmental or Benelux initiative aimed at new negotiations among the Six, that for the moment – he prophetically mentioned a period of five months – nothing should be done at all as far as European integration was concerned. Even after the ratification of the Paris Agreements, he argued, the room for manoeuvre would remain dependent on the willingness of at least six countries to accept the supranational idea. He therefore wanted to "wait for better weather", he said, and made clear that government would refrain from initiatives on the European front as long as the Mendès-France Government remained in power.[14] In accordance with this policy line the Dutch government kept a low profile on European affairs during the next three months. Unlike the Belgians they refrained from theoretical discussions about the future of European cooperation and/or integra-

---

13 NA, MR (400), Notulen Ministerraad 25.10.1954, 1.11.1954 and 22/23.11.1954. Archief van het ministerie van Economische Zaken Den Haag (*Archive of the Ministry of Economic Affairs, The Hague*) (henceforth: EZ), directoraat-generaal van de Buitenlandse Economische Betrekkingen (henceforth: BEB), No. 2482 (Benelux: vergaderingen van de voorzitters van de Raden): (Frans-Duitse samenwerking), 18.11.1954.

14 NA, MR (400), Notulen Ministerraad 20.9.1954. *Handelingen 1954-55. TK*, 630-631.

tion. Also they enthusiastically participated in the torpedoing of the French ("fake integration") plans for a European Armaments Pool.

Although some kind of Armaments Secretariat was set up within the WEU framework, the final result fell far short of the initial French proposals.[15] Also, when in January 1955 Pella, the President of the ECSC Council, made a tour of the Western European capitals in order to investigate the possibilities of further integration, Beyen urged him not to launch an initiative aimed at an extension of the ECSC, because of the threat to the supranational character of the Community, such renegotiation of the ECSC treaty would imply.[16]

III. New Policy Formulation in Belgium and Benelux

In Belgium, meanwhile, reactions to the failure of the EDC project were of a more activist nature. Almost immediately Baron Snoy et d'Oppuers, a senior civil servant of the Ministry for Economic Affairs, started informal talks on the future of European integration with colleagues in both the Belgian and Dutch administration.[17] By November 1954, Victor Larock, the Belgian Minister for Foreign Trade, presented a number of "propositions d'ordre économique pouvant servir à une action politique à entreprendre par les pays de Benelux" in order to arrive at a "relance d'intégration européenne". He suggested a joint Benelux initiative aiming at the creation of a (Western) European Free Trade Area, limited to certain products, mainly manufactured goods, namely those for which the total factor costs were more or less equal in the participating countries. For those products alone tariffs and quantitative restrictions within the area would be abolished, while trade policies with regard to third countries remained to be decided upon by each individual government. The Larock Plan also comprised proposals for cooperation in public work projects and a common European plan for road construction. A common Fund for Restructuring would help to defray setbacks and distortion caused by increased competition.[18] Larock's proposals did not

15 NA, MR (401), Notulen 10.1.1955, 17.1.1955 and 24.1.1955. NA, MR (510): 'Wapenpoolbesprekingen, oprichting van een bewapeningscomité in de WEU', 27.4.1955 and: "Draft Decision of the Council of the Western European Union as Adopted by the Organisation Committee on Thursday 21st April 1955".

16 NA, MR (401), Notulen Ministerraad 17.1.1955.

17 J. Ch. Snoy et d'Oppuers, "Un témoin raconte: Du plan Schuman aux traités de Rome", in: *30 jours d'Europe*, No. 285 (avril 1982), pp. 23-24.

18 Archief van het ministerie van Buitenlandse Zaken, Buitenlandse Handel en Ontwikkelingssamenwerking Brussel (*Archive of the Ministry of Foreign Affairs, Foreign Trade and Development Cooperation, Brussels*), (henceforth: Min. BZBrus), 17.771/4 (Notes du Department), "Comment reprendre le problème de l'intégration économique" (undated); Min. BZ, II, 913.100, No. 164. "De Belgische integratieplannen", 24.3.1955 and "Relance de l'integration européenne. Propositions d'ordre

get far. Foreign Minister Spaak and his advisors were of opinion that the international political situation in Europe had to be handled with care and did not allow for daring initiatives of this kind. They refused to put the Larock Plan on the Benelux agenda.[19]

Spaak, indeed, thought along different and more cautious lines. During the last months of 1954 he had a series of talks with Monnet, the President of the ECSC High Authority, who intended to draw up a plan of action to put new life into his ideal of a united and supranationally governed Europe. Spaak was his main interlocutor. Possibly, Monnet's role in what later was called the "European Relaunch" has been somewhat exaggerated in the literature. Nevertheless, there seems to be little doubt that he exerted considerable influence on both the ideas and policies of at least this Belgian statesman.[20]

Monnet and Spaak shared the belief that 'something' had to be done, to get out of a possibly indefinite impasse. At the same time, however, they were well aware of the fact that whatever initiative was taken the state of affairs of European politics called for the utmost caution: "Il fallait avant tout éviter un nouvel échec", wrote Spaak afterwards.[21] This meant that whatever the form of the eventual proposals they would have to be acceptable to the governments concerned. In fact, like Beyen, Spaak did not believe in the possibility of a successful move forward as long as Mendès-France and his adherents dominated French foreign policy. Consequently the Spaak-Monnet talks during the winter of

---

économique pouvant servir à une action politique à entreprendre par des pays de Benelux" (undated). Larock's proposals for a common European plan for road construction may well have been inspired by US president Eisenhower's plan for a nationwide interstate highway system resulting in the Federal-Aid Highway Act of 1956.

19 Min. BZBrus, 17.771/4 (Notes de Departement): "Note pour le dossier 'Accords Franco-allemands'", 22.12.1954. In March 1955, after the fall of the Mendès-France government in France, the Larock Plan was revived by the Belgian administration and obtained Spaak's official support. Not for long, however; soon its central idea, the estblishment of an European Free Trade Area, survived as main aim in the Snoy et d'Oppuers Plan, drafted in the spring of 1955 and thus constituted the basis for the Free Trade Area negotiations of 1957. The Dutch supported the Free Trade Area idea; they considered it, however, a typical OEEC project and did not entertain much hope that it would ever be realized. (Min. BZBrus, 17.771/4 (Notes du Departement): memo Snoy et d'Oppuers to Gérard, 24.3.1955; memo Gérard to Snoy, 30.3.1955; "Note pour la Direction Générale de la Politique", 1.4.1955; R. Dingemans and A.J. Boekestijn, "The Netherlands and the enlargement proposals 1957-1963", in: A. Deighton and A.S. Milward (eds.), *Widening, Deepening and Acceleration: the European Economic Community 1957-1963*, Baden-Baden: Nomos, 1999, pp. 215-241 (p. 235).

20 P. H. Spaak, *Combats Inachevés, II. De l'espoir aux déceptions*, Paris: Fayard, 1969, pp. 61-62; R. Mayne, *The Recovery of Europe, from Devastation to Unity*, London: Weidenfeld and Nicolson, 1970, p. 220.

21 Mayne, *Recovery of Europe*, p. 220.

1954/55 were in the nature of preliminary theoretical discussions about what might be done in the future. Monnet managed to convince Spaak of the desirability of proceeding by extending the powers of the ECSC to related sectors, especially transport and energy. Moreover, inspired by the views of his collaborator Armand, Monnet proposed the creation of an entirely new High Authority for common research on, and the production of, atomic energy for civil purposes. In his "Atoms for Peace" address before the UN General Assembly in December 1953, US President Eisenhower had raised the perspective of sharing American technology and know-how, as well as nuclear materials (fissionable materials), with other countries for the sake of civil power programmes. Also, because of the recent scientific developments in this field Monnet expected atomic energy to lead to a "new industrial revolution". Therefore, both he and Spaak regarded this sector as a promising nucleus for European integration in general: since the continental European countries lacked the facilities to develop the potentialities of atomic energy individually, there was a natural community of interests to arrive at close cooperation in the field.[22]

The Spaak/Monnet reasoning was bound to conflict with Beyen's ideas, as the Dutch Minister had, as early as 1952, argued against the sector approach and had favoured a *general* approach to economic integration by means of creating a Western European customs union instead. For the moment, however, both Spaak and Beyen shared the negative consensus that time was not yet ripe for a new initiative.

Benelux co-operation would turn out to be of the essential. Shortly after the Drees' Government's decision, Beyen went to Brussels for a political "tour d'horizon" with his Benelux colleagues, Spaak and Bech. The downfall of EDC had seriously affected intra-Benelux foreign policy cooperation. By the end of 1954 mutual consultation and policy coordination had reached something close to zero. During the final phases of the EDC negotiations in August when Spaak had launched a proposal containing far-reaching concessions to the French demands without having consulted his Benelux partners previously, lack of cooperation became blatantly obvious.[23] During the subsequent WEU negotiations the Benelux delegations had worked together again, but no fundamental discussion on the future of European cooperation and integration had taken place at the Benelux level. As a consequence, Spaak had embarked upon a course considerably different to that pur-

22 *Ibidem* and F. Duchêne, *Jean Monnet. The First Statesman Of Interdependence*, New York: W. Norton & Companie, 1994, pp. 264-265.

23 A.E. Kersten, *Maken drie kleinen een grote? De politieke invloed van de Benelux, 1945-1955*, Bussum: Van Holkema & Warendorf, 1982, pp. 10-15; NA, MR (400) Notulen Ministerraad 30/31.8.54.

sued by Beyen. Right from the beginning Spaak had had little sympathy for the free trade area idea generated by Snoy and his supporters in the Belgian Ministry of Economic Affairs. Contrary to the opinions of most political actors and observers at that time, Spaak had initially been in favour of a new effort to create a politically integrated Europe. Also he had considered the newly founded WEU a suitable organisational nucleus for such an attempt, an opinion which caused Beyen some anxiety. Apart from that, Spaak's ideas corresponded with those of his Dutch colleague to the extent that he too was more than sceptical on the question of whether it would be possible to bring about any progress whatsoever as long as the Mendès-France Government remained in power.[24] At the Benelux summit of 25 November 1954 Spaak, Beyen and their Luxembourg colleague, Bech, agreed on a passive stance on the European integration issue.[25]

For no apparent reason, Dutch sources on this Beyen-Spaak-Bech summit are rather vague. Beyen afterwards reported to the Cabinet that on "the most important points" an agreement had been reached. By this he meant that Spaak had explicitly distanced himself from his earlier ideas about using the WEU as a starting point for new integration initiatives. In the course of the discussions Spaak presented his new ideas about an extension of the field of activity of the Coal and Steel Community but interestingly enough he did not limit himself to that: he also raised the question whether a common market "in a wider sense" would be worth considering. When his Dutch colleague referred to the Netherlands' proposals on this topic as embodied in the Beyen Plan, he learned to his astonishment that Spaak was uninformed about them. An exposition by Beyen of his train of thought on this theme was followed by a more general discussion on the perspectives of economic integration.[26]

The available sources do not reveal any clear-cut decisions taken by the three. The fact, however, that Beyen reported agreement "on the most important issues" to his government seems to indicate that the Benelux ministers at least agreed that the time was not yet ripe for a new initiative among the Six. That at any rate was what Beyen told the Dutch Parliament in December.

---

24 NA, MR (400), Notulen Ministerraad 18.10.1954; Min. BZ, GS1, 913.10, inv. No. 663, Codetelegram Beyen/ Luns – Washington, 8.11.1954; H.J. Küsters, *Die Gründung der europäischen Wirtschaftsgemeinschaft*, Baden-Baden: Nomos, 1982, p. 66.

25 Min. BZ, 1, GS, 913.10, No. 663: codetelegram Beyen 216, 25.11.1954. NA, MR (400), Notulen Ministerraad 29.11.1954.

26 Min. BZ, GS1, 913.10, inv. No. 663, Codetelegram Beyen 216, 25.11.1954; NA, MR (400), Notulen Ministerraad 29.11.1954.

IV. Spring 1955: the Origins of the New Beyen Plan

During the first months of 1955, the centre of the diplomatic stage was dominated by the Saar-problem, the French proposals for a European Armaments Pool, Germany's return to sovereignty and the plans for French-German economic cooperation. On a more or less "subterranean" level, however, the discussions on the future of European integration continued. It was clear that at some point the Western European Governments would have to decide on the future and form of the European integration process, if any. The most suitable occasion for common reflection, it seemed, would be the forthcoming meeting of the Council of Foreign Ministers of the ECSC when the member countries were to decide on a successor for Jean Monnet as president of the High Authority. For various reasons, however, this meeting, originally scheduled to take place in February when Monnet's term of office would expire, was postponed time after time. At first the French Government did not want to jeopardise the ratification of the Paris Agreements by the *Conseil de la République* by agreeing to a new ministerial meeting on the European issue. Then, after this ratification on March 27, it was the Germans who asked for a delay, firstly because of their wish to negotiate Europe's future only after a complete restoration of (West) German sovereignty, and secondly because they hoped to find a way out of their domestic differences between Chancellor Konrad Adenauer and his Minister of Economic Affairs Ludwig Erhard over the stance to be taken by the Federal Republic.[27] The period up to June 1, 1955, when the meeting finally took place, has been baptised the "Period of Constructive Opportunism". Indeed, throughout Western Europe, blueprints for future integration were drawn up and discussed. In the Low Countries alone, at least five distinct concepts for a European "relaunch" can be identified. These were fuelled by resistance against the sectoral and supranationalist aspects of Monnet/Spaak approach. First of all there was the plan by Baron Snoy of the Ministry of Economic Affairs for an OEEC Free Trade Area. Of more practical political importance, however, seems to have been the initiative of Belgian Minister of Foreign Trade Larock. He presented a number of "propositions d'ordre économique pouvant servir à une action politique à entreprendre par les pays de Benelux" in order to arrive at a "relance de l'intégration européenne". Larock's proposals originally dated from the fall 1954. In March 1955 he obtained some kind of official governmental support for his ideas which were now referred to, at least by the Dutch administration, as "the Belgian propos-

---

[27] NA, MR (401), Notulen Ministerraad 11.3.1955; Min. BZ, II, 913.100, No. 20, 'Conferentie Ministers van BZ K.S.G.', 15.4.1955; Min. BZ, II, 913.100, No. 134, memorandum Chef DWS to M., 15.4.1955; Min. BZ, II, 913.100, No. 134, – 'Ons K.S.G. initiatief en de O.E.E.C', 16.4.1955.

als". Like in November 1954, Larock suggested the creation of a Free Trade Area limited to certain products, mainly manufactured goods, namely those for which the total factor costs were more or less equal in the participating countries. For those products alone tariffs and quantitative restrictions within the Area would be abolished. Trade policy with regard to third countries would remain within the competence of the individual states.

Institutionally the Larock Plan was based on the principle of intergovernmental cooperation (supranationality, Larock suggested, might be introduced later on, on the basis of a common agreement) and in connection with this the Belgian minister hoped for British participation. For France he suggested an empty chair policy: if necessary this country would be allowed to join in a later stage when it considered that its economy was strong enough. Apart from the Free Trade Area idea, the Larock proposals were concerned among other things with a common Western European public works policy and a common plan for road construction. A common Fund for Restructuring would help to defray setbacks and distortions caused by the increased competition.[28]

In addition to these two more or less governmental initiatives the Belgian ex-minister Van Houtte launched, on March 17, a plan which resembled the Snoy concept. He argued for a Benelux initiative within the OEEC for the formation of a group of countries which would be willing to accept a gradual tariff reduction over a period of ten to fifteen years and the simultaneous abolition of quantitative trade restrictions up to 100%.[29] Last but not least, the Dutch Member of Parliament Blaisse drew up a "pre-integration programme", published in February 1955. It took the line that, for the present, the political situation was not ripe for real economic integration. Free movements of goods, capital, labour and services between the Western European countries would require a preliminary European development programme aimed at the removal of both the economic and psychological barriers to integration. Among other things his programme comprised suggestions for an intergovernmental plan for the development of Southern Italy, a common project on agricultural productivity, and one for the construction of atomic energy and natural gas plants, and technical and financial cooperation in the

---

28 Min. BZ, II, 913.100, No. 164, memorandum Sous-Chef DWS to M, 21.3.1954; and: "De Belgische integratieplannen", 24.3.1955; and: "Relance de l'intégration européenne. Propositions d'ordre économique pouvant servir à une action politique entreprendre par des pays de Benelux".

29 Min. BZ, II, 913.100, No. 131, "Analytische vergelijking van de verschillende plannen voor Europese economische samenwerking", 29.3.1955.

field of housing. The Council of Europe was, according to Blaisse, the most suitable institution to start action along these lines.[30]

Moreover, this sudden accumulation of integration plans was not limited to the Low Countries. Also, in the Strasbourg Parliament, the OEEC and the European League for Economic Cooperation, more or less original proposals were formulated. In Western Germany the 1953/54 debate between Adenauer and Erhard and their adherents was getting into full swing again: As Adenauer supported a political orientation towards Western Europe and therefore, preferential economic relations with that part of the Continent; whereas Erhard as his disciples advocated a fundamentally liberal policy without discriminatory elements aimed at world-wide free trade and hence frowned upon regional block formation.[31]

Finally, Spaak continued and even intensified his deliberations with Monnet. The latter, who would remain President of the High Authority until a successor was appointed, was by now busy writing a declaration in which he embodied his ideas concerning an extension of the supranational powers of the ECSC to the energy sector (oil, natural gas and electricity) and to the transport sector (land, water and air transport including the railways). Moreover, inspired by the views of his collaborator Armand, he now proposed the creation of an entirely new High Authority for common research on, and the production of, *atomic* energy for civil purposes. Because of the recent scientific developments in this field Monnet expected atomic energy to lead to a "new industrial revolution". Therefore he regarded it as a promising nucleus for European integration in general: since the European countries concerned lacked the facilities to develop the potentialities of this atomic energy individually, there was a natural community of interests to arrive at close cooperation in this field.[32]

Certainly, all this planning for the future of Europe was reinforced by the fall of the Mendès-France government on February 5, 1955. The subsequent formation of the Faure Cabinet, in which the "anti-European" (i.e. anti-integration) Gaullist element was considerably weaker and in which the pro-European M.R.P. now held important posts, contributed to a resurgence of pro-integration hopes and expectations. In fact, Faure's inaugural address to the *Conseil de la République* suggested that the new French Government would take a more positive stance than its predecessor. But the real objectives of French government policy remained as yet unclear; new supranational institutions

---

30 *Ibidem.*

31 *Ibidem.*

32 For a final draft see: Min. BZ, II, 913.100, No. 19, "Projet de Declaration"; Min. BZ, II, 913.100, No. 139, Letter Beyen to Spaak, 14.4.1955.

would probably be impossible. As a result, the "new optimism" of February/March 1955 was a cautious one.

It is noteworthy that all the schemes for general (or "horizontal") economic integration discussed took the line that some form of intensified intergovernmental cooperation was the best, or at least the most realistic, goal to be aimed at. Faure too stated that the French interest would be primarily concentrated on "cooperation" in the fields of electricity, transport and atomic energy; sectors which corresponded with those chosen by Jean Monnet for his sectoral supranational approach. Clarification of French intentions was to be delayed until the French Parliament had ratified the Paris Agreements.[33]

Nevertheless, a new political situation had developed with new hopes and European integration plans "springing up like mushrooms", as Beyen commented at the end of March 1955.[34] The Dutch minister himself and the Dutch Government in general, however, were not so easily affected by the winds of change. The change of tack came in March, sparked off by the Spaak-Monnet talks.

The fall of Mendès-France, the emergence of the Faure Cabinet and the development of a more optimistic climate in general had not failed to impress both Spaak and Monnet. During the last weeks of February the latter arrived at the conclusion that his declaration on the future of Western European integration – originally meant to be his valedictory address and the programme of his projected pressure group for the United States of Europe – might serve in the near future as the basis for a joint communiqué to be issued by the six community governments.[35]

---

33 Min. BZ, II, 913.100, No. 19: "Notes" (GS No. 46999-175t). Min. BZ, II, 913.100, No. 139, codetelegram ambassador Paris, 14.4.1955. Min. BZ, II. GS, 913.10, "Europese Integratie IV": "Toezeggingen door Faure aan de M.R.P. gedaan tijdens zijn kabinets-formaties", 15.3.1955.

34 Min. BZ, II, 913.100, No. 19: "Nota inzake de Europese integratie" accompanying letter 24.3.1955.

35 During the first months of 1955 diplomatic sources suggested that the French government was unwilling to renew Monnet's mandate as President of the ECSC's High Authority. Consequently, faced with the unlikelihood of a second term, Monnet pondered on alternative ways to carry the European integration project forward. On 13 October 1955 he launched his Action Committee for the United States of Europe, bringing together the major political parties and trade unions of Western Europe in a combined effort to exert pressure on the national governments for the sake of European integration. P. Winand, *Eisenhower, Kennedy and the United States of Europe*, New York: St. Martin's Press, 1993, pp. 72-73; Interview with Max Kohnstamm in: A.G. Harryvan, J. van der Harst and S. van Voorst (eds.), *Voor Nederland en Europa. Politici en ambtenaren over het Nederlandse Europabeleid en de Europese integratie, 1945-1975*, Amsterdam: Boom, 2001, pp. 81-117, (pp. 101-102); J. Monnet, *Mémoires*, Paris: Fayard, 1976, pp. 475-488.

When the Benelux Foreign Ministers met on March 10, 1955, in order to discuss the problem of Monnet's successor, Spaak proposed to hold a meeting of the Ministers of Foreign Affairs of the ECSC countries shortly after the ratification of the Paris Agreements by the French Parliament. At such a meeting the French could be invited either to produce, or to agree to, a declaration of intent on the future of European integration. Such a joint statement, Spaak argued, would serve as a basis for further governmental action. Also, if the French thus explicitly committed themselves to a new more positive European policy, the effect might be that Monnet would reconsider his resignation as President of the High Authority.[36]

Beyen's reaction had been prepared. Armed with the news of the new Monnet-Spaak policy line Theo Bot, the Director of the Western Cooperation Section of the Dutch Foreign Ministry, had produced a preparatory note for the Benelux summit in which he implicitly suggested that the time had come to change tack and take a more active stance on the issue of Western European integration. The note briefly summarized the traditional Dutch objections against further sectoral integration either within or without the ECSC[37] and taking into account these objections, a different course was suggested contrary to the one Monnet advocated:

> In our opinion it would be preferable to pursue further integration by reverting to the basic ideas of the Beyen plan (gradual realization of a tariff community, the elimination of trade restrictions, the creation of a European Fund) and to prepare for its realization by a gradual ripening of both the European political climate and European economic conditions.[38]

The wording of this note was cautious. Beyen however, now obviously convinced of the necessity to embark upon a new and more active policy, did not limit himself to "gradual ripening". At the Benelux summit he approved of Spaak's plan to aim at an ECSC conference in order to provoke a clarification of French intentions. But, as he pointed out emphatically, this did not mean that he took sides with Monnet's particular proposals for sectoral integration. On the contrary, within a

---

36 NA, MR (401), Notulen Ministerraad 11.3.1955, J. Monnet, *Mémoires*, Paris: Fayard, 1976, p. 47.

37 Implicit in the extension of the existing community, he argued, was the danger that the administration of the new sectors concerned, might be dominated by, and subordinated to, the interests of the coal and steel sectors. The objection against sectoral integration in general was that the distinct fields of economic activity were so closely connected with each other that the sector approach as compared with the general approach could not really work: the sectoral divide could only be artificial and would create problems of its own.

38 Min. BZ, II, 93.100, No. 139: "Bijeenkomst Benelux-Ministers van Buitenlandse Zaken", 8.3.1955.

fortnight Beyen drew up a discussion paper for Cabinet in which he proposed nothing less than a Benelux initiative for new intergovernmental negotiations, aimed at the creation of a Western European Economic Union. The Beyen plan had thus been resurrected. Once again, the Dutch would launch an initiative for *horizontal* integration on a *supranational* basis in Western Europe.[39]

Beyen's bold proposal was based on several motives, most of them mentioned by Beyen in his note or presented during the Cabinet discussions. He referred to the recent changes in France and the subsequent mushrooming of integration and cooperation plans. He discussed briefly the ideas of Larock, Monnet, van Houtte, Blaisse, the European Movement and the activities of the Strasbourg Parliament and concluded that there was the imminent danger of enormous confusion. It would be most unfortunate, he argued, if the Dutch found themselves in a position in which they could only react to proposals put forward by others. Such a situation would weaken the Dutch position considerably. Consequently, in cooperation with the Benelux partners the Government should take a positive stand of its own. Stating the policy goals which should be embodied in this stance, Beyen defined in a rather classical way the combination of commercial self-interest and European idealism, which seems to have governed Dutch European policy during the 1950s: "We aim at a real intensification of cooperation between the European Countries and at the development and stabilisation of the European market (for our exports)".[40]

In view of all this, the course then proposed by many advocates of European integration was hardly attractive for the Dutch. The choice against further sectoral integration, embodied in the Luxembourg resolution, was still as valid as ever and thus the objection against the Monnet approach still held. Moreover, he deprecated the general opinion that horizontal economic cooperation in Europe for the present would only be possible on an intergovernmental basis and cooperation on a supranational basis would only be possible for specific sectors, related to those administered by the ECSC.

As things stood, Beyen wrote, such general statements about Europe's potential in the field could neither be proved nor refused. Admittedly, the gusto for horizontal integration on a supranational basis, especially in France, was not particularly impressive. He refused, however, to take for granted that the fate of the EDC had proven that Western Europe was not ripe for supranational institutions *in general*. More-

39 NA, MR (401), Notulen Ministerraad 11.3.1955. Min. BZ, II, 913.100, No. 19: "Nota inzake de Europese integratie", accompanying letter 24.3.1955.

40 Min. BZ, II, 913.100, No. 19: "Nota inzake de Europese integratie", accompanying letter 24.3.1955.

over, the many supporters of integration who, boasting of their "realism" and now advocating intergovernmental schemes or sectoral integration, were under an illusion; neither of the two would, as such, lead to general economic and political integration of Western Europe. In brief: "The ruining of the EDC project has not affected the approach of the Dutch Government". Therefore, there was no reason whatsoever why the Dutch should not try to revive the EPC-negotiations, and to aim at a new European Community, now with an exclusively economic task on the basis of the Beyen Plan.

The first Dutch goal should be a Benelux initiative along these lines. So far Spaak had not gone deeply into the problem. Given their previous discussions, however, it was quite feasible that he would sympathize with the proposed idea, Beyen argued. Also, such an initiative would not necessarily be incompatible with possible extension of the ECSC to transport and energy. As before, the Dutch would not fundamentally resist proposals to that end. And again, as before, they would not accept integration schemes for the WEU. Finally, in order to improve its chances of realization, the Benelux proposal should allow for a special transitional period for France in order to enable that country to modernize its economy, as well as a system of exceptive clauses for agriculture.[41]

Beyen's proposal gave rise to an extensive debate within the Dutch Government. Prime Minister Drees spoke in plain terms of his scepticism. He and his policy advisors were of the opinion that there was not much chance of making a success of the proposal. The other European countries would not forego the possibility of protecting their national economies. Hence, in view of the former EPC negotiations, there was a serious risk that a new supranational institution without real administrative powers would be the lamentable result. He would not disapprove of a supranational institution if a real customs union were to be realized, but he did not think that feasible, also because his Ministry seriously foresaw the return to power of Mendès-France. Drees' advisors were inclined to regard Beyen's proposal as a rather unhappy result of parliamentary pressure. The Prime Minister himself would prefer an approach along the lines of the Van Houtte Plan, i.e. aiming at a Western European market without the clutter of supranational organs and joint policies. All things considered, he was in favour of an attempt to investigate possibilities for common action at the Benelux level.[42]

The extreme opposite stance was taken by Sicco Mansholt and his Ministry of Agriculture, a stronghold of die-hard supporters of the

---

41 *Ibidem*.

42 NA, MR (509), letter Fock to Drees, 25.3.1955. NA, MR (401), Notulen Ministerraad 21.3.1955 and 28.3.1955.

"institutionalist" and/or "federalist" approach to European integration. Here the Foreign Minister's proposal for a Benelux initiative equally met with a kind reception. Beyen's ideas with regard to the contents of such an initiative however were considered "an error". Once more, it was argued, the accent was laid on the traditional Dutch interest, the furthering of intra-European trade and the creation of a customs union. France, Italy and Germany would not go along with this approach. EPC experience, they reasoned, had made clear that general economic integration could not be created on the basis of intergovernmental negotiations: new talks on the formation of a customs union would once again lead to endless discussions about elementary preconditions like the harmonisation of fiscal, social and monetary policies. Complex problems of this magnitude should not be dealt with by intergovernmental negotiations and an intergovernmental treaty. They needed to be resolved gradually by supranational organs. Therefore the Dutch initiative should aim at the creation of a *political* community administered by a supranational institution with powers for the gradual development of a joint economic policy. Political integration should be the basis and starting point for a development towards economic integration (exactly the reverse of Beyen's thinking).[43]

In spite of this strategic difference of opinion, Beyen and Mansholt engaged in what can well be called a tactical coalition throughout the 1952-1956 period. Mansholt, by his relentless hammering in the Cabinet on his undiluted federalist anvil and by preaching a European institutionalist approach, provided Beyen with political leeway. Claerly, in comparison with Mansholt's conceptions, the Beyen plan was much more geared towards the Dutch national interest than Mansholt's European idealism. Hence, Mansholts extremism helped Beyen gaining ground for his approach, even – and significantly so – with Prime Minister Drees. This state of affairs was no coincidence. Mansholt and Beyen engaged in regular consultations and appear to have decided on a "good cop" versus "bad cop" division of labour within government deliberations. Mansholt, who did not suffer fools gladly, conversily held Beyen in high esteem, thought him a *grand monsieur*, as well as an ally and an inspirator. When Beyen left the Foreign Ministry in the fall of 1956 this constituted a severe blow for Mansholt, both politically and

43 Archief van het Ministerie van Landbouw en Visserij Den Haag (henceforth: Min. Landb.), GS archief 5.631 Eur. integr. bespr. 1955-56: Note by Van der Lee for Mansholt, 25.3.1955. Min. BZ, II, 913.100, No. 19: letter Mansholt to Beyen, 26.3.1955. Thiemeyer analyses Mansholt's "vast vertrouwen" (great confidence) in European cooperation and the latter's conviction that the creation of supranational European institutions was "onontkoombaar" (inevitable). Guido Thiemeyer, 'Sicco Mansholt and European Suprantionalism', W. Loth (ed.), *La gouvernance supranationale dans la construction européenne*, Brussels: Bruylant 2005, pp. 39-53 (pp. 46-47).

personally. Mansholt briefly considered the option of trying to succeed Beyen as Foreign Minister, then projected his ambitions on the nascent European Commission.[44]

Zijlstra, the Minister of Economic Affairs, basically agreed with Drees in that he emphasized the importance of the aim of arriving at a customs union. With regard to supranationality he was more positive than the latter: referring to the Benelux experience he underlined that for the final aim, i.e. a fully-fledged economic union, supranational institutions would be inevitable for the formulation of common policies. For the first phase – a "simple" customs union – one could, however, do without such common institutions. Here too Benelux could serve as an example. More generally Zijlstra showed interest in the Larock concept of horizontal integration limited to a selected number of sectors and products.

In March 1953, Mansholt was not present at the discussion in Cabinet. Consequently Beyen found himself in a rather isolated position when he tried to defend the values of a supranational stance as such. The Foreign Minister "had a hard time" reported Mansholt's substitute. According to the latter Beyen had to give in, in that he was made to accept the primacy of the customs union aim over the supranationality goal, now willing to regard the latter as the coping-stone. Beyen also had to deal with severe criticism of his suggestion concerning a special set of clauses for France. This was considered a premature concession which might be misused by the French negotiators. Generally speaking the reactions in Cabinet can be characterized as rather sceptical. Nevertheless, it was agreed that Beyen would continue the preparations for a Benelux initiative "to moot the question of economic integration".[45]

V. The Benelux Memorandum for a European Relaunch

On April 4, 1955, Beyen sent Spaak a note, basically an abridged version of his cabinet paper, suggesting a joint Benelux initiative. The time had come, he wrote, for a "prise de position commune nettement définie de la part du Bénelux". The three Benelux governments should work together in order to launch an initiative for the forthcoming ECSC Foreign Ministers Conference. The aim of such an initiative would be the creation of "une communauté supranationale, ayant pour tâche de réaliser l'intégration économique de l'Europe au sens général en passant par la voie d'une Union Douanière à la réalisation d'une Union Econo-

44 Interview with Mansholt's *chef de cabinet*, dr. J. van der Lee, 14.5.2007, The Hague.

45 Landb., GS archief 5, 631 Eur. integr. bespr. 1955-56; "Aantekening voor de heer Minister: betreft Ministerraadsvergadering van 28 Maart – Benelux initiatief voor hervatting Europese integratiebesprekingen", 28.3.1955. NA, MR (401), Notulen Ministerraad 28.3.1955.

mique".[46] Beyen realized, he wrote, that proposals of this kind "pourraient rencontrer une opposition assez sérieuse de nos amis français". That however was not sufficient a reason for withholding those proposals. Also he underlined the compatibility of general integration with further sectoral integration and suggested that the new Community would be a most suitable institution for carrying out the development programme and the other "interesting suggestions" of Larock.

Meanwhile, the French Parliament had ratified the Paris Agreements and Spaak, who was still in close contact with Monnet, had reached the same conclusion: that the time for action had come. On April 2, 1955, without prior consultations with the Benelux partners, he sent the Foreign Ministers of France, Germany and Italy a proposal for a joint declaration on European integration for the forthcoming ECSC meeting (which at that time was scheduled to take place in late April). Spaak proposed that the six countries should express their common intention to pursue the process of integration by an extension of the powers of the ECSC into the sectors of transport and conventional energy; they should create a new organ for atomic energy, linking it to the ECSC. In order to draw up a treaty to this end a governmental conference should be organized, presided over by Monnet.

The Spaak proposal, which did not mention anything concerning horizontal integration, was not received favourably. The French had not yet made up their mind and did not want to pursue such a direct course of action. Also, Prime Minister Faure felt little sympathy for Monnet and would not agree to a European relaunch presided over by the latter. The Germans were still occupied with their domestic differences and did not like the idea of integration in the field of nuclear energy. The Italian reply was vague; the Rome Government did not want to commit itself.[47]

This disappointing experience may have contributed to Spaak's interest in the ideas of his Dutch colleague. His reaction to Beyen's note was positive although at the same time pessimistic. He would gladly support Beyen's cause, he wrote, but doubted seriously if the proposal would be acceptable to the French. Nevertheless, he agreed with Beyen that they ought to give it a try.[48] Still, in his opinion, it would be advisable to make sure that there would be a possibility of "orderly with-

46 Min. BZ, II, 913.100, No. 19: "Note", (GS No. 46999-175t).

47 Spaak, *Combats Inachevés II*, pp. 62-63, Snoy et d'Oppuers, "Un témoin", pp. 23-24.

48 As he wrote in his letter of April 7, 1955: "Les idées que vous (...) défendez me paraissent excellentes et fondamentalement, je suis d'accord avec vous. Mais je me demande si la politique que vous préconisez a quelque chance de succès. Je me demande, notamment, si le Gouvernement français peut l'accepter. Peut-être et je serais prêt à me rallier à cette idée devons-nous faire l'expérience", II, 913.100, No. 19: letter Spaak to Beyen, 7.4.1955.

drawal" (*position de repli*); a suggestion which can hardly have been encouraging for Beyen. Referring to the latter's statement on the compatibility of general/sectoral integration Spaak proposed to combine tactics: "On peut mener à la fois la lutte, pour obtenir un grand marché européen et en même temps tâcher de régler certains problèmes par secteur".[49]

Both approaches could be embodied in a Benelux proposal, he concluded. He continued by an exposition on the Monnet approach, stressed the importance of a governmental conference to draw up a Treaty for further sectoral integration (!), and voiced his expectation that a development along these lines would make Monnet reconsider his resignation and stand for a second term of office. Obviously Spaak did not have great faith in the possibility of a governmental conference on the formation of a customs union.

Beyen wrote back on April 14. He concluded that agreement had been reached and emphasized: "Je ne m'oppose nullement à l'idée d'une extension des compétences de la C.E.C.A.". Such an extension might be useful, Beyen agreed, although it would not enhance political solidarity in Europe and as such would not lead to European unification. Moreover, Beyen wrote, on a more practical level he had some doubts if all subsectors of transport and energy could be administered by a sectoral authority in a viable way. For oil, for instance, such an administration might be rather difficult to realise. As far as electricity was concerned, he was not sure that this sub-sector would really need supranational organisation. Also, there was no denying that transport integration was urgently needed: but was the ECSC the best framework for such an operation, he wondered.[50] In spite of this criticism Beyen's reply constituted a landmark, in paving the way for a joint Benelux proposal, comprising suggestions for both general and sectoral integration.

Meanwhile, within the Dutch Government, the discussion on the customs union approach continued. In practice this meant that several

---

49 Min. BZ, II, 913.100, No. 19: letter Spaak to Beyen, 7.4.1955. Min. BZ, II, 913.100, No. 139: codetelegram embassy Brussels to Beyen. 5.4.1955.

50 Min. BZ, II, 913.100, No. 139: letter Beyen to Spaak, 14.4.1955. Beyen's doubts reflected the results of the discussions in the Dutch Cabinet on the advantages and disadvantages of the sectoral approach: Oil should be omitted, it was argued, in order not to jeopardise relations with the oil companies. Moreover there was the fear that "oil-integration" within the ECSC would lead to extra levies on this product (meaning higher consumer prices) in order to finance a low coal price policy. Equally, responsibilities for the ECSC concerning transport did not seem a good idea, because this would probably lead to low costs of railway carriage policy and a corresponding need for government subsidies – both contrary to Dutch railway policy. Finally, with regard to electricity, cooperation at OEEC level had, according to the Cabinet, produced satisfactory results. NA, MR (401), Notulen Ministerraad 12.4.1955.

attempts were made to change Beyen's mind and to convince him of alleged errors and risks attached to his initiative.[51] For starters, the Foreign Minister had to deal with severe criticism within his own department. Beyen had written his March 24 cabinet paper alone and apparently without using preliminary drafts of civil servants. Consequently, the Directorate-General for the Economic and Military Aid Programme (DGEM) could, taken by surprise, only react after its discussion in Cabinet. In the beginning of April DGEM director Van der Beugel produced a note in which he denounced the new Beyen Plan as unrealistic. Referring to the experiences of the EPC negotiations and the lessons which could be drawn from Benelux, he stated that a custom union administered by a supranational organ would not be acceptable, neither for France, nor for the other ECSC countries: this initiative could only lead to lengthy discussions. Likewise, in his opinion, there was a real danger that the Beyen scheme would be used as the grounds for creating a supranational organisation without any real power. The institutionalist approach of Mansholt's Ministry of Agriculture provided a convincing illustration! An extension of the Coal and Steel Community competence, on the contrary, was feasible and this could be the alternative the Dutch should aim at. Admittedly, the traditional objections against sector integration were still valid as far as the creation of new pools was concerned; he argued that they would be considerably less valid in case of an extension of the already existing ECSC. The sole use of stressing horizontal integration would be that it would provide an opportunity to expose the Dutch long-term goals. Beyen himself replied that he failed to see why he should *not* moot the question of a customs union – "What are we afraid of?" he asked his fellow ministers – and reiterated that he would not resist an enlargement of ECSC powers.[52]

Beyen's conviction could not hide the fact that in his own Ministry only the Western Cooperation Section of the Foreign Ministry showed itself committed to the New Beyen Plan. Apart from the traditional economic arguments, this section presented a number of typically political motives, most of which concerned Germany. Horizontal integration and supranationality, for example, were deemed to be considered

51 Min. BZ, II, 913.100, No. 139: "Nota betreffende Benelux-initiatief tot hervatting van de integratie-besprekingen", 14.4.1955. Min. BZ, II, 913.100, No. 19: letter Beyen to Mansholt, 22.4.1955. Min. BZ, II, 913.100, No. 139: letter Mansholt to Beyen, 28.4.1955. Min. BZ, II, 913.100, No. 19: letter Spierenburg to Beyen, 27.4.1955. Min. BZ, II, 913.100, No. 131: letter Zijlstra to Beyen, 27.4.1955.

52 Min. BZ, II, 913.100, No. 19: memorandum No. 775 from Van der Beugel to Beyen, 5.4.1955. Min. BZ, II, 913.100, No. 134: memorandum No. 815 from Van der Beugel to Beyen, 12.4.1955. Min. BZ, II, 913.100, No. 151: "Europese economische integratie", 7.4.1955.

in order to avoid both the political neutralization of Western Germany and resurging nationalism in that country.[53]

Beyen, however, stuck to his guns. An official of the Ministry of Agriculture informed minister Mansholt about Beyen's position in no uncertain terms:

> Van der Beugel informs me that Minister Beyen clings with desperate tenacity to the customs union idea as the starting point for the new talks. Allegedly nothing can put the scheme out of his head, although both supporters and antagonists of integration at his Department do not agree with the customs union approach.[54]

Reactions from outside the Foreign Ministry were hardly more encouraging. At the Agricultural Ministry two notes were drawn up to demonstrate the desirability of aiming at the creation of common institutions, with initially rather limited powers on the one hand, and a lack of feasibility of the customs union idea on the other.[55] Spierenburg, the Dutchman on the High Authority, sent the Foreign Minister the most recent draft of Monnet's "Declaration". In the accompanying letter he wrote that in his opinion the ECSC countries would be able to agree with one another only on the point of sectoral extension of the existing Community. Minister Zijlstra of Economic Affairs sent Beyen an essay of his own hand on the merits of the Larock Plan.[56] Various observers and advisors pointed to recently started Franco-German negotiations on intensified economic cooperation between those two countries, seemingly predicting a return to bilateralism rather than a move forward to supranationalism. Serious blows to Dutch trade could be the consequence.[57]

---

53 Min. BZ, II, 913.100, No. 19, memorandum Van der Beugel to Beyen, No. 775, 5.4.1955; Min. BZ, II, 913.100, No. 134, memorandum Van der Beugel aan Beyen, No. 815, 12.4.1955; Min. BZ II, 913.100, No. 151, "Europese economische integratie", 7.4.1955.

54 Landb., GS archief 5, 631 Eur. integr. bespr. 1955-56: note Van der Wee for Mansholt, 19.4.1955.

55 Min. BZ, II, 913.100, No. 139, 'Nota betreft Benelux-initiatief tot hervatting van de integratie-besprekingen', 14.4.1955; with accompanying letter Mansholt to Beyen, 20.4.1955; BA., 11, 913.000, No. 19, Letter to Mansholt, 22.4.1955; Min. BZ, II, 913.000, No. 139, Letter Mansholt to Beyen, 28.4.1955.

56 Min. BZ, II, 913.100, No. 19, letter Spierenburg to Beyen, 27.4.1955; Min. BZ, II, 913.100, No. 131, letter Zijlstra to Beyen, 27.4.1955.

57 Min. BZ, II, GS, 913.10, Europese integratie deel IV, "Toezegging door Faure aan de M.R.P. gedaan bij zijn kabinetsformatie", 15.4.1955; and: Codetelegram, Van Boetzelaer – Den Haag, 19.4.1955; Min. BZ, II, 913.100, No. 139, Codetelegram Van Boetzelaer – Den Haag, 13.4.1955; 3.Z., 11, 913.100, No. 19, "Notitie over de economische aspecten van de Frans-Duitse samenwerking", March 1955.

All in all, the sources suggest that Beyen within his own Ministry as well as in Cabinet and Benelux, was in an isolated position in that he was one of the few who was actually convinced of both the desirability and the feasibility of his scheme.[58] Indeed, notwithstanding a general lack of encouragement, Beyen stuck to his point of view. On April 21, in a speech before the Council of the European Movement he made his proposals public, thus confronting the opposition against it, within as well as without the Foreign Ministry, with a *fait accompli*.[59]

The Benelux Foreign Ministers met on April 23, in The Hague. Bech, who had been informed by Spaak about the latter's discussions and correspondence with Beyen, had not been able to come to the meeting (but would approve of the results afterwards). Beyen and Spaak had discussions on the basis of the latest draft of Monnet's declaration. Initially, the President of the High Authority had frowned upon Beyen's customs union's proposal: "Il ne croyait pas opportun de heurter de front par l'idée d'un Marché Commun les puissantes traditions protectionistes de la France".[60] And only the final draft of Monnet's paper allowed for something that could be described as a second phase, i.e. after the enlargement of ECSC competence, in which the member countries would begin to "fixer les conditions et le programme d'une intégration générale".[61] From Beyen's point of view the Monnet proposal was embarrassing by its lack of ambition. In accordance with what they had decided upon, the Benelux ministers chose for a different course: sectoral and horizontal integration could be combined to complement one another and were to be equally proposed. On the basis of their instructions a team of Dutch and Belgian civil servants drew up a joint "Memorandum des Pays Benelux aux Six Pays de la C.E.C.A." for the forthcoming Foreign Ministers conferences of the Six. The argument of the document was that the moment had come to enter a new phase in the process of European integration and that such integration had to be realized first of all on the economic level: A unified Europe could be created by means of developing common institutions, the progressive fusion of the national economies, the establishment of a great common market and the progressive harmonisation of social policies. This was worked out in a set of practical proposals for sectoral integration in the fields of transport, classical energy and atomic energy (prepared by the Belgian administration) and one for the establishment of an economic community based on a common market along the lines of the Beyen Plan (prepared by the Dutch administration). Also, the harmonisation of

58 Min. BZ, II, 913.100, No. 131: memorandum Bot to Beyen, 7.4.1955.

59 Winand, *Eisenhower, Kennedy*, p. 73.

60 Snoy et d'Oppuers, "Un témoin", pp. 23-24.

61 Min. BZ, II, 913.100, No. 19: "Projet de Déclaration".

social policies (regulations on the length of the working week and holidays, overpay and nightwork etc.), was mentioned as an indispensable aim in its own right. An intergovernmental conference should be charged with studying these projects and the drawing up of a treaty. The Memorandum was carefully worded: In the institutional proposals neither the idea of "supranationality" nor the concept of a "High Authority" were mentioned. Nevertheless, for both the Atomic Pool and the Common Market "common authorities" were suggested, for classical energy and transport on the other hand an 'organism' would do. Clearly, Spaak and Beyen did not want to awaken the strong anti-supranational sentiments in France and elsewhere. The institutional framework therefore, they proposed, should be worked out by the above mentioned intergovernmental conference. Also, the Common Market proposals, although based on the original Beyen Plan, were much more open-ended and flexible than the rigid set of detailed regulations the Dutch had so vehemently stuck to in 1953/54. Generally, the document was characterized by a "certain vagueness", which, according to Beyen, had the advantage that it facilitated the adherence of the other governments to the basic idea of organizing a conference on the issues raised by the Benelux. Equally, the mentioning *expressis verbis* of the need to harmonize social policies meant an important recognition of traditional French claims on this issue, suggesting a new Dutch policy line.[62] Benelux experiences appear to have played a part on this issue (see Chapter 3).

The Beyen/Spaak Memorandum was not favourably received by the Dutch Government. The diluted New Beyen Plan proposals and, generally, the "hybrid" character of the Memorandum met with criticism. Unfortunately for the critics, the dual approach which it embodied was an inevitable consequence of the way it had come into being, i.e. as a compromise between the Benelux partners. Consequently, only a few minor changes were introduced. On May 9, 1955, the Dutch Cabinet grudgingly consented the official presentation of the Memorandum to the French, West German and Italian Governments.[63]

VI. Getting Down to the Brass Tacks at the June 1955 Messina Conference

In spite of the careful tactics underlying the Benelux initiative, it did not receive an ecstatic welcome in the Western European capitals. The Paris government, diplomatic sources revealed, would continue to block any decision by the Six which would force it to submit a new European

---

[62] Min. BZ, II, 913.100, No. 139: "Memorandum des Pays Benelux aux six pays de la C.E.C.A." and: codetelegram Beyen/Luns to Washington, 23.5.1955.

[63] NA, MR (401), Notulen Ministerraad 6.5.1955 and 9.5.1955.

treaty for parliamentary approval in the short run, i.e. before the 1956 elections. And on the general economic integration proposal a lengthy Parisian debate resulted in the conclusion that the establishment of a common market had to be considered as a very long-term project which could create considerable problems for the French economy and which was closely connected with the problem of the future of the French overseas territories.[64] In Bonn the Benelux proposals led to a revival of the conflict between chancellor Adenauer and economics minister Erhard and their respective allies. For Adenauer, primarily concerned with making the Bundesrepublik a full-fledged partner in the Western Block, European integration in general was of the utmost importance. Erhard and his supporters, however, considered European economic integration potentially dangerous for trade liberalization on a worldwide scale, because it would lead to regional protectionism and state dirigisme. Erhard had denounced the Beyen Plan ever since 1953. The Bonn memorandum for the forthcoming Foreign Minister's conference, written in reply to the Benelux one, thus bore the marks of a difficult compromise, showing that within Germany the reticent forces were still strong.[65] True, the German memorandum subscribed to the principal ideas of the Benelux proposal and, as Küsters points out, constituted a landmark in that for the first time general (or horizontal) integration was explicitly accepted as an end of German foreign policy.[66] The point of departure of the German reasoning, however, remained the work done in GATT and OEEC, the primacy of which was equally explicitly stated. Liberalizing measures between the Six in fact would have to allow for the gradual establishment of a common market. New institutions, let alone supranational ones, were not envisaged: within the ECSC a consultative organ had to be charged with the elaboration of practical proposals for cooperation.

In Brussels and The Hague the conclusion was drawn that the *Bundesregierung* would not give its support to new supranational initiatives. In fact, German reticence on this issue reflected not just anti-integrationist and anti-supranational sentiments in the Bonn government itself, but also the wider spread opinion that since France, like before,

---

64 Min. BZ, II, 913.100, No. 131: "Rapport uit Parijs inzake Europese integratie", 25.4.1955. Min. BZ, II, GS, 913.10 Europese integratie IV: codetelegram Paris 5.5.1955. Min. BZ, II, 913.100, No. 134: codetelegram, Van Boetzelaer, 27.5.1955.

65 Min. BZ, II, 913.100, No. 139: "Memorandum der Bundesregierung über die Fortführung der Integration", accompanying letter 27.5.1955.

66 Küsters, *Wirtschaftsgemeinschaft*, 118. The German Memorandum even complemented its Benelux counterpart in proposing the gradual introduction of free movement of labour within the future common market, the drafting up of a set of rules for fair competition and the creation of a capital fund for promoting productive investments.

was the potential stumbling block for new integration efforts, no proposal should go beyond what the French government could accept.[67]

Faced with these discouraging reactions Beyen and Spaak decided to present their proposal in an even more open and flexible fashion. Before the proposed intergovernmental conference would start drafting up treaties, Beyen suggested, the ground should be prepared by an experts conference: these experts should explore independently from their national governments the room for common action on the issues singled out by the forthcoming ministers conference. Their report should then serve as a basis for the actual treaty negotiations. Also, the experts' conference should occupy itself with all possible kinds of future cooperation in Europe, intergovernmental schemes included; this would enable countries from outside the Six, especially the UK, to participate in the proceedings. All this, Beyen reasoned, would facilitate a positive French reaction while the need for supranational solutions would nevertheless be demonstrated. Spaak agreed, adding the suggestion that the secretary-general of this expert's conference should be a "political personality". Clearly the Belgian minister had in mind the unsatisfactory results of the 1953/54 EPC conferences when national experts had been unable to come to terms with each other. In the new set up the political personality's chairmanship should squeeze a maximum of agreement out of the delegates, he reasoned. Thus, in reaction to the alleged French and German reticence the original Benelux proposal was extended with a procedural supplement.[68]

Indeed, the last weeks before the ministers' conference, which was finally scheduled to take place at Messina (Italy) during the first two days of June 1955, the perspectives for the Benelux initiative seemed to be far from certain. This induced Spaak, Beyen and Bech to adopt a minimalist stance: discussing tactics on the morning before the start of the conference they decided not to oppose their colleagues' choice, be it in favour of sector integration or the common market approach. Instead they would throw in all their political weight for getting the Benelux procedural proposals accepted.[69] The minutes of the Messina conference

67 Min. BZ, II, 91.3.100, No. 139: codetelegram Lamping, 27.5.1955. II, GS, 913.10 Europese integratie IV: codetelegram, Van Boetzelaer, 5.5.1955.

68 Min. BZ, II, 913.1000, No. 20: "Betreft Conferentie van Ministers van Buitenlandse Zaken der Zes op 1 Juni 1955", 19.5.1955; Min. BZ, II, 913-100, No. 19: posttelegram Van Harinxma, 25.5.1955. Min. BZ, II, 913.100, No. 134: memorandum Chef DWS, 25.5.1955. Min. BZ, II, 913.100, No. 21: "Projet de Resolution", accompanying letter 25.5.1955.

69 Snoy et d'Oppuers, "Un témoin", pp. 23-24, J. Snoy et d'Oppuers, "Le rôle du Benelux dans la relance européenne en 1955": in *Belgisch buitenlands beleid en internationale betrekkingen. Liber amicorum, Prof. Gui de Raymaeker*, Leuven, 1978. p. 232, J. Snoy et d'Oppuers, "Les étapes de la coopération européenne et les négo-

show that this turned out a wise approach. Both the French Foreign Minister Pinay and the German assistant secretary of state Hallstein, though both pro "European" themselves, made clear that their room for manoeuvre was extremely limited. Pinay stated that his government was in favour of an effort at sector integration for energy and transport. With regard to the common market proposal, however, he would not be able to bind his country to any clear cut commitment:

> Après l'échec auquel a abouti le Traité de la C.E.D., lui semble-t-il opportun de ne pas s'engager dans la voie de ce qui paraitrait idéalement souhaitable, mais de rester sur le terrain de ce qui est pratiquement possible. [...] Par conséquent, M. Pinay estime qu'il y aurait avantage à procéder d'abord par secteurs, parce que cette méthode permettrait un départ immédiat et une action rapide, tandis qu'une intégration générale postulerait l'harmonisation progressive des conditions économiques et sociales dans les six pays.[70]

Hallstein showed himself more in favour of the common market approach. On the institutional issue, however, the federal government did not want to go further, at least for the moment, than a consultative organ, he told his colleagues. And generally, as far as new organizations were concerned "le Gouvernement fédéral est d'avis qu'il faut éviter de créer de nouvelles institutions européennes".[71] These statements showed that no far reaching decisions were to be expected and both Spaak and Beyen, though stressing their fundamental belief that without supranationality no real solution could be expected, made clear that they were aware of this and underlined the openness and flexibility of their proposals. Spaak explained that he, "more desirous to obtain concrete results than to defend a theory" had considered it wise to put the emphasis on sector integration. If the meeting, however, preferred to embark on the more "audacious" course of general integration as well, so much the better... And Beyen frankly stated that his government did not expect the meeting to come up with real decisions or even statements of principles. For the moment what could be done was to indicate the issues and to organize an intergovernmental conference to work them out.

It was along these lines, in fact, that the deputies under the chairmanship of Belgium's Snoy et d'Oppuers finally worded the compromise which was accepted by the ministers early in the morning of the 3rd of June: The so-called Messina declaration envisaged an intergovernmental conference prepared by an experts conference under the chairmanship of

ciations relatives à une zone de libre échange" *Chronique Politique Étrangère* 12 (1959), pp. 569-623, p. 590.

70 Min. BZ, II 913.1000, No. 21: "Projet de procès-verbal de la réunion *C.E.C.A.*, des Ministres des Affaires Étrangères des États membres de la C.E.C.A. Messine 1er et 2 juin 1955", Luxembourg, 13-6-1955.

71 *Ibidem.*

a "political personality" as suggested by the Benelux countries. Moreover, the Declaration was heavily based on the Benelux memorandum in that it mentioned all its proposals for both sectoral and general integration. However, it did not mention them as aims on which agreement had been reached but explicitly as objects of study and possibly negotiations. Also, the Benelux wordings had been robbed of the last clear-cut policy content they had. Particularly its institutional suggestions were suppressed; even with regard to atomic energy, an issue on which everybody seemed to agree that a common effort would make sense and for which the Benelux had proposed a "common authority", the Declaration stated nothing more than the intention to "study" the creation of a "common organization". Yet, under the circumstances this was the best possible result for the Benelux countries and it was recognised as such by both Spaak and Beyen.[72]

VII. Discussion

From a Dutch foreign policy point of view the so-called *Relance européenne* was not so much a European relaunch rather than a continuation of existing national policies. Ever since 1952 the main aim of Dutch Euro-policy had been an economically integrated Western Europe along the lines of the Beyen Plan, i.e. a non-protectionist customs union or common market administered by a supranational institution.

The failure of the EDC and EPC marked a temporary setback for these aspirations but did not undermine or alter them significantly. Fear of "fake integration" and resurgence of French-German bilateralism, as well as the awareness that no concrete results were within reach made Beyen originally adopt a defensive stance. The fall of the French Mendès-France government then fulfilled the most important condition for a more active policy. The desire to take the initiative instead of being obliged to follow others acted as an extra inducement in making the Dutch Foreign Minister aspire to get the Beyen Plan back on the European negotiation table.

Beyen's position, however, turned out to be an isolated one: in both the Dutch Cabinet and Benelux, as well as in his own ministry, few were convinced of both the desirability and the feasibility of his proposal. The conviction that, whatever the contents of a future initiative, common Benelux action was to be regarded a *conditio sine qua non* for its success, made Spaak and Beyen arrive at a political compromise. The Benelux memorandum for the Messina conference combined Spaak's

72 *Ibidem*; NA, MR (511): "Résolution adoptée par les Ministres des Affaires Étrangères des États membres de la C.E.C.A., réunis à Messine les 1er et 2 juin 1955". Min. BZ, II, 913.100, No. 21: codetelegram Beyen/Luns to Washington, 8.6.1955.

Monnet-inspired proposals for sectoral integration with a relaunching of the Beyen Plan for general economic integration.

Its "hybrid" character, though, may well have been decisive in making the Benelux proposal a success at Messina: it had something to offer for everybody and yet pinned no party down on drastic commitments. The importance of the Messina Conference and Resolution, therefore, has been exaggerated in the political and historical literature. For some they have even got mythical proportions. The primary documents suggest a more detached approach. What basically happened at Messina is threefold: firstly, it put European integration back on the negotiation table; secondly, it was decided that the new talks would be on *economic* integration and thirdly, a certain *method* for these talks was agreed to.

Thus Messina created the conditions for successful negotiations, rather than being a decisive break-through in political terms. Beyen's "desperate tenacity" changed the mindsets of his Ministry, of the Dutch government as well as of his Benelux-colleagues. Combining their forces, Beyen and Spaak managed to exert substantial engineerial influence which, with the wisdom of hindsight, changed the agenda of the Six fundamentally.

Much of the Messina effect is to be attributed to Spaak and the way he subsequently put the Messina bridgehead to use. Securing appointment as the "Political Personality" in charge of the negotiations enabled him to split the expert talks in the fall of 1955 into two main groupings, one on Euratom and one on the Common Market. Time and again he would tell the delegates in the latter forum that their task was to work out a method how to realise the common market, not to pass judgement on its desirability. Looked upon from this angle, of all his efforts during the Relance Beyen's success in gaining Spaak's support for relaunching the common market ideal may have been the most significant.

CHAPTER III

Between Example and Spectre

The Impact of Benelux on the Netherlands' European Policy and the Making of the 1957 Common Market Treaty

Introduction

The significance of Benelux for the process of European integration during the 1950s and 1960s is stressed in the historical and economic literature in a twofold manner, both suggesting valuable resources for exerting engineering influence by the Smaller Powers concerned. In the first place, Benelux is portrayed as a precursor to the European Economic Community, which came into being from 1957 onwards. The economic and political experiences gained by Belgium, the Netherlands and Luxembourg as part of their Benelux co-operation are supposed to have played an important role in their negotiations with France, Italy and the Federal German Republic to achieve a broader based economic unity. The fact is that Benelux embodied the first actually realised attempt to come to regional-economic bloc formation in post-war Western Europe. Thus it acted as a *test laboratory* for European integration, a laboratory which pioneered real life and practical examples for both academic theory and political practice of economic integration processes. The lessons drawn from the Benelux experiment could be used in the 1950s for stands and stances of both the Benelux delegations themselves and those of their future EEC partners during the intergovernmental talks on the foundation of a European Political Community (EPC) and the subsequent EEC negotiations.

Secondly, foreign policy cooperation on European integration among the Benelux countries is emphasized. By streamlining their mutual positions as much as possible, Belgian, Dutch and Luxembourgian delegations are supposed to have succeeded in talking in near unison during the European negotiations fora as a result of which they were able to acquire a disproportionately large influence in their talks with their French, German and Italian colleagues.[1]

In the publications of the policy makers who were involved in EEC negotiations at the time great significance is given to both aspects of the role of the Benelux. Looking back, Dutch Foreign Minister Stikker (1948-1952) wrote in his memoirs: "Benelux during this initial period of European economic organization and cooperation, served as an inspiring model for the idea of unification". Benelux, "as a unit" gave "much greater power to Belgium, Luxemburg and The Netherlands than they could possibly have had as individual states".[2] Former permanent secretary of the Department of Economic Affairs in Brussels and co-signer of the EEC treaty, J.C. Snoy et d'Oppuers says: "C'est ainsi que dans la rédaction du Traité de Rome, un grand nombre de formules qui ont été finalement adoptées, étaient inspirées par l'expérience des pays de Benelux".[3]

Likewise, discussing the impact of Benelux during the 1950s and 1960s, Woyke draws the following conclusion: 'Das internationale Gehör, das sich Kleinstaaten durch Integration in Europa verschafft haben, steht in keinem Verhältnis zu ihrer tatsächlichen Bedeutung'.[4] According to him, Benelux has managed to retain this political significance up until the 1960s. Only at the time of entry by Denmark, Ireland and the United Kingdom in 1973 the Benelux countries are supposed to

---

1 In Grosbois' analysis, this foreign policy empowerment aim was the most important one: "car la création de cette organisation régionale n'avait pas pour objectif premier la réalisation d'une intégration économique entre les trois pays signataires. En exil à Londres, les pays membres de l'union Benelux y ont adhéré *avant tout* dans le but de créer une sorte de groupe de petites nations de l'Europe occidentale, afin que, dans les négociations internationales, leur point de vue soit désormais pris en compte par les grandes puissances", (emphasis mine, AGH), Th. Grosbois, "La Belgique et le Benelux: de l'universalisme au régionalisme", in: M. Dumoulin, Geneviève Duchenne and Arthe van Laer (ed.), *La Belgique, les petits états et la construction européenne*, Brussel: P.I.E.-Peter Lang, 2003, pp. 59-91 (p. 60). Although distinct, Hirsch argues, the two power resources, to wit the test laboratory experience and foreign policy cooperation, were far from separate. Benelux, precisely by using "seine eigene Erfahrung als Integrationslaboratorium" tabled "Memoranden [...] die sich als wegweisend erwiesen". M. Hirsch, "Benelux ist mehr als nur ein geographischer Begriff: Ein Motor der europäischen Integration", in D. Kneip and E. Stratenschulte (eds.) *Staatenkooperaton in der EU*, Opladen: Leske&Budrich, 2003, pp. 43-50 (p. 49).

2 D.U. Stikker, *Men of Responsibility*, New York: Harper and Row, 1965, pp. 178, 181.

3 J.C. Snoy et d'Oppuers, "Les étapes de la coopération Européenne et les négociations relatives à une zone de libre échange", in: *Chronique de Politique Étrangère*, Vol. XII, 1959, (pp. 569-623), p. 584.

4 W. Woyke, *Erfolg durch Integration – Die Europapolitik der Benelux-Staaten von 1947 bis 1969*, Bochum: Brockmeyer, 1985, p. 387.

have had to let go of their common power stance within the European Community.

More recent integration studies, based on primary source material from Western European negotiations in the 1950s, fine-tune this image of an influential and far-reaching Benelux co-operation. On the one hand, the importance of the role of the Benelux states in the EPC and EEC negotiations comes more and more to the fore. In these studies there is specific reference to the initiatives worked out by the Dutch Foreign Minister J.W. Beyen and to his blueprint for a future customs union between the six ECSC states. (see Chapter 1). The successful relaunch of the Beyen Plan in 1955 at the Messina conference, where the foundation for the actual EEC negotiations was set down, also receives much attention in more recent historiography. Yet we also find that the successes of the Benelux countries could only, to a certain degree, be attributed to a really effective Benelux co-operation. On many an issue during negotiations the points of view of Belgium, the Netherlands and Luxembourg diverged considerably. The intended co-ordination of their foreign policies was often inadequate. Personal disputes between the ministers concerned and interdepartmental struggles within national delegations hampered concerted actions. Where and when the Benelux delegations did act successfully, for example, when presenting their memorandum for the Messina conference, this did not so much reflect a unity as regards content but rather a painstakingly achieved tactical compromise (see Chapter 2).[5] Thus, diplomatic successes of the Benelux states were only in a moderate way the result of a concerted Benelux policy on European integration.

Such dressing down of external concerted actions of the Benelux encounters a parallel in the historiography on the internal development of Benelux co-operation. Here, more than ever, the difficulties on the road to the eventual 1958 Economic Union-treaty are emphasised. The many exception clauses and secret protocols of the Benelux agreements of the late 1940s and early 1950s evoke an image of Swiss Emmentaler cheese. In lieu of an intrepid integration attempt and an important predecessor of the EEC, Benelux rather proves to have been an awkwardly functioning intergovernmental collaboration on sub-sectors of

---

[5] See for instance: A.E. Kersten, *Maken drie kleinen één grote? De politieke invloed van de Benelux 1945-1955*, Bussum: Van Holkema & Warendorf, 1982; R.T. Griffiths and A.S. Milward, "The Beyen Plan and the European Political Community", in: W. Maihofer (ed.), *Noi si mura. Selected working papers of the European University Institute*, Florence: E.U.I., 1986, pp. 595-621; A.G. Harryvan and A.E. Kersten, "The Netherlands, Benelux and the Relance européenne 1954-1955", in: E. Serra (ed.), *La relance européenne et les traités de Rome*, Brussels: Bruylant, 1989, pp. 125-157.

economic policy. In extremis[6] we are presented with the image of a Benelux which went bankrupt internally as an integration concept, although, was bailed out for the sake of an external facade for purposes of foreign policy. It so happened, as the argument goes, that the "Benelux myth" proved to be a convenient vehicle both in acquiring a considerable sum of Marshall aid as well as in strengthening the concerted positions at the European bargaining tables.

Quality ideas, when they are both inspiring and catching on, are among the most effective instruments a Smaller Power finds in its foreign policy tool kit when aiming at engineering influence. Following up on the strong indications that the Benelux countries put their regional integration experiences to good use in their European policies, we scrutinise in this chapter academic analysis and political practice of the Benelux lessons on regional economic integration, as well as the way these results of the "Benelux research station on regional integration", were incorporated and put to use into the Netherlands' policies on Europe.

I. The Benelux Lessons

From the beginning, expectations that Benelux could function as a research station were voiced by many. As early as 1946 *The Economist* spoke of a new model of democratic international co-operation.[7] Following Kuin, Weisglas referred to it as an "example and laboratory" towards a European customs union.[8] In 1949 Bareau described Benelux as a practical test case, on which every instrument in the economic laboratories of Europe should be focused.[9] Robertson also alluded to the Benelux as the equivalent of a laboratory experiment in economic integration.[10] In 1960 Gay and Wagret portrayed Benelux as a "laboratoire du marché commun".[11]

The notion that Benelux actively played such a role is emphasised by Hartog who, in his *Nederland en de Euromarkt* from 1971, states: "In all

6 A.J. Boekestijn, "Een nagel aan Adam Smiths doodskist. De Benelux-onderhandelingen in de jaren veertig en vijftig", in: E.S.A. Bloemen (ed.), *Het Benelux-effect*, Amsterdam: NEHA, 1992, pp. 143-168.

7 *The Economist*, 17-8-1946; cited in: M. Weisglas, *Benelux, van nabuurstaten tot uniepartners*, Amsterdam/Brussel: Elsevier, 1949, p. 341.

8 Weisglas, *Benelux*, p. 339.

9 P. Bareau, "Rifts in the Benelute", in: *The Spectator*, 9-9-1949, (pp. 319-320), p. 319.

10 W. Robertson, "Benelux and problems of economic integration", in: *Oxford economic papers*, (new series), Vol. 8, No. 1 (pp. 35-50), p. 35.

11 Fr. Gay and P. Wagret, *Le Benelux*, Paris: Presses Universitaires de France, 1960, p. 115.

probability, without Benelux there would have been no EEC".[12] In Hartog's opinion, trying out economic integration on a small scale has been the Benelux states' most important contribution towards the materialisation of the EEC. Moreover, as Belgian economist Samoy puts it, Benelux has not only been "the pioneer, the lab", it also continued to play this role well into the 1970s.[13]

From the late 1940s onwards we can discern an epistemic community of academics and civil servants aimed at monitoring and analysing Benelux' economic and political lessons. This epistemic community comprised some thirty individuals sharing a common policy enterprise, to vid monitoring and sharing analysis of Benelux' economic development and its concomittant policy experiences, as well as drawing conclusions from the latter in terms of academic insights and policy lessons for the Netherlands, Benelux and potential wider regional-economic cooperation frameworks. Three leading economic journals, *Zakenwereld*, *De Economist* and above all *Economische-Statistische Berichten* provided the participants in this epistemic community with vessels to divulge experiences and discuss findings and opinions.

High-ranking civil servants played a key rol in this exchange of views: Hans Hirschfeld, the powerful government commissioner for Marshall Plan Affairs, Jaap Kymmell as the minister's economic advisor at the Foreign Ministry, Jozias Wemelsfelder as director at the Ministry of Economic Affairs and F.W. Dirker a regional economics expert at the same ministry, G. Brouwers and J.E. van Dierendonck in similar positions at the Ministry for Social Welfare, H. van Blankenstein was the economic integration specialist at the Ministry of Finance, W.P.H. van Oorschot was the trade specialist of the Directorate-General for External Economic Relations (BEB) in the Ministry of Economic Affairs. M. Weisglas headed the Press Service of the same ministry, to mention some of the more prominent policy practitioners.[14]

A second caucus consisted of the network of Jan Tinbergen, the founder and director of the *Centraal Plan Bureau* (CPB), the Netherlands Bureau for Economic Policy Analysis. This group comprises Petrus Verdoorn, Tinbergen's deputy, Groningen economics professor F. Hartog, co-founder of the CPB, as well as IMF economist Jacques Polak (J.J. Polak). Like Tinbergen Polak had worked as an economist

---

12 F. Hartog, *Nederland en de Euromarkt*, Leiden: Stenfert Kroese, 1971, p. 10.

13 A.G. Samoy, "Benelux, de Europese pionier", in: *Belgisch buitenlands beleid en internationale betrekkingen. Liber amicorum prof. dr. Omer de Raeymaeker*, Leuven: s.n., 1978, (pp. 221-225), p. 221.

14 For an overview of the policy competences and division of labour among the various governmental departments see "A Note on the Making of the Netherlands' European Policy during the 1950s and 1960s" at the end of this book.

with the League of Nations during the 1930s. Under Tinbergen's direction the CPB developed in an authoritive interface between Academia and policy making on a whole range of questions, among which the Benelux issue.[15]

A third group consisted of various other academics and publicists like Pieter Kuin, a Unilever Director and personal acquaintance of Foreign Minister Beyen, as well as monetary and fiscal expert H.W.J.A. Vredegoor.

The groups were closely interrelated. Kuin e.g., aside from being a business director had been president of the *Raad voor de Economische Unie* (Benelux Central Council)[16] until the late 1940s. He had taken a PhD in economics and published on – among other issues – transport problems and the relation between universities and business life.[17] Many of the participants were either trained or teaching at the Rotterdam School of Economics.[18] The community appears to have been a relatively open one, with a reading knowlegde of Dutch being the only hard condition for participation. A few Belgians participated, like the pro-Benelux Cl. De Bièvre as well as L.L. Sermon, who was of a rather Benelux sceptic persuasion. Research findings were communicated to a larger public (Wemelsfelder, Hartog) and published in larger international fora by, above all, Kuin, Wemelsfelder and Verdoorn, where they were picked up and recycled by Meade and Balassa.[19]

The outcomes of the "Benelux laboratory" relevant to European economic integration as discussed by the epistemic community and in the

15 As F. Hartog worded it in 1970: "When the CPB has spoken all possibilities are still open, but we know to what extent". J. Passenier, *Van planning naar scanning. Een halve eeuw planning in Nederland*, Groningen: Wolters Noordhoff, 1994, p. 363. In 1968 Tinbergen was honoured with the first Nobel Prize for economics.

16 H.G. Schermers en H.A.H. Audretsch, 'De instellingen van de Benelux', in: *Benelux in de kijker, 50 jaar samenwerking*, Tielt: Lannoo, 1994, p. 138.

17 P. Kuin and H.J. Keuning, *Het vervoerswezen*, Utrecht: Het Spectrum, 1948; P. Kuin, *Universiteit en bedrijfsleven*, Rotterdam: Unilever, 1952.

18 The *Nederlandsche Handelshoogeschool* was founded in 1913, renamed as *Nederlandsche Economische Hogeschool* (NEH) in 1938 and created a name for itself by its innovative contribution to econometrics. H.P. van Dalen and A. Klamer, "De Rotterdamse econoom tussen wetenschap en handel", *ESB* 24.12.1999, pp. 958-960.

19 P.J. Verdoorn, "A Customs Union for Western Europe – Advantages and Feasibility", *World Politics*, July 1954, pp. 482-500; P. Kuin, "Lessons of Benelux", *Progress*, autumn 1953, p. 160; J Wemelsfelder, "Benelux. An Experiment in Economic Integration", *Economia internazionale: revista dell'Istituto di Econmia Internazionale* 1955, pp. 543-557; J.E. Meade, *The Theory of Customs Unions*, Amsterdam: North-Holland Publishing Cy., 1955; J.E. Meade (ed.), *Case Studies in European Economic Union. The Mechanics of Integration*, London: OUP, 1962; B. Balassa, "Trade Creation and Trade Diversion in the European Common Market", *The Economic Journal*, Vol. 77, No. 305, March 1967, pp. 1-21.

academic literature of its days basically concern three areas: development of trade between the participating countries within a customs union, the role of economic and social policies within the integration process and, finally, the consequences of integration for the structures of the economies concerned and the adjustment problems consequently encountered. We will discuss these issues *seriatim*.

A. Development of Benelux Trade: the "Elasticity Pessimists" versus the "Benelux Effect"

Initially politicians and economists were reluctant to answer the question apropos the consequences for internal trade between Belgium, the Netherlands and Luxembourg as a result of the 1948 Benelux customs union. It was deemed certain though that abolishing tariffs and quantitative restrictions to regional trade would have positive effects on trade. However, it was much more difficult to determine the extent of accompanying trade and expected GDP growth. Comparable examples of experiments with regional economic bloc formation dated from the 19th century and more recent experiences with the Belgian Luxembourgian Economic Union (BLEU) dating from 1921 and the customs union between Liechtenstein and Switzerland (1923) did not quite comply with the Benelux state of affairs which, in terms of economic weight of the participating states, was on a more equal footing.[20] The shaping of theories on regional integration had only just begun – Jacob Viner would publish his "The Customs Union Issue" in 1950 – and where calculations were produced they dampened expectations: eliminating tariffs would, on average, make Dutch products on the BLEU market cheaper by approximately 7% and Belgian-Luxembourgian products exported to the Netherlands by some 10%. No great illusions were harboured about the price elasticity as to how import demands would react to such developments. At a broadening of demand by two per cent points at each per cent in price decrease, increase of trade volume would be restricted to 20% at the most.[21] Academics and policy-makers were

[20] The other experiments in European regional economic integration during the Interbellum were a result of the post WW I peace treaties or otherwise politically tinged, like the customs unions between Danzig and Poland (1920-1939), the Saar territory and France (1920-1935), the Memel territory and Lithuania (1923-1939), Albania and Italy (1939-1943). All of these were relatively short-lived and collapsed when they lost their political relevance. Hence, Kohr observes, Benelux (1948) constituted "the first major common market to be established in the twentieth century". L. Kohr, "The History of the Common Market", *Journal of Economic History*, Vol. 20, 1960, pp. 441-454 (p. 444).

[21] P. Kuin and P.J. Verdoorn, *Welke zijn de achtergronden en vooruitzichten van de economische integratie in Europa en welke gevolgen zou deze integratie hebben, met name voor de welvaart in Nederland* (Praeadviezen Ver. Voor Staathuishoudkunde), 's Gravenhage: Nijhoff, 1952, provides us with a "pessimistic" calculation of trade

largely in the dark, though, with regard to the *dynamic* effects of the customs union, the long-term effects of the expansion of the market and the possibilities of ongoing division of labour.[22]

Be that as it may, by Dutch policy makers Benelux was considered of great importance, in that it could provide the country with an enlarged home-market and thus – at least partly – compensate for the loss of the traditional export markets in Germany and Indonesia. Equally, Benelux was deemed an important catalyst for the ambitious national industrialisation policy, aimed at a substantial increase in industrial exports. From the Dutch point of view, Weisglas argued in a resounding 1948 PhD analysis, complementarity of the two economies (the Netherlands as a predominantly agricultural economy and Belgium as a quintessentially industrial one) was anything but a *conditio sine qua non*.[23]

In order not to lose the political credit with the United States gained through the Benelux initiative and the subsequent chances for large Marshall financing, Benelux-expectations were opportunely stretched in a considerable way. The most optimistic prognoses are to be found in the "Second memorandum concerning the long term program of the Benelux countries" of October 1948 drawn up for the OEEC. The United States had asked the Marshall countries to each draw up a long-term program in which they were to outline exactly how they thought to arrive at a viable economy and a stable balance of payments by the time of the projected end of Marshall aid in 1952. The Americans thought that reducing European dollar shortages called for a resurgence of intra European trade. To further this aim, one or more European customs unions would be of great importance. They were served hand and foot with the Dutch Benelux-expectations (see Table 1). Cabinet reports stated that trade in the Benelux in both directions would be doubled around 1952/53 in comparison to its 1947 volume. It remained entirely unclear how this development was to be realised in the real world. Government's Marshall-plan chief Hirschfeld was none too happy about the speculative figure juggling carried out to make target figures converge with American expectations. He tartly noted that these kinds of "negotiation schedules" were not founded on well-considered economic policies.[24]

---

effects of a customs union between the six Coal and Steel Community countries, based on an assumed elasticity of -2.

22 Weisglas, *Benelux*, pp. 15-17.

23 *Ibidem*.

24 "Tweede memorandum betreffende het programma op lange termijn van de Beneluxlanden", in: *Handelingen van de Tweede Kamer der Staten-Generaal*, 1948/49, 16-12-1948, 1021-2. P. van der Eng, *De Marshall-hulp. Een perspectief voor Nederland, 1947-1953*, Houten: De Haan, 1987, pp. 69, 76-77.

Table 1. Development of Intra-Benelux Trade 1948-1953, as foreseen in the Second Benelux Long Term Program of December 1948 (in Millions of US Dollars)

	1936-38	1947	1948-49	1949-50	1952-53
Export Netherlands to BLEU	171	105.7	140	186	213.7
Export BLEU to Netherlands	221.3	181.1	192.5	267	370.7

Source: *Tweede Memorandum betreffende het programma op lange termijn van de Beneluxlanden*, 3 in: Handelingen van de Tweede Kamer der Staten Generaal 1948/1949, 1021-2 (16 december 1948). The figures for the period 1936-1938 have been corrected for the 1948 price level by a 3.75 multiplier. In 1948 the fixed exchange rate between guilder and dollar was 1 $ = *f* 2,65.

The actual developments in intra-Benelux trade, however, exceeded the most optimistic expectations. From the late 1940s onwards, exchange of goods in both directions rose explosively. Within a few years exchange of goods between Benelux countries rose to a previously unseen high level both in value and in percentage of its entire import and export packages. The import-export series, deflated by the price index-figures also showed a *doubling* of trade volumes for the period 1948-1952. Where Belgian imports from the Netherlands before the war amounted to 9% of total Belgian imports, this figure had risen to 13,8% in 1953 (see Table 2). Trade in the opposite direction was even more telling: before the war Belgium's share of Dutch imports moved around 11%; during the early 1950s this had risen to around 17 to 18%.

Table 2. Intra-Benelux Trade 1948-1960 in Millions of Guilders at Current Prices and as Percentages of Total Imports.

Year	Export Netherlands to BLEU		Export BLEU to Netherlands	
	Value in millions of guilders	As % of total BLEU imports	Value in millions of guilders	As % of total Dutch imports
1948[1]	435	8.2	732	14.7
1949[2]	491	9.3	761	14.3
1950[3]	743	10.1	1.437	18.4
1951	1.058	10.9	1.774	18.3
1952	1.232	13.3	1.451	17.2
1953	1.263	13.8	1.556	17.2
1954	1.297	13.4	1.841	17.0
1955	1.430	13.3	2.205	18.1
1956	1.624	13.1	2.680	18.9
1957	1.847	14.1	2.816	18.1
1958	1.868	15.7	1.459	17.8
1959	2.065	15.8	2.747	18.3
1960	2.234	14.9	3.155	18.3

[1] 1000 Bfr. = f. 60.50.

[2] 1000 Bfr. = f. 64.80.

[3] 1950-1960: 1000 Bfr. = f. 76.00.

Source: Benelux Economische Unie. *Documentatie*, s.l., s.n., s.a., p. 7.

In two articles in *Economische Statistische Berichten* in September and December 1953, Hartog ascribed the sharp increase in bilateral trade between Benelux countries to the "Benelux effect". According to Hartog, the tariff advantages which were brought about by the realisation of the customs union had a greater effect than the "elasticity pessimists" had expected. Rather than the expected -2, the value of substitution-elasticities for Belgian and Dutch import markets turned out to be around -5, according to his calculations. Extrapolating Benelux results, he calculated a substitution elasticity of about -4 for the customs union between France, Italy, West Germany and the Benelux countries as proposed in the Beyen Plan. This meant that the establishment of such a customs union on a broader European scale would entail important consequences for multilateral trade between participating countries.[25]

Hartog's findings did not remain uncontested. Thus, Polak observed a general increase in the exchange of goods between medium-sized West European trading nations for the period 1945-1952. For example, exports from Benelux countries to Italy and Switzerland had risen in percentages comparable with those of intra-Benelux exports. Therefore, broadening of trade within the Benelux area did not appear to be a phenomenon specifically attributed to the customs union but rather part of a more general development.[26]

Polak's findings, in turn, were challenged by Tinbergen. The latter argued that, in light of the relatively high starting level, trade development between Benelux countries, on the basis of growth percentages, could not be accurately compared with trade increases with, for example, the Scandinavian countries. Also, because of this high starting level "reduced surpluses" were to be expected in the relative growth figures.

He concluded that, in comparison with pre-war patterns of trade flows, Benelux trade, in both directions, had undergone a more than average increase. The Benelux effect had most definitely played a role in this.[27] Calculations by Kristein, in spite of his criticism of Hartog's methods, supported the latter's findings about the significance of this Benelux effect: half of all Dutch imports from the BLEU was to be attributed to the Benelux customs union.[28]

Economic and historic literature of a later date puts the significance attributed to the "Benelux effect" into perspective. Development of

---

25 F. Hartog, "Het Benelux-effect", in *Economisch-Statistische Berichten (ESB)*, 23.9.1953, pp. 747-749. F. Hartog, "Naschrift", *ESB*, 16.12.1953, p. 1012.

26 Letter to the editor by J.J. Polak, *ESB*, 16.12.1953, pp. 1010-1012.

27 J. Tinbergen, "De economie der Beneluxlanden voor 1940 en na 1945. De invloed van Benelux op het bedrijfsleven", *Zakenwereld*, 1956, No. 17. (pp. 27-32), p. 30.

28 Marvin Kristein, *Benelux. Son influence sur les exportations belges à destination des Pays-Bas*, s.l.: Comité Benelux, 1956, p. 10.

Dutch trade with BLEU during the first post-war years was predominantly the outcome of governmental policies[29] on the basis of political-monetary considerations under extraordinary circumstances such as, for example, the temporary loss of West Germany as the Netherlands' most important supplier of capital goods. Tariffs played a part in this, albeit on a minor scale. Only with the sharpening of intra European liberalisation policies, within the framework of the European Organisation for Economic Co-operation (OEEC) did tariffs recapture their trade political edge.[30] In light of ex-post calculated elasticities for the bilateral trade development of EEC member states, Hartog's estimate seems to have been on the high side.[31] This does not alter the fact, that, in accordance with Hartog's later claim, the prosperous development of intra-Benelux trade and the recognition of a Benelux-effect may have been important weapons in the battle against "elasticity pessimism". Indeed, the Benelux-effect appears to have played a role in Beyen's campaign for establishing a customs union on a broader European basis, in constituting an empirically based argument in its favour.[32]

B. Liberalisation and Harmonisation: The Role of Economic Policies

The substantial growth of intra-Benelux trade had a troubling drawback: At the time of the commencement of the so called *Voor-Unie* (Pre-Union) in 1950, the Dutch deficit on the bilateral balance of trade with

---

29 In reality, until the end of 1949, the Dutch-Belgian border was "the toughest frontier in Europe to move anything across", according to M. Hoffman in the New York Times of 31 July 1949, as quoted in J.E. Meade (ed.), *Case studies in European Economic Union. The mechanics of integration*, London: OUP, 1962, p. 152. Actual liberalization of Dutch imports from Belgium started only with the coming into effect of the Benelux Pre-Union Treaty in October 1949 and initially covered a limited 30% of Dutch imports from the BLEU. "If we conclude an attractive trade deal with Switzerland or the South Pole, we do not pretend to have given birth to a 'pre-union' either", sneered Belgian economist Sermon. (L.L Sermon, "Benelux, test de l'unification économique de l'Europe?", in: *Revue générale belge*, No. 49, November 1949, pp. 110-123, p 110.

30 R.T. Griffiths, "The abortive Dutch assault on European tariffs 1950-1952", in: M. Wintle (ed.), *Modern Dutch Studies. Essays in honour of Peter King*, London: The Athlone Press, 1988, pp. 186-208, (pp. 188-189).

31 Cf. P.J. Verdoorn, "The intra-block trade of the Benelux", in: E.A.G. Robinson (ed.), *Economic Consequences of the Size of Nations*, London: MacMillan, 1960, pp. 291-332. Eliminating all other factors, Verdoorn attributes 22% of intra-Benelux trade expansion to the customs union. Likewise, Bela Balassa, "Trade creation and diversion in the European common market: an appraisal of the evidence", in: B. Balassa (ed.), *European Economic Integration*, Amsterdam: North-Holland, 1975, pp. 79-118. According to Balassa's calculation for the periods 1953-1959 and 1959-1970 elasticities of intra-trade among the Six were, respectively, 2.4 and 2.6.

32 F. Hartog, *Nederland en de Euromarkt*, Leiden: Stenfert Kroese, 1971, pp. 12-13.

Belgium, which on a monthly basis had already grown from around 10 million guilders to more than 20 million guilders between 1946 and 1949, rose to DFL 80 million per month in 1950. It so happened that the Netherlands had had a substantial structural deficit with Belgium before the war. Back then, this could be compensated for with Dutch income from third countries, as well as oil revenues from the Dutch East Indies. During the first post-war years, however, the Dutch balance of payments was in deficit on all fronts due to war damages as well as the loss of German trade and loss of income from the Dutch Indies. This resulted in The Hague having to pay for the deficit with Belgium with *ad hoc* means of financing such as Belgian credits, Marshall funds and, as of 1950, the use of Dutch credit margins within the European Payments Union (EPU). This situation gave rise to sharp criticism. In the ideal world of a fully-fledged economic union, which the Benelux partners were striving to achieve in order to satisfy the criteria of the *Voor-Unie* treaty, such a financing problem would not present itself. The guilder and the Belgian franc would be mutually convertible, or at least the economic policies of the two partners would be aligned in such a way that deficits of such proportions could be prevented. None of these options proved feasible because, and here one fundamental weakness of the Benelux construction came to light, in the real world of the early 1950s, economic and monetary policies of the Netherlands and those of the BLEU differed considerably and, in some respects, were even aimed in opposite directions: Belgian economic policies were pre-eminently liberally orientated leaving wages, prices and investments by and large to market forces, whilst in its monetary and budget policies the Belgian government pursued a tight monetary policy and small budget deficits. The Dutch government, on the other hand, in its pursuit of economic recovery and industrial expansion, emphatically kept a tight rein on wages, prices and investments. It maintained a low interest rate while running a substantial budget deficit.

This contradiction in policies would prove to be an important obstacle for the prosperous development of Benelux into a genuine economic union. In the opinion of some it undermined the credibility of Benelux co-operation and, at the same time, its potential as a role model for European co-operation on a broader scale. Belgian monetarist Sermon described Benelux as a classic example of how things should not be done: the Benelux partners should have begun by making their currencies mutually convertible and by co-coordinating their monetary policies. A stable trade balance and convergence of prices and wages were to be considered salutary consequences of, rather than conditions for, regional economic integration. He argued that Benelux, in its dependency on an agreement to international payments at a European level, in no way could be seen as a definitive test for Europe's economic unification. It was more the other way round: a case of a European monetary agreement being a necessary precondition for further Benelux development.[33] Towards the end of 1951, Kymmell wrote, in similar vein, that such a monetary agreement, which in the meantime had been realized in the form of the EPU, had been the foundation and precondition for everything that had been achieved within the Benelux framework. Conversely, Benelux had been more of a hindrance than an advantage to the EPU. The extreme debtor position of the Netherlands as a result of intra Benelux liberalisations and Belgium's extreme creditor position had threatened EPU's ability to function. Also, he argued, Benelux failed to qualify as a trade political trump card for its member-states' relations with the United States. Kymmell reasoned that from an international monetary and trade political viewpoint, EPU was much more interesting than Benelux. He drew the conclusion that "the fact that postponing the Benelux economic union would be a blow to European integration, for which pursuance this union was supposed to be a shining example, is an argument which only very few will dare to uphold".[34] Along with Kymmell, various other authors likewise stressed the dependency of Benelux' unimpeded functioning on facilitating European constructions. In 1954 for example, even Hirschfeld seems to have lost confidence in an independent pioneering role for Benelux. According to him, the only way towards completion of Benelux Economic Union was within the framework of international co-operation on a larger scale.[35]

In 1951 and 1952, continuation of Dutch economic recovery and a deflationary change in government policies led to a considerable improvement in the national balance of payments. The country's debtor status within EPU changed to a creditor status and, through a combination of substantial increases in Dutch exports to Belgium and a decline of Belgian-Luxembourgian exports to the Netherlands, the intra Benelux deficit was reduced considerably. The boom reversal, instigated by the Korean War, in an otherwise mild recession formed an important background to this development. Because of deflationary restraints on domestic demand Dutch production became available for international markets at attractive prices, hence the reward of the Drees government's restrictive policies on wages and prices. Conversely, the Belgian export package had become relatively expensive, due to considerable wage increases made possible by Brussels' liberal-economic policies. At the

33 Sermon, Benelux, "test de l'unification", p. 121.

34 J. Kymmell, "De economische unie; reculer pour mieux sauter?", *ESB*, 18.4.1951 (pp. 292-293), p. 292. J. Kymmell, "E.P.U. en Benelux", *ESB*, 5.12.1951, pp. 892-894.

35 H.M. Hirschfeld, 'Benelux en de wijdere Europese samenwerking', *Internationale Spectator*, 1954, pp. 643-660.

Benelux level, this meant that, in a number of branches of Belgian industry Dutch competition had made a heavy impact. Notably, layoffs and business closures in Belgian textile, leather, tobacco and furniture industries resulted from the supply of inexpensive Dutch products on the Belgian market. For the first time in the history of the Benelux process, economic interest groups found themselves actually harmed by Benelux liberalisation. This provoked serious reactions in Belgium: in general, employers' organisations and trade unions blamed low Dutch wages and social security rates and the subsequent difference in competitiveness as being the cause of Belgian problems. Dutch "wage dumping" ought to be overcome by mutual adjustment of economic-social policies of the Benelux countries.[36] Politically this stand was translated into Belgian claims on escape clauses, by means of which threatened sectors, through levies and import restrictions, were to remain protected from "unfair" and "destructive" Dutch competition. With regard to the future development of Benelux the basic assumption among Belgian politicians was that further liberalisations in trade should go hand in hand with a full mutual alignment of the two partners's wage and price policies. From Brussels' point of view, a considerable measure of socio-economic equality was a precondition for free trade among the Benelux-countries.

In the Netherlands increased self-confidence translated into firm insistence on further liberalisation of trade within Benelux. In the academic and political debates on the "Belgian problems" the importance of "directorial" Dutch wage policies and their impact on competitiveness were played down:[37] Looked upon on a European scale, Dutch wages were not extremely low. Belgian wages, rather, were extremely high. In the analysis by Dutch academics the blame lay with the Belgians themselves who, because of a highly overvalued Belgian Franc, exorbitant indirect taxes, an inflationary budget policy and a general lack of planning, appeared to have priced themselves out of the international markets. Harmonisation of policies was surely advisable, but it was up to Belgium to adjust to Dutch policies and not the other way around. Furthermore, such a harmonisation should not be put forward as a precondition towards further liberalisation of trade. On the contrary, the

---

36 Cl. de Bièvre, "Economische Unie tussen 'le miracle belge' en 'le miracle hollandais'", *ESB*, 24.9.1952, pp. 724-728. Meade, *Case Studies*, p. 129.

37 Wrongfully so, as Van Zanden demonstrates. J.L. van Zanden, "Geleide loonpolitiek en de internationale concurrentiepositie van Nederland, 1948-1962", *Maandschrift Economie*, 52, 1988), (pp. 464-477), pp. 473-474. According to Van Zanden in 1947-1953 Dutch businesses experienced a substantial improvement in competitiveness mainly as a result of government policies. Among these, two offensive devaluations played a part. Generally, low and declining costs of living facilitated wage controls. Declining costs of living, in their turn, were a consequence of government keeping fixed rents in place and a successful cheap food policy.

former ought to be a consequence of the latter. Wage levels, price levels and the underlying policies of the two countries should converge driven by the mechanisms already in place within the Benelux common market.[38]

In accordance with Belgian demands a "Protocol concerning co-ordination of economic and social policies" was agreed upon between the Benelux-countries in July 1953. It provided for a system of escape and arbitration clauses whereby, by virtue of joint consultations between both the governments and representatives of the various industries in the three countries, protection on a temporary basis could be given to branches of industry which were heading for a crisis. Nevertheless, the underlying fundamental differences were not solved by this agreement. Against the Belgian demand for overall harmonisation of policies as a precondition for further liberalisations, the Dutch government put its willingness to agree to limited co-ordination in those specific cases where this would prove to be desirable. With regard to the problem of policy harmonisation in general, however, only a few common fundamental principles were formulated with which the national policies of the three countries should be in line. The Secretary General of the Brussels Department of Economic affairs, J.C. Snoy et d'Oppuers, observed that these fundamental principles left ample space for "essential differences".[39] They did not offer any perspective for a political solution concerning the problem of uneven competition within the Benelux. With this, the core of Dutch policy remained intact: trade liberalisation was the first and foremost means to accomplish economic interweaving between the Benelux partners. Full co-ordination of economic policy was seen as a work lasting years and years which "in the end [was to] give maximum effect to meanwhile accomplished integration".[40]

The controversy on policy harmonisation proved to be the most important restraining factor towards further development of Benelux co-operation into a full-fledged economic union. Further agreement on a more freely cross-border exchange of production factors was now largely dependent on the extent to which – as a result of a change in

38 G. Brouwers, "Prijzen en lonen in Nederland en België", *ESB*, 14.5.1952, pp. 372-374; H.W.J.A. Vredegoor, "België en Benelux na 'le miracle hollandais'", *ESB*, 27.8.1952, pp. 648-652; J.E. van Dierendonck, "Komt er een 'miracle Benelux'?", *ESB*, 15.10.1952, pp. 784-786; H.W.J.A. Vredegoor, "Versterking van de Belgische internationale concurrentiepositie als voorwaarde voor 'un miracle Benelux'", *ESB*, 22.10.1952, pp. 805-808; Meade, *Case studies*, p. 171.

39 J.C. Snoy et d'Oppuers, "Benelux, doelstelling en taak", in: *Zakenwereld*, 1956, No. 17, (pp 25-26), p. 26. A. Rom Colthoff, "Benelux-stapvoets voorwaarts", *ESB*, 4.8.1954. Meade, *Case studies*, pp. 131-135.

40 G. Brouwers, "Benelux", in: *ESB*, 2.9.1953, (pp. 681-684), p. 683.

politics or changing international circumstances – wages, prices, interest rates and tax rates would converge. At the time when, in 1954, both interest and budget policies of Belgium and the Netherlands had converged considerably, it proved possible to greatly liberalise the transfer of capital within the Benelux on this basis. On the other hand, liberalising trade in agricultural produce, much sought after by the Netherlands, was rendered practically impossible due to great differences in production costs and price guarantee schemes. Likewise, on the matter of harmonising excises and other indirect taxes, also propagated by the Netherlands, progress was very slow, so that until 1958, the would-be economic union still operated custom checks even at its internal borders.

In the literature, various conclusions are drawn from the Benelux experiences with the liberalising of cross-border exchanges of goods, services, capital and labour and concomitant policy harmonisation. There is an undisputed observation that the input of economic co-ordination, necessary for achieving an economic union, proved to go considerably beyond what the concerned governments had initially presumed adequate to meet the case. Meier, and many with him, blamed failing policy harmonisation for trade liberalisation turning out to be a tiresome and often stagnant process. In this respect, he concludes, the development of Benelux "renders a clear picture of the dangers which an inadequate co-ordination of social-economic policies produce".[41] Such failing to tune up diverging national policies is often connected with the absence of supranational institutions within Benelux-co-operation with their own powers. Taken from this viewpoint the lack of a common political basis made the future of Benelux a hazardous affair, remaining entirely dependent on the political willingness and the opportunities of successive national governments to implement, consolidate and extend the Benelux integration experiment.[42]

Others, however, have drawn attention to Benelux' manifold accomplishments, the many things that *were* accomplished, despite the absence of supranational bodies and inadequate policy harmonisation. Thus

---

41 E. Meier, *De Europese economische integratie*, diss. Tilburg 1958, Leiden: Stenfert Kroese, 1958, p. 47.

42 W. Robertson, "Benelux and problems of economic integration", in: *Oxford economic papers*, (new series), Vol. 8, No. 1 (pp. 35-50), p. 50. In 1959, Benelux secretary-general, Van Lynden, emphatically advocated a long-lasting debut of intra-Benelux economic policy harmonization, lest "lines that now converge will start diverging again". That such divergence was not manifest yet, he reasoned, was to be attributed to good fortune, rather than to intergovernmental policies and cooperation. C.D.A. van Lynden, "De Benelux-integratie als voorbeeld voor de integratie van Europa", in: *De huidige economische ontwikkeling/Benelux* Verslag Accountantsdag AVA 19.11.1958, Nijmegen: Taylor, Efficiency-Bureau voor Administratieve Organisatie, 1959, pp. 53-64, p. 59.

Heilperin thought Benelux a profoundly encouraging precedent for the EEC in the making, precisely because the Benelux experiment proved to be successful in spite of the absence of both supranational institutions and monetary integration, in combination with a limited policy harmonisation.[43]

Hartog drew the conclusion from the Benelux practice that important differences in economic and social policies proved to be compatible with a large degree of economic freedom in inter-Benelux trade. "Apparently the main emphasis of economic policies within an integrated economic area can remain with the national governments".[44] The same was to be expected for integration on a larger scale than Benelux, says Hartog. Again, the national level of economic policies would remain by far the most important.

C. *Structural Changes and Adaptation Problems in the Benelux Economies*

At the implementation of the Pre-Union Treaty in 1949, Weisglas predicted that the economic structures of Belgium, the Netherlands and Luxembourg would not undergo any fundamental changes due to the formation of Benelux. Precisely the fact that these economies were not mutually complementary meant there would be little chance of one-sided specialisation and conflicts of interests which could hamper the due convergence of economic policies.[45] The history of Benelux development during the 1950s would indeed demonstrate that the transfer of national markets into the larger encompassing Benelux market took place – albeit not without hitches – without serious structural changes for the economies concerned. Eliminating trade restrictions resulting in increased competition led in some industries to loss of capital and loss of jobs. In general, however, such adjustment problems were limited and of a temporary nature.

In the literature up to now various causes are illustrated for this mild character of the Benelux adjustment process. During the decades before 1949, the economies concerned were protected by relatively low tariffs, so that mutual competition was not a completely new phenomenon.[46] The fact that all three countries already experienced a relatively high level of industrialisation could also have been the reason for deep cutting shifts as a result of comparative cost benefits "staying at a

43 M. A. Heilperin, "Europe edges toward a Common Market", in: *Fortune*, September 1956, (pp. 142-165), p. 142.

44 F. Hartog, *Het economisch wereldbestel*, Amsterdam: J.H. de Bussy, 8th ed., p. 121.

45 Weisglas, *Benelux.*, p. 10.

46 Notwithstanding bilateral trade and payments agreements seriously hampering such competition during most of the 1930s.

minimum".[47] The fact that a particularly sensitive sector, to wit agriculture, was largely excluded from the Benelux integration process, equally played a major part.

However, of similar great importance was the fact that division of labour and economic specialisation resulting from Benelux liberalisations were not so much manifesting themselves *between* but more *within* the existing branches of industry. Thus Dirker noted in 1954 that the union partners were complementing each other more and more in their mutual trade. While Dutch industrial export to the BLEU was applying itself more to finished consumer products, the growing Belgian outlet on the Dutch market specialised in raw materials and, particularly, in semi manufactured products.[48] This trend reflected the success of the Dutch industrialisation campaign. In 1938, the share of industrial end products in Belgian imports from the Netherlands had been 16%; in 1953 this had increased to 45%. Keen competition edged Belgian employers into productivity improvement and further specialisation. Thus, Dutch industrial expansion was not at the expense of Belgian economic development. In the textile industry, for example, Belgian companies opted for specialising in the export of yarns and fabrics. Their Dutch counterparts put their comparative advantage to use by specialising in fabrics and manufactured end products. Both groups reaped the profits of such a division of labour. In 1938 the Netherlands and the BLEU each exported 13% of their total textile exports to each other; in 1953 this amounted to 25%. In the steel industry, where Belgian employers were specialising on the production of capital goods, a similar development occurred.[49]

Although the problems stemming from liberalisation were generally manageable, they did necessitate some adjustment of production pre-sets and management. In the view of Dutch politicians and economists, such an adaptation to Benelux relations should, as mentioned before, take place on the Belgian side. In a much quoted article from 1954, "Benelux as an example of economic adjustment" Wemelsfelder describes as the core of the Belgian adjustment problem the necessity to force back the disproportional development of wages between the consumer goods sectors on the one hand and, the capital goods sectors on the other. Here the advent of Benelux had sharpened a previously existing problem. The moral of Benelux experiences for future regional integration was that governments and trade unions should practise self-discipline, if need be

---

47 Meade, *Case studies*, 10.

48 F.W. Dirker, "De ontwikkeling van het handelsverkeer tussen de B.L.E.U. en Nederland", *ESB*, 7.4.1954, pp. 271-274.

49 Robertson, *Benelux and Problems*, p. 40.

accepting wage reductions, to let inevitable adjustment processes run their course as smoothly as possible.[50]

In the practice of Benelux development during the second half of the 1950s, it was not so much reduction of Belgian wages rather than Dutch wage *increases*, which diminished the difference in competitive conditions between the two economies. In 1954-1955, as a result of the favourable economic situation and improved Belgian labour productivity, many of the protective measures meant to shield Belgian branches of industry against excessive Dutch competition could be withdrawn, whereby the problem lost a great deal of its acute character.[51]

Hence, in the literature regarding the Benelux adjustment process, both the before mentioned intra-sectoral specialisation and the so-called dynamic effects of Benelux integration are emphasised. The Dutch industrialisation miracle and the Belgian capacity for *reconversions remarquables* constituted an acknowledgement of the wholesome effect of increased competition caused by Benelux liberalisation. Integration in a broader European context was expected to benefit from a similar mechanism: The dynamic effects of regional integration could be relied upon to greatly diminish differences in competitive production conditions.[52]

II. Impact of Benelux Experiences on Dutch Policies on Europe, 1952-1954

The assumption that experiences gleaned from the functioning of Benelux have had a significant impact on Dutch and Belgian policies with regard to regional economic integration in a broader European context is plausible in view of the large overlaps between the groups of policy makers involved. As we argued in the previous section, many of the higher placed civil servants involved in the political and academic debate on Benelux played an equally prominent part in determining the Netherlands' policies on the EPC and EEC negotiations. In the Dutch case Hirschfeld, Kymmell, Wemelsfelder, Brouwers and Van Dierendonck, Van Blankenstein, Van Oorschot, mentioned in the previous section, all occupied influential posts, be it as senior civil servants or as departmental advisors to the ministers of Foreign Affairs, Economic Affairs, Social Welfare, and Finance, respectively. On the Belgian side,

50 J. Wemelsfelder, "Benelux als voorbeeld van economische aanpassing", *ESB*, 23.6.1954, pp. 492-496.

51 W.P.H. van Oorschot, "Enige aspecten van de ontwikkeling van de intra-handel en de buitenlandse handelspolitiek van de Beneluxlanden sedert de laatste oorlog", *Zakenwereld*, 1956, No. 17 (pp. 261-264), p. 263.

52 Gay en Wagret, *Le Benelux*, pp. 125-126. Hartog, *Euromarkt*, pp. 13-17.

notably high-ranking civil servants Snoy et d'Oppuers and Van Tichelen, both from the Belgian Department of economic affairs, left their marks equally on Belgian Benelux policies as on the country's European integration policies.

At the ministerial level too, Benelux formed an important background for the thought process behind European policies. This was the case in Belgium, when in 1954, Spaak once again took charge of the Brussels Ministry of Foreign Affairs. During the war years, he had taken part in the London talks of the exiled Belgian and Dutch governments and thus had stood at the cradle of Benelux. After 1945, he had also been closely involved in developing those wartime treaties. The most important lesson he had learned from the "Benelux adventure", Spaak argued in his memoirs, had been a political one: problems of international integration could not be solved by expert conferences and technical working groups, but, solely through the political willingness of the responsible decision makers at the top. And with that, he criticised those West European politicians who, in their endeavours towards West European integration, had hidden themselves behind technical problems put forward by their civil servants, dodging their political responsibilities for cutting the knots. Without the primacy of political will, of the *volonté politique*, nothing would have become of the Benelux, he said. This *volonté politique* would indeed become the anvil on which Spaak, in his role as political leader of EEC negotiations during 1955-1957, would incessantly pound.[53] Like Spaak, Dutch Foreign Minister Beyen had been actively involved in the wartime negotiations on Benelux. Hence, although he did not bear direct responsibility for Benelux-matters, (these resided with his fellow Minister without portfolio Luns), this did not prevent him, on several occasions, from putting Benelux at the forefront as an example of the possibilities as well as problems that would occur with regional integration. In that, he rushed himself in order to forestall criticisms: the fact that the Benelux countries had succeeded in overcoming important problems even without supranational institutions was by no means a guarantee for institutional success with integration on a broader scale. He stressed the geographical size of the three countries, their common history and an alleged mutual solidarity among the Benelux nations, propitious conditions which could not be counted upon in the case of regional integration among the Six. On no account did Beyen want the Benelux co-operation experience to

[53] Min. BZ, II, 913.100, No. 52: "Projet de procès-verbal de la réunion de ministres des Affaires étrangères des États membres de la C.E.C.A., Noordwijk, 6 septembre 1955", 28.9.1955. Paul-Henri Spaak, "La Relance européenne", *Société Belge d'Etudes et d'Expansion*, 159, 1956, (pp. 132-153), pp. 147-148.

be used as an argument against his Beyen Plan towards West-European economic integration on a supranational basis.[54]

Throughout the drawing up and fine-tuning of the Beyen Plan, Benelux conceptions and experiences were put to use in interdepartmental discussions and decision-making. When, at first, there was considerable confusion as to the formula, i.e. the concrete politico-economic concept by which the intended regional economic integration between the Six should be achieved, in the final wording of the Beyen Plan the endeavour was presented as a customs-union to subsequently evolve into a common market.[55] Beyen's chief economic advisor, Van der Beugel, advocated the customs union concept as a concrete goal that would appeal to the public, as Benelux had demonstrated.[56] Whether the integration enterprise of the six countries would be sufficiently strong to realise a customs union was an entirely different question. Blankenstein, the economic integration specialist of the Department of Financial Affairs thought that, particularly in the light of Benelux experience, there was little hope in this matter. It was far from evident that the problems like those which prevailed in Benelux could be solved in a projected grouping of the Six.[57]

The debate within the Dutch policy-making elite on the pros and cons of a West-European customs union concentrated on the consequences such a co-operation framework would have on the development of the Dutch economy in general, and its foreign trade in particular. In this discussion the above-mentioned "elasticity- pessimistic" analysis of Verdoorn played an important role. Many policy makers, amongst whom Prime Minister Drees, feared that the trade expanding effects as set down in Beyen's customs union, would be undone by the expected damage in trade relations with third countries. After all, the common external tariff by which the customs-union would operate could well turn out to be substantially higher than the current Benelux tariff, as a result of which the Dutch price level would rise considerably. If the worst came to the worst the Dutch economy would end up being locked up in a protectionist trade block. Beyen himself thought this possibility to be improbable and found himself supported by calculations by

---

54 See e.g.: Min. BZ, II, 913.100, No. 132, "A survey of the development of European integration". A report presented by Beyen at the European Movement's Rome conference, May 1957, p. 26 and *passim*.

55 In the terminology confusion of those years, a customs union was often labelled as a "tariff community", even though a customs union along the lines of GATT, article XXIV was meant. Min. BZBrus, 17.771, "Note pour monsieur le ministre des affaires étrangères", 26.5.1953.

56 Min. BZ, II, 913.100, No. 14, Van der Beugel to Beyen, 12.11.1952.

57 Min. Fin., Gen.Thes., BBV, 1262-8, H. van Blankenstein, "De verschillende plannen tot verlaging der tarieven", 20.3.1953.

Wemelsfelder and the *Centraal Plan Bureau*, which showed that even if the external tariff would rise from the Benelux average of 8% to the "Schuman-average" of 13%, the Dutch price level would increase by no more than 3%.[58]

Drees' opposition was not targeted at the idea of a West European customs union as such. On the contrary, the Prime Minister thought regional-economic liberalisation and integration of the utmost importance for the Dutch economy. Nevertheless, he feared that the framework of EPC would either lock up the Netherlands within a protectionist continental grouping or turn out to be politically unfeasible, leading to nothing at all. Be that as it may, Beyen's creed, "no political integration without economic integration", garnered enough support within the Cabinet to carry this statement.[59] Once the *Ministerraad* had given the green light to Beyen's policies, Drees supported them completely, in spite of some differences of opinion between the two men on the strategies which were to be pursued. During the years leading up to the signing of the Treaty of Rome, Drees would make the realisation of a West European customs union and common market a precondition for Dutch participation in further European integration. With that, in his opinion, Benelux remained an example, albeit not in every way shining, yet surely worthy of emulation. After all, as Drees would argue in February 1956, Benelux' rugged course notwithstanding, its common market was definitely an asset: "there is a common external tariff and, except for agriculture, hardly any barriers to trade left".[60]

The suggestions which, in 1953, were put to the other EPC countries in the wordings of the Beyen Plan reflected a vision of integration also pursued by the Netherlands on Benelux level. Vital to these proposals, economic integration was largely identified with liberalisation, whereby the liberalisation of cross-border exchange of goods was put at the forefront. Should liberalisation lead to serious disruptions in economic life then, the country concerned was to apply for a temporary lifting of treaty obligations with the supranational executive body, to be granted on the basis of an escape clause. The Dutch proposals did not provide for obligations in policy harmonisation. As in Benelux, mutual align-

58 NA, MR, Notulen Ministerraad, 29.4.1953. Min. BZ, I, 913.100 No. 66, "Nota betreffende eerste voorlopige uitwerking van het door Nederland gedane voorstel inzake een Europese tariefgemeenschap", 25.3.1953, 14-17. Min. BZ, I, GS, 913.10 'Europese integratie deel II': "Rapport van de Economische Sub-Commissie" 22.4.1953, with annex: "Enkele zeer voorlopige calculaties omtrent de gevolgen van een tariefgemeenschap voor Nederland". J. Linthorst Homan, *Europese integratie. De spanning tussen economische en politieke factoren*, 's Gravenhage: Nijhoff, 1955, p. 158.

59 See Chapter 2.

60 NA, MR Notulen Ministerraad 27.2.1956.

ment of economic, social and monetary policies would have to come from liberalisation of trade.[61]

In Belgium and Luxemburg, Benelux experiences too had had an impact on formulating national policies with regard to European integration, albeit in quite a different way. The importance of regional economic integration was fully underscored by the Belgian policy makers. Less obvious, in their view, was the road along which this aim was to be achieved, according to the Dutch proposals, to wit, the tariff community/customs union construction. In Belgian policy considerations, the unsatisfactory Benelux experiences in the field of interstate finance, fierce Dutch wage competition and the related problem of policy harmonisation came predominantly to the fore. In its analysis of the Beyen plan, the Brussels Department of Foreign Affairs criticised the one-sidedness of the Dutch drive for liberalising trade. The lack of enthusiasm shown by The Hague for liberalising capital movements in Benelux, something which the Belgians had emphatically called for, and "le redoutable problème de l'harmonisation des salaires"[62] were seen as important and dangerous omissions in the Beyen plan. Referring to the fortunes of EPU, a solid settlement of the balance of payments problems was deemed necessary if further regional integration was to be realised. Thus the conclusion was that regional integration without thorough preliminary work on these issues "ne peut conduire qu'à des déceptions semblables à celles qui attristent à présent les plus ardents protagonistes de Benelux".[63]

These negative Benelux connotations were predominantly present in Belgian preparations for the EPC negotiations. The most outspoken point of view was worded by Blero of the Department of Agriculture. Basing himself on Benelux experiences, he wondered whether regional integration with countries where producers worked in conditions quite different from Belgian ones was possible or at all desirable. Generally, Belgian policy makers were of the opinion that the starting point for regional economic co-operation was to be set up on rather a broader basis than was foreseen in Beyen's proposals in order to avoid the problems experienced in Benelux. In the Belgian way of thinking, instead of a customs union, a fully-fledged common market, based on the "four freedoms", was to be preferred, whereby free trade in goods would be complemented by free movement of labour, services and capital. The problems of adjustment which liberalisation would bring about were not so much to be *solved* by means of escape clauses, as

---

61 See Chapter 2.

62 Min. BZBrus, 17.771/1, "Note pour monsieur le ministre des affaires étrangères. Etude du 3e Memorandum néerlandais concernant la Communauté Européenne".

63 *Ibidem*.

hitherto proposed in the Beyen Plan, but rather *prevented* through co-ordination of the economic, social and financial policies of the member states. It was generally acknowledged that for such a major operation considerably more institutional leverage was needed than, as Van Tichelen of Economic Affairs described it, the "rudimentary" Benelux organisation. A readjustment fund, clear agreements on the timely realisation of the treaty obligations in time, rights to appeal to a European Court of Justice and a supranational authority were deemed indispensable.[64]

During the EPC negotiations, which took place from the summer of 1953 onwards, the Netherlands proved to be in an isolated position with regard to its trade in goods centred approach. With the exception of France, which did not want any economic integration whatsoever within the EPC framework, the participating delegations preferred the grand scheme of a common market over the Dutch concept, in which a customs union was projected as a first base on the road to the four freedoms, and they attached great value to a mandatory agreement on the alignment of policies and common policy competences for an envisaged supranational institution. Preventive harmonisation rather than repressive escape clauses were to make the integration process bearable.

Whereas the Netherlands, in the Benelux co-ordination protocol of 1953, had managed to hold the ship of harmonisation at bay, European-wise it had to give way. Throughout 1953 The Hague defended the position that the supranational authority should not go beyond issuing non-binding recommendations to the EPC member-states' governments on matters of economic policy alignment. In March 1954 the Netherlands withdrew its reservation on this issue. This meant that, in certain cases to be defined subsequently, supranational competencies resulting in binding directives became conceivable. Whether this concession, for which Beyen had to take a lot of flack from the Ministry of Financial Affairs, would suffice to secure an agreement among the Six remains doubtful.[65] Be that as it may, due to the problems concerning the ratifica-

64 Min. BZBrus, 17.771/1 "Réunion du groupe de travail du lundi 1er juin 1953"; Min. BZBrus, 17.771/1, "Rapport", with accompanying letter Daufresne de la Chevalerie to Scheyven, 6.6.1953. In the former document Van Tichelen commented on Benelux as something from the past: "Le Benelux *était* une organisation assez rudimentaire". (emphasis mine, AGH). In fairness, Benelux too was equipped with a Readaptation Fund (1954) and a Court of Justice (1958).

65 Min. BZ, I, GS, 913.10, No. 663: "Conférence pour la Communauté Politique Européenne, Rapport aux Ministres des Affairs Étrangères". Min. Fin., Gen. Thes., BBV, 1262-9, "Algemene beschouwing over de economische besprekingen ter Parijse studieconferentie E.P.G. van 7 januari tot 8 maart 1954", 6.3.1954. Min. Fin., Gen. Thes., BBV, 1262-9, "Vergadering Commissie-Beyen inzake Europese Politieke Gemeenschap op 12 maart", W. Drees jr. to minister Van de Kieft, 12.3.1954.

tion of the EDC treaty by France, the EPC talks were put on the back-burner. Eventually, the rejection of the EDC treaty by the French *Assemblée Nationale* entailed their final demise.

III. The Benelux Factor in the EEC Negotiations 1955-1957

For the Benelux countries, the negotiations taking place from July 1955 to March 1957, leading to the European Economic Community (EEC) Treaty of Rome, unfolded under a decidedly more fortunate ascendant than the previous 1952-1954 EPC talks. Grip on the agenda, hitherto unsuccessfully sought for, made for much of the difference. Belgian Foreign Minister Spaak appointed by the Six as political director of the negotiations, exerted decisive leadership throughout the negotiations. Also, immediately after his appointment, invoking Beyen's pioneering role on the issue, Spaak secured chairmanship of the Common Market committee for the head of the Dutch negotiation team, Verrijn Stuart.

The Common Market Upgraded, to Dutch Delight

The Common Market issue, as will be recalled from chapter 2, came to the post-Messina negotiation table in Brussels as one among the many subjects to be scrutinized and reported upon by the national delegates. At Messina, one can argue, the topic was "smuggled in" by means of Beyen-Spaak salami tactics,[66] together with apparently more promising and less controversial looking issues, to wit integration in the areas of transport, classical energy and above all the proposed new nuclear energy integration effort Euratom. As Spaak himself candidly put it at Messina, deliberations on the Beyen Plan could be useful, if and to the extent that they *would not delay* "des résultats plus limités, mais plus rapides, dans des secteurs économiques particuliers".[67]

This *de facto* secondary status, however, did not last long. At the Noordwijk ministers' conference, after three months of negotiations Spaak, admitting his change of view explicitly, drew the conclusion that "le véritable progrès qui a été fait à Messine a consisté à donner, comme hypothèse de travail, la réalisation du marché commun, l'ensemble des

---

66 Jean Monnet Oral History Project "Vraaggesprekken met Nederlandse beleidsmakers inzake Europese integratie", "Addendum bij het gesprek van drs. R.P.B.A. Dingemans en drs. J. Schram met Dr. E.P. Wellenstein", Den Haag/Groningen, 2001, p. 4.

67 Min. BZ, II 913.1000, No. 21: "Projet de procès-verbal de la réunion *C.E.C.A.*, des Ministres des Affaires Étrangères des États membres de la C.E.C.A. Messine 1er et 2 juin 1955", Luxembourg, 13.6.1955, 20-21; Min. BZ, II, 913.100, No. 52, "Beknopt verslag eerste bijeenkomst Messina Studie Commissie te Brussel, 9 Juli 1955 o.l.v. Minister Spaak", DWS to Beyen, 11.7.1955.

autres efforts à réaliser en vue de l'intégration économique européenne devant s'ordonner autour de cet objectif principal".[68]

Spaak's observation hit the nail on the head. Between June and September 1955, to the delight of the Dutch delegation in Brussels, the Common Market issue indeed made a remarkable transformation from additional topic to principal objective of the economic integration negotiations.

The Belgian Foreign Minister himself had been the chief operator in bringing about this spectacular upgrading. Spaak's conversion from accepting to actually embracing the Beyen side of the Messina-agenda was greatly enhanced by a report of a young economist by the name of Pierre Uri representing the ECSC's High Authority at the conference: "Note sur l'intégration économique génerale d'après l'expérience de la Communauté Européenne du Charbon et de l'Acier (présentée par le représentant de la Haute Autorité)", as presented to the Brussels conference on 27 July 1955. The Uri report, analysing the High Authority's experiences in regional integration and summing up the lessons to be drawn from the latter for future horizontal integration, was an immediate and outstanding success with Spaak and among the Brussels' negotiators and their political bosses at home. Even today, more than half a century after its publication, it is not difficult to acknowledge its remarkable qualities: written in a crystal-clear French, the report addresses the quintessence of regional-economic integration and discusses the political choices to be made in the process in an amazingly thought provoking way. Political economy at its best. Spaak went for it hook, line and sinker, singing its praise, declaring it "compulsory reading" for the delegates, dominating the discussions on its conclusions and instructing the national delegates in the classical energy, transport and other sectoral commissions to ensure that their reports fitted in with those of the Common Market Committee. "The Common Market issue is to dominate all other issues of the Messina resolution" Dutch chief negotiator Linthorst Homan reported to Beyen, "not only according to the wishes of the Dutch delegation, but now also in the view of mister Spaak in his capacity of chairman of the negotiations".[69]

[68] Min. BZ, II, 913.100, No. 22, "Verslag van de Conferentie der Ministers van Buitenlandse Zaken der zes landen, leden der E.G.K.S., gehouden te Noordwijk op 6 september 1955"; "Projet de procès-verbal de la réunion des Ministres des Affaires étrangères des États members de la C.E.C.A. Noordwijk, 6 septembre 1955", Brussel 28.9.1955.

[69] Min. BZ, II, 913.100, No. 47, "Note sur l'intégration économique générale d'après l'expérience de la Communauté Européenne de Charbon et de l'Acier (présentée par le représentant de la Haute Autorité) 27 juli 1955"; Min. BZ, II, 913.100, No. 89, Homan to Beyen, 22.8.55 and Kymmell to Van der Beugel, 24.8.1955.

Thus, the Dutch delegation in Brussels as well as The Hague's foreign policy elite had ample reason indeed to be pleased as punch with the Uri report and its recommendations. Most importantly, it provided the Dutch *and* Spaak with a convincing academic as well as political argument for establishing a Western European customs union and common market along the lines of the Beyen Plan. As the Dutch delegation in Brussels put it: "In its general approach document No. 65 is entirely in line with the Beyen Plan and it usefully expands on a number of aspects of the latter on the basis of the ECSC experiences". Amongst such useful expansions was the argument, helpfully in line with Dutch Benelux-based claims, that cross-border differences in wages and social security expenses had to be regarded like other comparative cost advantages and disadvantages and as such should *not* justify or give rise to a general harmonisation of wage policies nor one of social policies in general.[70] The Uri report proved indeed most helpful in keeping preliminary policy harmonization at bay. Overall levelling of wages and social securities advocated by the French and Belgians and much feared by the Dutch, stopped being an issue. Dutch negotiator Linthorst Homan was adamant: "What we strived for all these years, what we failed to gain victoriously in Paris, what we advocated to no effect in Benelux, [has] now been achieved rather to our own surprise, above all because of the academic and political strength of Document no. 65 of the Coal and Steel Community on this issue". Consequently instead of a *precondition* for the projected customs union entering its crucial second phase, social policy harmonisation entered the EEC Treaty as a long-term *aim* of the horizontal integration process.[71]

Thus, already in an early stage of the talks, it became clear that a breakthrough could be achieved on this matter in the sense that, apart from the French, all delegations agreed that policy harmonisation should not be aimed at total levelling or unifying policies and pre-sets for

---

70 Min. BZ, II, 913.100, No. 89, Homan to Beyen, 22.8.1955. Min. BZ, II, 913.100, No. 47 "Note sur l'intégration économique générale d'après l'expérience de la Communauté Européenne de Charbon et de l'Acier (présentée par le représentant de la Haute Autorité) 27 juli 1955", 9, Min. BZ, II, 913.100, No. 52, Linthorst Homan to Van der Beugel 11.10.1955 (with accompanying letter Van der Beugel to Beyen 14.10.1955).

71 Min. BZ, II, 913.100, No. 53, Linthorst Homan to Van der Beugel, 2.11.1955. Spaak made Uri a permanent member of the negotiations' steering committees, in which he was to play an influential role as Spaak's confidant and in the actual drafting of the Rome Treaties. On the harmonisation issue this was not unhelpful to the Netherlands' interests. H.J. Küsters, *Die Gründung der europäischen Wirtschaftsgemeinschaft*, Baden-Baden: Nomos, 1982, p. 328; Min. BZ, II, 913.100, No. 52, Van der Beugel to Tuyll van Serooskerken, 21.8.1955. Marcel Ermers & John Kragt, "Tussen tradities en traktaten. Minister Beyen en de Europese integratie 1952-1956" (MA thesis, History Department of the University of Nijmegen, August 1988), p. 150.

competition and should instead be restricted to a "correction de distortions". Nevertheless, before a final agreement on this basis including France became possible the Netherlands had to take a further step down in the form of a sizeable concession to the French demand for an "effort special" to level labour conditions. Amongst others, harmonisation of the number of days' vacation per employee and the principle of equal pay for men and women had to be accepted. On the basis of this last concession the famous Article 119 on equality between women and men in matters of employment and occupation became manifest, ultimately the corner stone of EEC emancipation policy.[72]

The new course of events in Brussels did not fail to impress Beyen's staff at the Foreign Ministry. Was the Beyen Plan going to be a success after all? "We were mistaken, all of us", Van der Beugel, previously Beyen's most outspoken critic amongst the minister's advisors, wrote to Van Tuyll van Serooskerken, the ministry's Secretary-General. "How were we to envisage that the French would be willing to pay the price of a customs union for getting the bomb?" Likewise, Ermers and Kragt observe a noticeable rise in Beyen's status amongst his staff. Their renewed association with their political boss entailed a more supportive and constructive attitude to his policy goals, as well as a conspicuous increase in the expression "our minister" in departmental correspondence.[73]

Of course, Spaak's agenda revolution in general and the upgrading and progress of the Common Market negotiations in particular did not take place in a diplomatic vacuum. From the start of the Brussels deliberations onwards Dutch diplomats observed a change in attitude and atmosphere in comparison with the 1952-1954 talks. France and the Netherlands, representing the extreme stances as before, appeared to have reconsidered their positions. France, although sticking to its "intégrer pour liberaliser" approach, in which alignment of economic, social, financial and fiscal policies were regarded as a precondition for trade liberalisation, from August 1955, gave indications of having lifted its overall ban on the customs union approach. At the September 1955 Noordwijk ministerial conference, when French Foreign Minister Pinay referred to the Common Market negotiations as "the most difficult" of

72 Min. BZ, II, 913.100, No. 54, "De Europese Gemeenschappelijke Markt en het probleem der sociale harmonisatie" with accompanying letter Van Dierendonck to Van der Beugel, 24.8.1956; and: "Nederlandse positie ten opzichte van sociale harmonisatie" 12.9.1956. Post-Nice (December 2000) article 119 was renumbered article 141.

73 Min. BZ, II, 913.100, No. 52, Van der Beugel to Tuyll van Serooskerken, 21.8.1955. Marcel Ermers & John Kragt, "Tussen tradities en traktaten. Minister Beyen en de Europese integratie 1952-1956" (MA thesis, History Department of the University of Nijmegen, August 1988), p. 150.

"the tasks at hand", this sanguine interpretation found – implicit – confirmation.[74]

The Netherlands, while adhering to its "libéraliser pour intégrer" stance, according to which liberalisation of cross-border trade constituted the logical road to economic and social policy alignment, equally engaged in renewed soul-searching. At the time, The Hague's above mentioned March 1954 concession allowing for binding directives on socio-economic policy harmonisation had come way too late to make any constructive difference at all. A year later, discussing the same issues on the basis of the Messina agenda, such an originally ill-timed concession obtained a second chance to bear fruit. In discussing the Dutch chances in Brussels with his Hague superiors, chief-negotiator Linthorst Homan did not mince his words: in view of the March 1954 concession "and recent Benelux development on this issue" the five partner countries expected the Dutch to take a more flexible stance than previously. With characteristic vehemence he worded this message in a letter to his superior, economics minister Zijlstra: A broadminded approach would be indispensable, he wrote, continuing in capital letters, *OM DE MARKT EN DE UNIE TE VERKRIJGEN* ("To get the market and the Union").[75]

---

74 Min. BZ, II, 913.100, No. 22, "Projet de procès-verbal de la réunion des Ministres des Affaires étrangères des États members de la C.E.C.A. Noordwijk, 6 septembre 1955", Brussel 28.9.1955, 15. Min. Fin., Gen. Thes., correspondentie en documenten Nederlandse delegatie t/m aug. 1955, D.C. Breedveld, 'Brusselse conferentie over integratievraagstukken', 9.8.1955. Bossuat too signals a fundamental change in the French government's attitude towards the Common Market issue, but somewhat later, in October 1955. "La conférence de Messine se tient, et on se rend compte, comme dit François Valéry, que Pinay, ministre des Affaires étrangères a 'l'intention de contracter' un accord mais n'a pas pris 'un engagement de contracter'. Les Français comprennent pourtant qu'ils ne peuvent maintenir une attitude dilatoire et en octobre 1955 proposent de s'engager dans un marché commun pour une première étape de 4 ans". Bossuat also stresses the role of the new Mollet government which came to power at the end of January 1956. From 1953 onwards Mollet had been in favour of striking a deal with the Dutch on the common market: "Pour comprendre l'attitude finalement positive de Guy Mollet sur le marché commun, alors que le gouvernement précédent (Edgard Faure), était, comme on le voit, très réticent, il faut mettre en avant ses choix européens en son adhésion au Comité d'action pour les États-Unis d'Europe. Ainsi, en 1953, sur le marché commun, estimait-il qu'il faudrait transiger avec les Hollandais". G. Bossuat, "La vraie nature de la politique européenne de la France (1950-1957)", in: Gilbert Trausch (ed.), *Die Europäische integration vom Schuman-Plan bis zu den Verträgen von Rom*, Baden-Baden: Nomos 1993, pp. 191-239 (pp. 220-221). In a conversation with the Dutch ambassador in Brussels, Spaak underlined French and German agreement with the common market concept as important results of the Noordwijk conference. Min. BZ, II, 913.100, No. 22, Netherlands' ambassador Brussels to Beyen, 14.9.1955.

75 Min. BZ, II, 913.100, No. 89, Linthorst Homan to Zijlstra, 21.7.1955. An additional factor in the Brussels agenda reshuffle appears to have been lack of progress on the

Failure of Benelux Cooperation

The Spaak presidency, although generally acknowledged as crucial for bringing about the Brussels' conference most important result, the European Economic Community Treaty of Rome (1957) did *not* translate into enhanced leverage for Benelux co-operation. On the contrary, in spite of intensive liaising between the three delegations, reaching common ground on important issues proved often impossible. Throughout the deliberations leading to the May 1956 Spaak Report as well the subsequent intergovernmental negotiations leading to the March 1957 EEC Treaty, Dutch negotiators in their reports to The Hague complained that precisely the Spaak presidency of the negotiations jeopardized reaching common stances with the Belgian as well as the Luxembourg delegation. Time and again, Benelux foreign policy co-operation remained inoperative, either because of Spaak explicitly instructing the Belgian delegation not to team up with their Dutch counterparts, or alternatively, due to fears on the side of the Belgian delegates, that supporting a Dutch point of view would not find favour with the Belgian Foreign Minister. "Like on more issues, on this one, a common stance of the Benelux-delegations has not been achieved", Linthorst Homan reported on the institutional file. "All efforts in this respect resulted in a horrible failure".[76]

Part of the blame, some delegates felt, was to be attributed to the coterie of French advisors with whom Spaak surrounded himself: Thirty years later, looking back on the EEC negotiations, Van der Beugel was adamant:

> The Common Market Treaty is a French treaty. And that is because Spaak was surrounded by the economists and legal advisors of the Quai d'Orsay[77], of the ministère des Finances, Uri, Van Helmont[78], Michel Gaudet[79], enfin, that entire crowd encircled Spaak to mind the French interests. And Spaak was obsessed by the idea to accomplish his mission.[80]

"technical issues". The transport committee was regarded by many delegates as an unnecessary duplication of the work done in the Conference Européenne des Ministres de Transport (CEMT). The general feeling in the classical energy committee was best described by the question "What are we supposed to be doing here?". Progress on nuclear energy proved difficult. Min. BZ, II, 913.100, No. 89, Linthorst Homan to Minister of Economic Affairs, 21.7.1955.

76 Min. BZ, II, 913.100, No. 53, "Mogelijkheden inzake het Spaak-rapport", 14.3.1956.

77 The French Ministry of Foreign Affairs.

78 J. van Helmont, High-ranking French civil servant, assisted Jean Monnet in the High Authority of the ECSC and in Monnet's Action Committee for the United States of Europe.

79 M. Gaudet, legal advisor of the ECSC's High Authority.

80 Interview with Ernst van der Beugel in: A.G. Harryvan, J. van der Harst and S. van Voorst eds., *Voor Nederland en Europa. Politici en ambtenaren over het Nederland-*

Relations with the other Benelux partner Luxembourg did not help things either. Like before, the Luxembourg delegation kept a low profile at multilateral negotiations among the Six. In the past, Luxembourgian enthousiasm for Dutch European plans had been lukewarm at best.[81] Wary of losing its national economic independence to some supranational construction had made the country originally reject the Beyen Plan. Thus, at the 1953 Rome conference, Foreign Minister Bech had opposed the Dutch "no political integration without economic integration" approach: "Il ne me semble pas indiqué, entre autres, que la réalisation d'un marché commun dans un délai nettement déterminé et suivant un plan arrêté préalablement, d'une façon définitive et automatique, devrait constituer une condition indispensable pour la création d'une autorité politique européenne".[82]

Two years later Bech, although in favour of a *relance européenne*, deemed the Common Market paragraphs of the common Benelux Memorandum for Messina unfortunate. Since their inclusion was at the heart of the Dutch-Belgium understanding, however, he could not resist them in principle. As Trausch worded it: "Solidarité bénéluxienne oblige!".[83]

---

se Europabeleid en de Europese integratie, 1945-1975, Amsterdam: Boom, 2001, pp. 31-61, p. 47. Upon publication Van der Beugel's observation was deprecated by Edmond Wellenstein, formerly of the High Authority, in no uncertain terms: "It is not correct to say that Spaak when drafting his Report and the Treaty was surrounded by civil servants from Paris (Quai d'Orsay and *Ministère des Finances*) sent by the French government. Quite the contrary, they were officials of an outspoken 'communitarian' persuasion, whom the president of the High Authority René Mayer, provided Spaak with at the latter's request". (Letter Dr. E. P. Wellenstein to the author, 3.8.2001). And likewise: "The same goes for Van der Beugel's remark 'It is a French treaty'. Yes, it is. But in the sense that Uri and his team were French nationals. 'French officers', they were not, quite the contrary. This misunderstanding permeates the entire interview text. […] I wrote to Van der Beugel, explained him my misgivings and ended 'In brief, I would hate to see that the four persons mentioned (Uri, van Helmont, Gaudet and the one I mentioned, Delouvrier) will go down into history as the managers of the French establishment. The opposite was the case'. Van der Beugel answered me jocularly: 'After such a long time, what a familiar sentiment to disagree with you!'". Dr. E. Wellenstein in a letter to the author, 12.9.2001.

81 J.W.L. Brouwer, "In het kielzog van Frankrijk? Enkele opmerkingen over het buitenlands beleid van het groothertogdom Luxemburg, 1945-1950", in E.S.A. Bloemen, *Het Benelux-effect, België, Nederland en Luxemburg en de Europese integratie, 1945-1957*, Amsterdam: NEHA, 1992, pp. 33-53, *passim*.

82 Archives Nationales Grand Duché de Luxembourg (*Luxembourg National Archives*), (henceforth ANLUX) régime AE (henceforth: RAE), No. 5960, Speech Bech at 1953 Rome conference.

83 G. Trausch, "Le Luxembourg face aux traités de Rome. La stratégie d'un petit pays", in: E. Serra (ed.), *La Relance européenne et les traités de Rome*, Brussels: Bruylant, 1989, pp. 423-459, (p. 428).

During the EEC negotations, such reticence was again a dominant force in the Luxembourg stance. By April 1956 Dutch observers even obtained the impression that Luxembourg would prefer to refrain from joining the Common Market, if such were practicably possible. Luxembourg head of delegation Schaus voiced his government's concern whether by the realization of such a far-reaching project as the Common Market Luxembourg would continue to exist as a small but independent state.[84]

This led to a negotiation behaviour of a decidedly defensive nature which has been judged by some observers as passive and unambitious. Such verdicts strike us as somewhat unfair, in view of the Luxembourgian interests at stake and the way the country was treated by its five partners.

First and foremost, Luxemburg's interests were of an economic nature. The country's agriculture and viticulture, both heavily protected by barriers to trade, were unlikely to survive competition within a common market amongst the Six. That is: unless some special regime providing the country with an exemption status would be created, comparable to special arrangements created for Luxembourg in BLEU, Benelux and GATT. Free cross-border labour movement would also constitute a problem for the country, in which by the mid-1950s, already 27% of the industrial workforce was of foreign extraction. Luxembourg policymakers entertained an understandable fear that in a liberalised cross-border labour market their country's prosperity and high salaries would attract even more foreign workers, possibly raising their numbers to socially and politically unacceptable levels.[85]

Primary material in the Luxembourg and Netherlands archives demonstrates how the Luxembourg delegation struggled for an exemption status for what they called a "limited list" of treaty articles and products.[86] This the Dutch delegation experienced differently: "The perennial so-called 'limited' list was tabled again, containing the products Luxemburg wants to protect. It lists just about everything: dairy, meat,

---

84 BZII, 913.100, No. 53, Kymmell to Beyen, 21.4.1956. This sentiment was more widespread: In the Luxembourg archives we found a copy of "Document de travail No. 4" of which the section on the abolishment of quota and tariffs has been embellished by a drawing of a tombstone with the legend "Luxembourg" surrounded by sardonic looking hobgoblins. ANLUX, RAE, No. 7695, "Document de travail No. 4 (2e rédaction)", 2.12.1955.

85 ANLUX, RAE, No. 9701, "Relance européene", Schaus to Bech, 3.11.1955, Annex 3 'Observations du Ministère du Travail au sujet du Document No. 338', 3.11.1955.

86 ANLUX, RAE, No. 7695, "Comité Intergouvernemental – Question agricole", Schaus to Bech, 13.3.1956.

grain, wine!"[87] In pursuing their campaign, the Luxembourg delegation, found themselves facing a dilemma: given the country's limited economic significance the other five delegations were willing to grant the *Grand-Duché* the special regime it requested, but then equally expected its delegation to refrain from pushing its views on the general character of the Common Market and the EEC Treaty. Luxembourg's refusal to go along with this expectation caused irritatation with, amongst others, the Dutch. A March 1956 report by Linthorst Homans to The Hague may serve as an example:

> [Luxembourg wants to be treated as] an exceptional case. In the past the Netherlands agreed not to object against this wish. As we said in Rome and Paris the Netherlands' point of view is that it is better to make an exception for Luxembourg, than drafting the articles in such a way that they end up more protectionistic for all countries concerned. Luxembourg, however, should not try and do both: trying to dilute the articles first and then apply for an exemption status on top of it.[88]

The biggest bully of all turned out to be Spaak's right hand Pierre Uri. Luxembourg's head of delegation, Schaus, reported the following quote: "Pour ma part, je voudrais qu'on vous donne tout de suite tout ce que vous demandez en particulier, mais qu'alors sur le plan général, vous nous laissiez tranquilles".[89]

For Luxembourg such treatment made questions on the *political* future of the country and its 300,000 citizens in a future Euromarket of some 150 million Europeans more pertinent than ever. The conclusion was drawn that sovereignty and independence could only be safeguarded if sufficient national representation in the new Community's institutions could be arrived at. Such representation was also deemed elementary since Luxembourg would have to pay its part of the Community's budget.[90]

In the end, Luxembourg obtained most of what is wanted, both in terms of its exemption regime and representation. The Dutch did not receive the support from their Benelux ally they had hoped for, due to conflicting interests as well the reticent Belgian stance. Additionally, a psychological element may have played a role: Dutch disapproval of and

---

87 Min. BZ, II, 913.100, No. 90, "Verslag van de besprekingen in de kring der Hoofden van Delegaties ter Brusselse integratie-conferentie op 7-9 maart 1956". 10-3-1956 (12).

88 *Ibidem*, 11.

89 ANLUX, RAE, No. 7695, Schaus, to Bech, 13.3.1956 (9).

90 Trausch, *Le Luxembourg*, pp. 442-448.

irritation with Luxembourg stances was sometimes tinged with arrogance.[91]

Institutions, the Fight for a Supranational Community[92]

The discussions on the institutional set-up of the new European cooperation framework provide us with a case in point regarding the break-down of Benelux cooperation: At Messina, Beyen and Spaak saw eye to eye on this issue. The Benelux countries, Spaak stressed, had gone to great lengths to avoid the expression "supranational organization". Nevertheless, alluding to "l'expérience acquise dans le fonctionnement du Benelux, il souligne la nécessité absolue de prévoir la création d'un organisme doté de certains pouvoirs d'autorité". In the same vein, Beyen told his colleagues, that the coming into existence of both Euratom and the Common Market necessitated a "supranational solution" and, hence, a strong "common executive".[93]

By late September 1955 this consensus was in jeopardy: Spaak's deputy, Snoy et d'Oppuers, candidly suggested his Dutch opposite number Van der Beugel that on the institutional issue Belgium expected the Dutch to pull the chestnuts out of the fire "since Spaak as chairman of the conference did not want to take a stance that would deter the French". Also, Snoy et d'Oppuers let on, Spaak had now grown much more aware of the many objections and misgivings in Belgian industrial circles against ECSC-like structures. The German delegation fully supported Spaak's institutional reticence: "we are not supposed to discuss supranationalism, because of the French", Linthorst Homan summarized their attitude. For Beyen, however, an ECSC-like structure with a strong executive and majority voting in the intergovernmental

---

91 A report by ministerial advisor Kymmel to Van der Beugel in March 1956 provides us with an example of such Dutch disdain: "We were presented by a lovely motto for the entire integration exercise out of the mouth of Luxembourgian ambassador Schaus, not a particularly talented person. Discussing Luxembourgian agriculture he told us that his government now had come to the conclusion that the time had come 'pour mettre frein à l'immobilisme' (loud laughter)". At a more general level, Brouwer and Pijpers observe, the Netherlands – itself a Smaller Power in Europe – when dealing with Luxembourg finds itself in the role of a Larger Power and tends to behave accordingly. Min. BZ, II, 913.100, No. 53, Kymmell to Van der Beugel 12.3.1956. J.W. Brouwer and A. Pijpers, "Nederland en Luxemburg: een grote en een kleine mogendheid?", *IS*, 53, 1999, pp. 31-36, p. 32.

92 In this section we will concentrate on the supranational issue during the EEC negotiations. Chapters four and five provide the reader with a more elaborate view of the Netherlands' stance on the institutional dimension of European integration.

93 Min. BZ, II, 913.100, No. 21, "Projet de procès-verbal de la réunion des Ministres des Affaires Étrangères des États members de la C.E.C.A., Messine 1er et 2 juin 1955", Luxembourg 13.6.1955, 12, 22.

forum was quintessential for the success and irreversibility of the entire horizontal integration enterprise.[94]

The Hague Foreign Office was not to be deterred and stuck to its guns. On the institutional issue, Beyen and Luns informed the Cabinet in late October, the Brussels conference had remained rather vague:

> Only our delegation, followed with a certain degree of doubt by the Belgians, have expressed themselves clearly, and above all in favour of, a supranational institution endowed with policy competences. We are of the opinion that this stance should be maintained. The Dutch point of view has been and will be in future that our co-operation framework with little Europe of the Six only makes sense if such co-operation is organized on a different footing than the one we are familiar with in international organizations. This fundamental difference must find expression in its institutional set-up and, first and foremost, by a transfer of policy competences [to the Community executive].[95]

This touched upon, as Beyen and Luns argued, an essential issue: "(...) to wit that supranational organization is, annex to other manifestations of co-operation in Europe, both desirable and feasible. Co-operation amongst the Six, however, *not* bearing the Community characteristics, is deemed not attractive to the Netherlands. It is [HM government's delegation]'s task to further this view".[96]

---

94 Min. BZ, II, 913.100, No. 157, Linthorst Homan to Van der Beugel, 17.9.1955 (quote); Min. BZ, II, 913.100, No. 52, Van der Beugel to Beyen, 21.9.1955. Van der Beugel's commentary: "If everybody is afraid to deter the French (also take note of the German stance) we are not going to make much progress". Van der Beugel is referring to the German stance on the institutional issue as exposed by the Federal Republic's representative to the Brussels' conference a few days before at the occasion of Belgian-Dutch-German dinner party: "Supranationality, according to the Germans, should not be a topic of discussion, because of the French. If the French did not exist, they responded to a pertinent question, the Germans would be willing to discuss supranationalism (...) Do we have to bring the matter up in Bonn with a view to getting more spunk into Ophuels? Any urchin would have gone beyond what Germany's new Ambassador in Brussels went yesterday" Min. BZ, II, 913.100, No. 157, Linthorst Homan to Van der Beugel, 17.9.1955.

95 NA, MR, Notulen Ministerraad 31.10.1955.

96 *Ibidem*; At the 4.11.1955 meeting of the Beyen Committee, Beyen once again stressed the importance of supranationalism for bringing about the common market. "If the French do not want supranationalism, it were better if they said so, even though that would mean that nothing would come of the plans currently under debate. If that is the case one can try and construe a new co-operation framework with Britain and the Scandinavian countries. If you were to argue than that supranationalism could not be arrived at in such an alternative framework, my response would be that – contrary to our efforts among the Six – it would not be strictly needed". [....] "He is of the opinion that the French efforts are directed at avoiding all initiative by a higher authority, while maintaining for themselves all freedom of action. It is rather parallel to aiming at a right to veto, something that has well outlived its course". Min. Fin., Gen. Thes., Corr. en doc. Nederlandse delegatie, sept.-dec. 1955, "het hoofd van de

And so they did. The March 1956 Spaak report turned out to be by and large in line with the Dutch wishes in terms of engineering influence. The proposed executive, the "European Commission" was to establish and subsequently manage the Common Market, a "Council of Ministers" was to be in charge of co-ordinating member-states governments' policies. This was a much better result than influential parts of The Hague's foreign policy elite had expected: In February 1956, for instance, the legal department of the Foreign Ministry had warned against the negotiations resulting in a *Societas Leonina*, in which the political influence of the larger member-states would – using an admittedly exaggerated metaphor – result in "economic annexation of the smaller countries under the pretext of integration".[97]

In comparison, the eventual outcome of the negotiations was a source of disappointment. In spring 1956 the institutional question came on the agenda again. Very quickly the conclusion had to be drawn that lacking Benelux-support the Netherlands was completely isolated on the issue. A sombre stocktaking showed that the perceived need to protect national interests meant that a major proportion of Community tasks was going to be assigned to the Council of Ministers. "The difference with intergovernmental co-operation is getting smaller and smaller", a tormented Van der Beugel reported to the Beyen Committee in November 1956: Decisions were going to express compromises between diverging national interests, in which process the interests of the larger countries could well prevail over those of the smaller countries. By November 1956 it became equally clear that the prospective EEC-member-states were definitely not prepared to endow the European Commission with the powers envisaged by the Spaak report. For months, the Netherlands kept battling for High Authority-like centrality of the European Commission in the decision-making of the projected European Economic Community. Then Beyen's successor, (since October 1956) Luns, settled for a Spaak-proposed compromise whereby the new Community would arrive at decisions by majority voting by the Council on the basis of Commission proposals.

Meanwhile, Dutch negotiators did succeed in limiting the negative aspects a little. In the EEC Treaty as signed on 25 March 1957, the cases where a qualified majority with weighted votes was required in the transitional period and thereafter were exhaustively listed. Equally important was the provision, embodied in article 149 EEC that in a

afdeling multilaterale zaken" (J. Grooters) aan de minister, via de Thesaurier-Generaal, 4.11.1955.

97 Min. Fin., Gen. Thes., Corr. en doc. Nederlandse delegatie, map 2 (landbouw, instituties), JURA, "Memorandum" 20.2.1956.

number of cases of importance, the Council could depart from the Commission's proposal only unanimously.[98]

These concessions were unable to satisfy the Dutch government. As it declared to Parliament: "Though one must certainly not underrate the importance of the Commission has taken on in the Treaty, the Commission's own decision-making possibilities are nonetheless limited, and more limited than the Dutch government would have wished".[99]

All in all, despite their persistent efforts, the Dutch did not succeed in empowering the European Commission as the EEC's central decision-making body. This came as a great disappointment to the leader of the Dutch delegation (since June 1956) at the intergovernmental negotiations, Linthorst Homan. Throughout the negotiations he aired his anxiety that in the absence of unity within the Council of Ministers, treaty agreements would be sabotaged: "What grief Benelux has already caused us on this matter".[100]

Trade with Third Countries

On an equally disputed issue, trade relations with third countries, Benelux co-operation failed in a similar fashion. Here, the common external tariff (CET) of the projected Common Market was at stake and hence its liberal, or protectionist nature. The Dutch took the low Benelux tariff as a starting point, counting on Belgium and Luxembourg to follow suit. Since France would insist on a high, even prohibitive CET, The Hague reckoned with a compromise in a later phase of the negotiations, along the lines of GATT Article 24 on the CET maximum, i.e. the weighted average of the tariff levels of the four constituting trade areas (France, Germany, Italy and Benelux). This proved an illusion. In November 1955, the Belgian and Luxembourgian delegations told their Dutch counterparts that they sided with the Dutch "in principle". However, since they did not dare to annoy Spaak in his attempt to arrive at a compromise their support for maintaining as much as possible of the low Benelux-tariff against the French demands could not be firm. Consequently, Linthorst Homan observed, in the subsequent talks the Netherlands would be "speaking on behalf of three countries, albeit that it is not at liberty to say so".[101]

---

98 Min. BZ, II, 913.100, No. 66, Van der Beugel to Beyen Committee, 1.11.1956 and 13.11.1956; Küsters, *Die Gründung*, pp. 398-399.

99 Handelingen van de Tweede Kamer der Staten-Generaal, 1956-1957, No. 4725, Memorie van toelichting, 4.

100 Min. BZ, II, 913.100, No. 53: "Mogelijkheden inzake het Rapport-Spaak", 14.3.1956.

101 Min. BZ, II, 913.100, No. 53, Linthorst Homan to Verrrijn Stuart, 25.11.1955.

Such fears proved well justified. Belgium and Luxembourg refrained from giving the Netherlands their formal support or tabling a common Benelux proposal. "They appeared to be under strong pressure from Mr. Spaak, who wants a unanimous report without dissident voices", Dutch diplomats reported.[102] Thus, as on previous occasions Benelux cooperation remained inoperative. Rather unexpectedly, in lieu of the Benelux partners, Germany became the Netherlands' principal ally in the struggle to keep CET as low as possible.[103]

Benelux Experiences in Regional Economic Integration, Model and Countermodel

Despite a number of crises, the 1955-1957 EEC negotiations went off in a considerably more constructive atmosphere than had been the case with the EPC talks. The enhanced flexibility of the French and Dutch delegations was of great importance in this matter. Apart from exchanging points of view, the negotiators engaged in free exchanges of ideas in which Benelux experiences were drawn upon numerous issues. Thus, in discussions on tax policies, internal and external trade policies, liberalisation of capital movements and agricultural problems, Benelux policy agreements were brought into the talks. This often happened on the initiative of one of the Benelux countries themselves. At times, however, Benelux references and comparisons were instigated by one of the other delegations.[104]

On the inevitably recurring question of harmonisation of economic policies, for instance, the other delegations made play with examples of Benelux experiences, examples which would supposedly show the necessity of far-reaching alignment of these policies.[105] The embarrassed Dutch, on the other hand, came up with empirical cases and arguments to the contrary from elsewhere. They provided, amongst others, figures

---

102 Min. BZ, II, 913.100, No. 39, Kymmell to Beyen, 26.11.1955. Elsewhere even more poignant: "Ze durven niet tegen de heer Spaak in te gaan" ("They don't dare to contradict Mr. Spaak"), "Weekbericht No. 11, 28 november – 4 december 1955".

103 Min. BZ, II, 913.100, No. 66, "Concept-nota aan de ministerraad inzake het buitentarief van de gemeenschappelijke markt", H.W. Maas, with annex, 28.11.1956. On this issue, Beyen was under considerable pressure from various Dutch business communities, stating that a low CET was an absolute condition for making a customs union among the Six attractive for the Netherlands. See, for example, Min. BZ, II, 913.100, No. 49, Chamber of Commerce Amsterdam to Beyen, 19.3.1956.

104 Some examples: Min. BZ, II, 913.100, No. 89: 'Algemeen overzicht der z.g. "eerste lezing", 5.8.1955, 4; *idem*: "Weekbericht No. 6", 4. Min. BZ, II, 913.100, No. 158, "Verslag van de besprekingen over de agrarische zijde der Douane Unie, Brussel, 11 januari 1956" with letter Linthorst Homan to Beyen, 13.1.1956, 3. Min. BZ, II, 913.100, No. 90: "Weekbericht No. 8. Periode 17 t/m 20 september 1956", 16.

105 Min. Landb., 's Gravenhage, GS5, 631, Europese integratiebesprekingen 1955, "Aantekening bij weekbericht No. 3".

showing the considerable differences in social standards between the various Swiss cantons without entailing any market disturbances whatsoever.[106]

A considerable sense of humour was indispensable in this line of work, Linthorst Homan wrote to Van der Beugel, passing on a new, "particularly fine example": While the Dutch delegation in the EEC negotiations was fighting tooth and nail against France's policy alignment claims, a Benelux ministers' conference one street away, equally in Brussels, produced a communiqué in which changes in the terms of intra-Benelux competition were called upon to justify certain social policy measures. "Tomorrow, at our conference I will get that flung into my face. I do understand of course that these bits of humour are inherent to political life. All the same there is a large number of issues on which we act differently in Benelux than we advocate in the wider [European] framework".[107]

Such divergence between Benelux policy and the Netherlands' stance on European integration was a source of concern for Van der Beugel, precisely because – as he wrote to Beyen "Benelux is rather important in our talks on European integration. We and our partners frequently refer to Benelux practices to underpin and underline what we deem desirable, or to illustrate what we consider necessary, or rather the opposite".[108]

In case of divergence between European aims and Benelux practice the Dutch delegation pursued a line of argument which we can summarise as follows: Of course, establishing a customs-union between three countries has a lot in common with getting the same job done for six countries. In theory one is dealing with the same set of problems. But that does apply to theory only, in that the difference between a merger of two economies (Netherlands and BLEU) on the one hand and a fusion of the Six on the other is enormous. Moreover, the strong political, cultural and economic ties between the Benelux countries are almost personal, which makes the Beneluxers realise that their history and geographic and strategic location gives them no alternative but to unify. Hence they can afford themselves an empirically oriented incremental approach, because they know they will reach their aim and know and understand each other inside out on this issue. Consequently, there is a world of difference between Benelux' concrete policy results and the virtually white sheet of paper the post-Messina conference of the Six has

---

106 Min. BZ, II, 913.100, No. 54, "Verschillen in sociale politiek in de Zwitserse kantons", with accompanying letter Linthorst Homan to Van der Beugel e.a., 16.5.1956.

107 Min. BZ, II, 913.100, No. 52, Linthorst Homan to Van der Beugel, 11.10.1955.

108 Min. BZ, II, 913.100, No. 130, Van der Beugel to Beyen, 16.11.1955.

to deal with. Thus summarised, Van der Beugel qualified this policy line as "a nice argument, containing a lot of truth on top of it"[109], but no longer adequate to cope with an increasing number of divergencies. In his letter to Beyen he discussed three of these.

Firstly, he recounted Linthorst Homan's experience on the issue. The Dutch view on policy harmonisation in Benelux was by and large countermarching the stance taken in the Messina negotiations.

> On the very same day we emphatically argued in Brussels that differences in wages and social security costs do not constitute a barrier to the establishment of a customs union, in the Benelux framework the ministers published a press statement, in which such differences were explicitly mentioned as competition affecting conditions.[110]

Secondly, whereas the Dutch delegation in Brussels declined a special treatment for agriculture, which it wanted to be dealt with as an integral part of the Common Market, agriculture within Benelux was routinely subject to special regimes.

Thirdly, and even more seriously, Van der Beugel deemed the differences on the institutional issue: In Benelux, although in its development way beyond the customs union discussed by the Six and preparing for perfection by the establishment of a fully-fledged Benelux Economic Union, nonetheless "even the slightest degree of supranationality (...) is dismissed as unimaginable" And yet, in the post-Messina-negotiations the Dutch strongly demanded supranational institutions as an absolute condition for bringing about a customs union.

After discussing these cases of extreme divergence ("I limited myself to three, many others could be brought up"), Van der Beugel wondered how they could be dealt with to make the Dutch position in Brussels less "unworkable". On the institutional issue, in particular, he argued that the ban on supranationalism within Benelux was historically rooted, in that supranationalism was unheard of when Benelux was conceived, i.e. during the Second World War. Van der Beugel's conclusion was clear: either divergence between Benelux policies and The Hague's stance on European integration had to be explained more convincingly, or, the divergence itself had to be tackled. With regard to the latter option, he would appreciate it, if, in the Benelux talks on Economic Union, "a rudiment of supranationalism could at least be on the agenda".[111]

Supranationalising Benelux as a means to save the Netherlands' face in Brussels! Van der Beugel's pressing letter, airing despair and seeking refuge in sarcasm, mooted a problem The Hague did not manage to

---

109 *Ibidem.*

110 *Ibidem.*

111 *Ibidem.*

solve; a problem that would hamper The Netherlands' stance in Brussels throughout the EEC negotiations.[112]

As reported by Van der Beugel, agriculture was one of the issues at stake. The delegations of France, Germany and Italy showed a keen interest in the Benelux regulations on agriculture. The latest Benelux agricultural agreement of May 1955 was distributed as a conference item much to the displeasure of the Dutch Agriculture Minister Mansholt who was not in the least satisfied with the slow rate of progress of Benelux liberalisation in the field. He proved himself anxious that the many protective stipulations in favour of Belgian producers and preferential arrangements, which he was trying to get rid of in the Benelux, would creep in again through the European back door. The Dutch delegates disassociated themselves from such Benelux practices and proposed a common agricultural policy along the lines of Mansholt's original "European Agricultural Community" proposals as launched during the early 1950s. Amongst themselves they referred to the emphatic interest of particularly the French delegates in Benelux agricultural arrangements as "extremely naughty". Thus, on agriculture too, the Netherlands was given a taste of its own Benelux medicine.[113] With foresight, Mansholt deemed that in order to give substance to the principles of a Common Agricultural Policy (CAP), the EEC was to avail of a means of pressure on the Council of Ministers in the form of an executive body with important supranational powers.[114]

Such a necessity to provide the new Community with a powerful supranational institution, equipped with powers of its own, was indeed a crucial underlying idea of the new Beyen Plan. After the downfall of the EDC and in view of French public opinion, this striving for supranationality was, at first, held back by the Benelux partners. However, from the Messina June 1955 conference onwards, Beyen, referring to the institutional problems in Benelux, had argued the *nécessité absolue* of such an institution.[115] Since then the Dutch delegates had frequently and with well-nigh-ritual references to the institutional weakness of Benelux advocated a strong executive.

---

[112] Min. BZ, 913.100, No. 25, Beyen to Prime Minister Drees, 15.5.1956.

[113] Min. BZ, II, 913.100, No. 158, "Verslag van de besprekingen over de agrarische zijde der Douane-unie, Brussel, 11 januari 1956" with accompanying letter Linthorst Homan to Beyen, 13.1.1956, 3. NA, MR, Notulen Ministerrraad, 4.3.1957. For Mansholt's early plans for a European Agricultural Community see: R.T. Griffiths and A.S. Milward, *The European Agricultural Community, 1948-1954*, Florence: EUI, working paper 86/254, 1987.

[114] NA, MR, Notulen Ministerrraad 19.11.1956.

[115] Min. BZ, II, 913.100, No. 21, "Projet de procès-verbal de la réunion des Ministres des Affaires Étrangères des États membres de la C.E.C.A., Messine, 1er et 2 juin 1955", 13.6.1955.

Euratom: a Red Herring?

If one takes a helicopter view of the Netherlands' policies on the 1955-1957 negotiations leading to the treaties of Rome one observation stands out: In comparison with the attention focused on – and energy invested in – the Common Market negotiations, the concurrent talks on the creation of a European Atomic community (EURATOM) were treated in a stepmotherly fashion. Of course, one can interpret this in terms of the Common Market project (or "realising the Beyen Plan") being the spearhead of Dutch diplomacy in Europe, absorbing means and man-power more than anything else. This explanation notwithstanding, this state of affairs also reflects the limited intrinsic significance Beyen and his successor, Luns, attached to the Euratom negotiations. Within the Dutch government this point of view was far from self-evident. Economics Minister Zijlstra and other members of the Cabinet repeatedly emphasized the potential importance of atomic energy for the Netherlands as the largest energy importer among the Six. Nevertheless, Beyen's view prevailed. He and his collaborators suspected that nothing much would come of the nuclear scheme: To which extent would the participating countries be willing to terminate their bilateral nuclear projects with third countries, like the Netherlands own nuclear cooperation project with Norway? How feasible was the projected Euratom monopoly on fissionable materials? Could one design an effective nuclear control regime, both acceptable to Germany and France, while the first was compelled to refrain from military use of atomic power and the second insisted on it? Would France indeed be willing to share its nuclear know-how with the Five? Would the American "Atoms for Peace" offer still stand if this were to facilitate France in developing a nuclear bomb? All of these were moot questions and Beyen's answers tended to be in the negative. Above all, Beyen deemed, Euratom would not work because, as yet another technical cooperation project, it "lacked psychologic appeal": hence it would not enthuse public opinion as the Common Market would.[116]

In pointing out these limitations to the Euratom project in comparison with the Common Market approach Beyen's stance was the complete opposite of both Jean Monnet and the American government on the issue. As Skogmar points out, talks with various officials among the Six made the US representative to the ECSC, Robert Eisenberg, estimate that the Common Market constituted "a pretty nebulous project".

---

[116] R.T. Griffiths and W. Asbeek Brusse, "The Dutch Cabinet and the Rome Treaties", in: E. Serra, *The Relaunching of Europe and the Treaties of Rome*, Brussels: Bruylant, 1989, pp. 461-493 (pp. 482-491). W. Asbeek Brusse, "Euratom", in R.T. Grifftihs, *The Netherlands and the Integration of Europe 1945-1957*, Amsterdam: NEHA 1990, pp. 209-224, (p. 209).

In their talks with American officials Monnet and his emissaries used exactly the same expression when explaining their preference for Euratom over the Common Market proposals. Hence, until well into 1956, official American government attention on the post-Messina negotiations was almost exclusively focused on the Euratom negotiations.[117]

American support for Euratom did remain intact, but otherwise Beyen's reservations were proven right. In January 1957 Luns told the government that Euratom's projected monopoly was seriously compromised, due to the French wishes to maintain Paris' independence on the matter, not least with a view to military applications.[118] Griffiths and Asbeek Brusse characterize feelings in Cabinet towards the eventual Euratom Treaty as "downright hostile".[119]

In spite of its doubtful and dwindling intrinsic value Beyen and Luns considered Euratom an important enterprise in *political* terms. From the relaunching of the Beyen Plan onwards, Euratom constituted the carrot that would keep the donkey moving, i.e. prodding France forward on the road that would lead her to accept the Common Market.[120] Considered this way, Euratom's downsizing in the course of the multilateral negotiations did not basically change the rules of the game. In this respect it was – bye and large – immaterial whether France wanted Euratom with a view to developing a nuclear bomb, or in order to prevent Germany from doing the same[121], or for domestic public opinion consumption as a sop for accepting the Common Market. For Beyen and Luns Euratom was the price-tag attached to realising the Beyen Plan. Tactically, the Hague supported the German *Junctim* which linked the signing of the Euratom Treaty to the EEC Treaty, thus ensuring that France too would live up to its part of the deal.[122]

In the greater scheme of things the question remains open as to which extent the EEC Treaty would have been ratifiable in France without a simultaneous Euratom agreement. Skogmar argues that if the nuclear issue had not been "solved in a way that was acceptable to France the result might have been international cooperation but not

117 G. Skogmar, *The United States and the Nuclear Dimension of European Integration*, Houndmills: Palgrave MacMillan, 2004, pp. 122-125 (p. 123). Winand, *Eisenhower, Kennedy*, pp. 83-87 (p. 83).

118 MR (405), 21.1.1957.

119 Griffiths and Asbeek Brusse, "The Dutch Cabinet", p. 492.

120 NA, MR (401), Notulen Ministerraad 6.5.1955.

121 Skogmar cites French chief Euratom negotiator Maurice Faure: "[...] If there were no Euratom, the Americans would have to make a bilateral treaty with Germany. Germany had already been allowed to have an army. With a powerful atomic industry she would have the fundamental elements of nationalism". Skogmar, *op. cit.*, p. 118.

122 Griffiths and Asbeek Brusse, "The Dutch Cabinet", p. 485.

integration".[123] In the same vein one can pose with Skogmar a second counterfactual question, i.e. whether the Common Market project would have survived, had it been opposed by the US.[124] This leads us to surmise that Euratom may have been a red herring, but from a European point of view it was a remarkably functional one.

IV. Discussion

Even if Benelux were a myth, it would be an illustrious myth. From the first steps on the road to regional integration up to our own times, politicians and academics of intriguing variety have derived inspiration from – and at times proved to be fascinated by – the impact of Benelux as a role model, pioneer and testing station for economic integration on a wider European scale. In economic and historical literature the experiences acquired within Benelux are presented as lessons to be learned for subsequent efforts in integration. The outcomes of this "Benelux laboratory for regional integration" are, however, ambiguous.

From the Dutch point of view, Benelux demonstrated that the benefits of regional economic integration, in terms of economic growth, went well beyond the forecasts of "elasticity pessimists". A substantial increase in intra-Benelux trade at low adjustment costs was imperative for advocating the application of the Benelux model as a model for economic integration among the Six. Likewise, The Hague's governing elite distilled from Benelux experiences the lesson that policy harmonisation could indeed be the result of, rather than a condition for, market liberalisation. On top of the tempestuous development of intra Benelux trade, the role of economic and social policies *vis-à-vis* that development, as well as the impact on the structures of national economies and the adjustment problems brought about by Benelux, provided insights which had their effects on national European integration politics of, in any case, the Benelux countries themselves. In the Netherlands, the success of Benelux liberalisation encouraged policy makers in their trade oriented liberal approach on European economic integration, whereas in Belgium, due to discontent with the unexpected side effects of Benelux, alternative integration models for Western Europe were advocated. During the negotiations leading to the Treaty of Rome, Benelux experiences acted as points of reference, sometimes as an example and sometimes as a spectre.

Benelux foreign policy cooperation did indeed play a vital role in Dutch diplomacy, for most of the period under discussion. As a source of engineering influence it provided The Hague with a leverage it could

---

123 Skogmar, *The United States and the Nuclear Dimension*, p. 252.

124 *Ibidem*.

never have had on its own. Spaak's presidency of the EEC negotiations (1955-1957), however, while crucial for bringing the hoped for Common Market into existence, also narrowed the chances of a Belgian-Dutch teaming up considerably. Lastly, since on essential issues Benelux was far from practicing what it preached, its diplomatic use as an empirical point of reference to support the Hague's European stances was never self-evident, at times even counterproductive.

Beyen and his successor (from October 1956 onwards) Luns did obtain the Common Market that had been the central goal of the Netherlands' European policy since 1952. Their prize-pig, coveted as it was, was a common market according to such specifications as the Six had agreed upon: overly protectionist in its relations with third countries, rather vague on its future policies on the Netherlands' most important export sector (to wit agriculture), an executive endowed with considerably less powers than the Hague had wished and coming at a steep price in terms of levelling labour conditions as well as (as will be dealt with separately in chapter 8) financial contributions to France's colonial development policies.

Looked upon this way, the story of the Netherlands, Benelux and the EEC negotiations is an awkward bedfellow for the school of thought which states that the 1957 EEC Treaty and its subsequent implementation constituted nothing but a diplomatic triumph for the Netherlands. External factors, above all Franco-German understanding on the major issues, severely limited the leeway for Dutch engineering influence.[125] The Uri report was decisive in bridging Beyen's economic abstractions and Spaak's perception of the political realities and economic possibilities of Europe in 1955. Also, our study corroborates Loth's conclusion that it is not exagerated "(...) die Römische Verträge als den Nach der Monanunion zweiten Akt des deutsch-französischen Friedensschlusses zu bezeichnen".[126]

For the Netherlands, however, the Rome treaties first and foremost meant the succesful realisation of a long-term goal of Dutch diplomacy, to wit the establishment of a common market amongst the Six. Indeed, as Griffiths demonstrates, without the constant pressure from the side of the Netherlands there might never have been a common market at all.[127]

---

[125] M. Segers, "Tussen verzoening en verval. De nationale standpuntbepaling van de Bondsrepubliek Duitsland gedurende de beraadslagingen en onderhandelingen over de verdragen van Rome" (PhD thesis Radboud Universiteit Nijmegen [2006]), *passim*.

[126] Wilfried Loth, "Deutsche und französische Interessen auf dem Weg zu EWG und Euratom", Andreas Wilkens (ed.), *Die Deutsch-Französischen Wirtschafsbeziehungen 1945-1960*, Sigmaringen, 1997, pp. 171-187, (p. 187).

[127] R. Griffiths, "The Common Market", in: R.T. Griffiths, *The Netherlands and the integration of Europe, 1945-1957*, Amsterdam: NEHA, 1990, pp. 183-208 (p. 204).

For exerting this pressure Benelux, both as a myth and as a reality, did serve as a valuable policy instrument.

Part II

Defending the Community

CHAPTER IV

Supranationality or Britain?

The Netherlands and the Fouchet Negotiations 1959-1962

Introduction

With hindsight, it could well be argued that the shipwrecking of the Fouchet proposals ranks among the Netherlands' important contributions to European integration in the 1960s. Indeed, the blocking of French president De Gaulle's proposals for an intergovernmental European Political Union, headed by a Council of Heads of State or Government in which the communitarian Brussels' institutions were to be integrated, reflected a strong support for the European Communities' institutions. This substantially delayed their "desupranationalisation", even though the latter could not be forestalled completely. Eventually, with what became known as the 1966 "Luxembourg compromise", European decision-making was – or appeared to be – set on a predominantly intergovernmental footing for over thirty years.[1]

During, as well as after, the Fouchet negotiations the plea for supranationalism in the Dutch stance was criticised as incompatible with that other basic aim of Dutch European policies, namely, British EC membership. Since the intergovernmental preferences of the United Kingdom were well known, such an extension would preclude political integration on a supranational basis, it was argued. After the breakdown of the negotiations the French President commented, clearly hinting at the Dutch position: "It is true that the proposals made by France met with two objections, which incidentally were entirely contradictory although put forward by the same critics".[2]

---

1 For the Netherlands' policy on the January 1966 "Luxembourg compromise" see Chapter 5. For a more elaborated discussion on the latter's impact see: J.-M. Palayret, H. Wallace and P. Winand (eds.), *Visions, Votes and Vetoes. The Empty Chair Crisis and the Luxembourg Compromise. Forty Years On*, Brussels: P.I.E.-Peter Lang, 2006.

2 *Towards Political Union. A Selection of Documents with a Foreword by Mr. Emilio Battista, s.l.: European Parliament*, 1964, p. 45.

This contradictory, or at least paradoxical, nature of Dutch European policy has been the subject of scholarly research as well as of political debate. In his study of the negotiations, Alessandro Silj argues that opposition by The Netherlands to the French plan was essentially motivated by The Hague's refusal to support De Gaulle's bid for French leadership of "Little Europe" as well as by their refusal to accept any form of European integration, except in the field of economic and social policies. According to the Silj analysis, the Dutch had always been lacking true enthusiasm for supranationalism and indeed when, as during the Fouchet negotiations, they put this concept to use, it was basically for window dressing purposes. In the Dutch view, the choice at stake was one between strong Atlantic ties with the USA, or a politically united Europe "having some of the ambitions of a third-world Power".[3] In a European foreign policy structure, apart from the Netherlands themselves, only Great Britain could effectively counterbalance anti-Atlanticist French policies. Nationalist Gaullist France and Atlanticist Holland had been the two poles around which, since 1958, the Community had been revolving, while the other member states, tried, for as long as possible, to avoid making a choice. In the end they did and were "punished" by De Gaulle's veto in January 1963 against British accession to the European Communities.[4] Robert Bloes, in his analysis of the Fouchet negotiations, also points to a 'choc idéologique franco-hollandais' as the latters' central issue. Bloes also argues that, while feigning to advocate "federalism" and "supranationalism", the Dutch government was in fact never disposed to go beyond functionalist economic institutions. Clearly, the Netherlands' transnational companies (Philips, Shell, Unilever, and AKZO) and other economic interest groups were influential in that they managed to gain domination for Atlanticsm even though such "pro-Americanism" was a trait of an economic elite rather than the population in general.[5] Susanne Bodenheimer, in her detailed and sophisticated study of the Fouchet negotiations, is slightly more positive about The Hague's supranationalism and Dutch views on European foreign policy cooperation and integration. Acknowledging that for the Dutch parliament "their principal concern was for the Communities, rather than for Britain" she pictures the government as dominated by

---

3 A. Silj, *Europe's Political Puzzle. A Study of the Fouchet Negotiations and the 1963 Veto*, Harvard: Centre for International Affairs, 1967, p. 60 "third-world power", one could argue, should be read as "third worldpower".

4 Silj, *Europe's Political Puzzle*, *passim* and particularly pp. 40-64. Silj's study of the Dutch stance, we should hasten to add, appears to be based solely on English language materials, which probably influenced his somewhat static if not monolithic rendition of the Netherlands' supranationality policy views.

5 R. Bloes, *Le Plan Fouchet et le Problème de l'Europe Politique*, Brugge: College of Europe, 1970, pp. 212-224.

"Atlanticists", who think of Europe in terms of what is appropriate for The Netherlands.[6] Admittedly, the country's claim to supranationalism finds recognition in her description of Dutch European policy in the latter half of the 1950s: while not accepting the federalist solution, the Dutch government recognized that future development lay in integration and became active advocates of supranationality within functional institutions. "They even cast their lot with the continental bloc, at the expense of ties with Britain". Nevertheless, like Silj and Bloes, Bodenheimer regards the duality of The Hague's stance as a figleaf for what boiled down to Atlanticst considerations. Dutch policy toward political union had been governed by the criterion of British participation, rather than that of "supranational institutions or Britain". By phrasing their policy as a set of two alternatives, the Dutch delegates left the impression that they wanted both, while actually insisting on one of them.[7]

More recent studies based in part on the extensive primary source material in the Dutch national archives present a somewhat different pathology of the "contradiction hollandaise". Nijenhuis, though confirming the primacy of Atlantic considerations over European aims in The Hague's policies and characterizing Dutch Fouchet policies as "extremely opportunistic", argues nonetheless that there was a clear-cut philosophy behind the Dutch "paradox": a united Europe of the Six was too limited for The Hague's political and economic purposes. Therefore, British EC membership was aimed at. If and as long as the UK did not join, the second best cooperation option among the Six should be of a supranational character and, so as not to cripple NATO, remain limited to economics alone.[8] And Riemersma, recalling that outsiders were often perplexed by how The Hague managed to square a predilection for supranational decision-making with the advocacy of British membership of the EEC, arrives at a similar conclusion. Dutch Foreign Minister Luns *cum suis* may have overrated the extent to which Great Britain would feel bound to the *acquis communautaire*, Riemersma argues, and Luns almost certainly felt too optimistic about the Dutch possibilities to play off the UK as a counterweight to the Paris-Bonn axis, "but it would be wrong to deny his course of action a high degree of pragmatism and

6 S.J. Bodenheimer, *Political Union: A Microcosm of European Politics 1960-1966*, Leiden: Sijthoff, 1967, *passim*.

7 *Ibidem*, 158. See also A. Cattani, "Essai de coopération politique entre les Six (1960-1962) et échec des négociations pour un statut politique", *Chronique de Politique Étrangère* (Brussels), 1967, pp. 389-400.

8 H. Nijenhuis, "De Nederlandse tactiek in de onderhandelingen over een Europese politieke unie (1960-1962): Nee tegen De Gaulle!", *Internationale Spectator*, January 1987, pp. 41-49, (p. 49).

logic".[9] This line of argument is carried forward by Bouwman, stressing London's 1958 declared agreement with majority voting on the ministerial council of the projected "Grand Design" free trade area. Bouwman depicts this policy statement as "London's Copernican Revolution". Therefore, Luns was quite right in assuming that the British government underwent a process of "socialisation" and realisation that in the era of interdependence, decision-making should move beyond the nation-state. Heath's October 1961 assertion that Britain was ready to accept and play its full part in the EEC institutions corrobated the Dutch minister's interpretation of a reformed British stance.[10] All in all, Dutch European policy of the early 1960s may have been seemingly paradoxical and as such detrimental to The Hague's credibility. Nevertheless, as we aim to argue in this chapter, considering the deeper motives behind Dutch Atlanticism and supranationalism, these policies appear to lose a lot of their apparent ambivalence.

I. The Netherlands' Policy on the De Gaulle Proposals

Concern and suspicion characterized the Dutch response to the 1960 French-Italian proposals for European political cooperation and the subsequent Fouchet proposals for a European Political Union. During the summer Foreign Minister Luns told his colleagues in the Cabinet that the country had to prepare itself for an isolated stance in resisting French hegemonic attempts. The Hague would probably stand alone in resisting proposals for institutionalized foreign policy cooperation between the six EEC-countries; proposals aimed at a revision of the Treaties of Rome, derobing the supranational Communities of their powers and subjugating them to a structure of intergovernmental committees within the framework of a European Political Union. Prime Minister De Quay argued that De Gaulle's apparent attempt at political leadership among the Six and the establishment of a 'third force' between the USA and the Soviet Union could equally lash back at France itself, putting Paris, rather than the Hague, in an isolated position. Much would depend, it was agreed, on the German stance and the extent to which Adenauer *cum suis* would be willing to stand up for supranationalism.[11]

---

9 R. Riemersma, "No European Military Integration: the Fouchet Plan", in: Ph. Everts and G. Walraven, *The Politics of Persuasion. Implementation of Foreign Policy by the Netherlands*, Aldershot: Gower/Avebury, 1989, pp. 175-188, (p. 186).

10 B. Bouwman, " 'Longing for London': the Netherlands and the Political Cooperation Initiative, 1959-62", in: A. Deighton (ed.), *Building Postwar Europe. National Decision-Makers and European Institutions, 1948-63*, Basingstoke/New York: Palgrave MacMillan, 1995, pp. 141-158 (p. 145, p. 155).

11 NA., MR Notulen Ministerraad 29.7.1960, 5.8.1960 and 19.8.1960.

Luns' vigilance was well grounded. In the months to come, the basic aims of Dutch foreign policy appeared to be at stake: the integrity and supranational character of the European Communities, Britain's EC membership and, last but not least, NATO unity and American leadership. Luns and De Quay turned out to be both right, in that, initially the Netherlands, but eventually France, was to find itself completely isolated. The Dutch-French argument on European political cooperation would turn out to be crucial for the outcome of the Fouchet negotiations.

The Hague's concern should be understood against the recent straining which Dutch-French understanding had undergone on essentials of European and Atlantic policy. As will be argued later on, serious doubts had left their marks in The Hague as to whether De Gaulle's assumption of power was a cure for, rather than an expression of, the ailments of the French Fourth Republic. More in particular, De Gaulle's September 1958 letter to Macmillan and Eisenhower, proposing a "triple directorate" of NATO consisting of the USA, the UK and France, had shocked The Netherlands' government as well as the nation's public opinion. The way France had been rebuffed by Washington and London had been a relief rather than a reassurance for the Hague government.

Traditionally, the scope, contents and room for manoeuvre of Dutch European policy were limited by the demands of NATO membership in general and the country's security dependency on the USA in particular. Awareness that, at the end of the day, only US conventional and nuclear military power could safeguard the Netherlands' territorial integrity made Dutch foreign policy makers judge every European policy option in the light of its possible consequences for the Dutch-American relationship and the functioning of NATO. European options threatening to damage NATO credibility and effectivity and possibly the Dutch-American understanding, were discarded for that very reason. NATO loyalty and the primacy of the transatlantic linkage were called into question *only* when they appeared to threaten the country's self image as a middle sized Power and Dutch colonial interests. Thus, president De Gaulle's attempts at "restoring French grandeur" in the world, were scorned by the Dutch policy makers as undesired competition for American leadership and a weakening of Western defence against the Soviet threat.

Moreover, since European policies had to fit into the Atlantic mould, Parisian initiatives aimed at bringing about a collective Western European foreign and security policy identity could, according to the Dutch, create leverage for the aforementioned French claims at co-directing NATO, and consequently result in undermining the Alliance. In view of the large differences in foreign policy views between the Six, Luns was convinced that "national ambitions rather than a European spirit" lay at the base of the 1960 Franco-Italian proposals for political consultations among the Six. Basically, as Silj worded it later, the proposed political structure was meant to enhance France's claims to address the world powers as the recognized representative and leader of the Six.[12]

Thus, a limited continental political grouping under French or Franco-German guidance was considered detrimental to Dutch interests. The Hague argued against such a block formation, for Atlantic, but equally for domestic reasons: The fact that Western Europe was economically split in two rivalling blocks, EEC and EFTA, was bad enough and should be corrected as soon as possible. An additional political division of Western Europe over and beyond the economic one should be avoided at all costs was the argument from The Hague. Therefore, Prime Minister De Quay and his government had ardently advocated enlargement of the EEC and during the unsuccessful "Grand Design" negotiations of 1958-1959, strongly resented Paris' *de facto* opposition to the establishment of a free trade area between the EEC and the UK and Scandinavian countries.

In June 1959, Foreign Minister Luns had worded Dutch irritation with France's policies during a formal conversation with the French ambassador in The Hague. He did not mince his words: Paris' attempts at forcing through French policies at the expense of the economic interests of other EEC member states would "sooner or later lead to fundamental difficulties between the two countries". The Dutch government was most concerned by the French refusal to further a wider association of European countries. As far as De Gaulle's suggestions for foreign policy cooperation among the Six were concerned, Luns was not amused. An economic *and* political division of Western Europe would be most unwelcome. If the French wished to play a leading role in Europe they should try more traditional methods rather than abusing the concept of "political integration", for which such intergovernmental continental alliance schemes did not have any meaning.[13]

While dining with his French counterpart Couve de Murville in July 1959, Luns clarified the Dutch position. The Netherlands would favour political integration as the final phase of a more comprehensive integration process in due time, to wit if and when truly communitarian decision-making would be *de rigeur*. Only a lengthy process of economic integration could bring about the community of interests which, in Luns' view, was to be considered a *conditio sine qua non* for such political integration to take place. Meanwhile, however, The Netherlands would oppose the establishment of "old-fashioned political alliances" under the

12 Min. BZ, II, GS, 913.10, Luns 28, 3.8.1959; Silj, *Europe's Political Puzzle*, p. 59.

13 Min. BZ, II, PV-EEG Brussel, 996.0 EEG, dossier Plan De Gaulle 1, Luns to Secr. Generaal, 4.6.1959. Min. BZ, II, GS 913.10, 1881, Luns 37, 11.7.1959.

cloak of "political integration", boiling down to the exclusion of the other European countries and detrimenting NATO.[14]

In the fall of 1959, after lengthy negotiations, the Six had managed to reach a compromise. The French obtained the regular consultations on matters of international policy between the EEC Foreign Ministers on which they had been insisting. The six ministers would meet every three months. According to Dutch wishes, however, the consultations would be conducted "without prejudice to consultations in NATO and the WEU" and, would be in no way binding, neither, in the absence of a common secretariat, "institutionalized".[15] Informal non-institutionalized exchanges of views between the Six fitted in very well with The Hague's concept of "silent", if not "secret" diplomacy.

Contrary to Dutch hopes, the 1959 compromise did not settle the political consultations' question for long. When, during the summer of 1960, Luns and his colleagues in Cabinet were informed of new German-French talks on foreign policy cooperation, this matter, as well the bilateral Franco-German basis, on which it was discussed, was viewed with suspicion. Of course, The Hague applauded smooth Franco-German relations as an important condition for effective European cooperation and integration. Intensive bilateral contacts between those two countries, on the other hand, when and if these lead to a *fait accompli* understanding between these two larger European states, through bypassing their European partners, were considered dangerous. Such bilateral understandings, it was argued, could well be to the detriment of the other EC member states and the European Communities as well as, according to some, foster hegemonic tendencies and even trigger off attempts at "leadership", underpin the formation of a "political directorate" *etcetera*. In this respect, the Adenauer-De Gaulle summit at Rambouillet caused anxiety among policy makers in The Hague.[16]

In the aftermath of the Adenauer-De Gaulle summit Luns consulted Benelux partners Belgium and Luxembourg and visited the Italian government in Rome. From the minutes of these meetings it can be learned that Luns' view of the world and the European policy situation had, apart from fundamental differences, a number of elements in common with the philosophy of De Gaulle. Like the French president, Luns was aware that the forthcoming American presidential elections

---

14 Min. BZ, II, GS 913.10, 1881, Luns to SG 22.7.1959.

15 *Towards Political Union. A selection of documents with a foreword by Mr. Emilio Battista*, s.l.: European Parliament, 1964, 5; Min. BZ, II, GS 913.10, 1881, Celer 92 to Luns, 8.9.1959 and Celer 57 to Bonn a.o., 24.11.1959.

16 Min. BZ, PV-EEG Brussel, 996.0, dossier Plan De Gaulle I, Luns 47, 18.6.1959 and Linthorst Homan 182, 4.7.1959; Min. BZ, II, GS, 913.10, 1884, Luns to Paris and Bonn embassies 1.8.1960.

paralysed US foreign policy, thus creating a temporary political leadership vacuum in the Western World. Likewise, Luns criticised the practical functioning of NATO and the executives of the three European Communities.

The Hague's philosophy on how to solve these problems, however, differed widely from that of De Gaulle. First of all, NATO should remain the main forum for coordinating the military and foreign policies of Western Europe's democracies. France's uncooperative Atlantic policies, rather than the absence of a Big Three directorate, were to blame for the Alliance's political malfunctioning. Luns welcomed a reinforcement of policy cooperation between the Six, but in a setting that would promote Dutch national interests, i.e. one respecting the Communitarian framework, rather than the intergovernmental anti-Communitarian set-up which De Gaulle had pleaded for and "which was bound to lead to a French policy for the whole of Western Europe". The French attitude in NATO had demonstrated that Paris did not truly wish to discuss her foreign policy problems with her allies; the creation of new institutions would not change this. Also, Luns pointed out, the Council of Heads of State or Government which De Gaulle now advocated would result in constitutional problems[17] and the proposed ministerial committees would undermine the European Economic Community. Instead of setting up these new institutions, the Six should act in order to avoid a wider economic and political division of Europe, tackle the problem of economic cooperation between the Six and the Seven, and, finally, adhere to the Treaties of Rome. To the Dutch government the institutional framework of the three European communities was sacrosanct: proposals affecting the Communities were to be scrutinized on their supranational calibre. The Hague did not oppose the extension of the "Community method" to other areas, but it fundamentally opposed discussion of issues within the realm of the Communities outside their executives and councils of ministers. Opposition to French moves that would undermine the supranational European edifice was called for. In short, The Netherlands judged the De Gaulle plans negatively.[18]

---

[17] In the Netherlands, the establishment of a Council of Heads of State or Government dealing with foreign policy would create a constitutional problem in that the Prime Minister of the Netherlands is a *primus inter pares* among his cabinet colleagues rather than a leader of government. Foreign policy and defence etc. are the primacy of the respective ministers rather than the Prime Minister's. See the note on the making of Dutch European policy at the end of this book.

[18] Min. BZ, II, GS 913.10, 1884, "Verslag der bespreking tussen Minister Luns en zijn Italiaanse ambtgenoot, Minister Segni, op 16 augustus 1960 in Venetië", 16.8.1960 and Luns to Secretaris-Generaal, 30.8.1960; NA, MR, Notulen Ministerraad 15.7.1960, 19.8.1960; Min. BZ, II, GS 913.10, 1887, Luns to Embassy Bonn 9.11.1960.

At the end of August 1960, the French proposals and the Dutch approach were directly confronted with each other during a meeting of President De Gaulle and Luns, the latter accompanied by Dutch Prime Minister De Quay, in Paris. Not surprisingly, the two views appeared incompatible. De Gaulle presented his well-known concept of the states as the representatives of the peoples and the pillars upon which Europe should be built. The French president criticised both NATO and the EEC for not sufficiently representing the national identities of the participating countries and advocated a stronger say by the national governments, which should not forego their responsibilities as the most important carriers of authority, in these organisations; whereas Luns stressed the importance of supranationality, the core-role of the Communities as a nucleus for further economic and political integration and the undesirability of creating new institutions. The problems of the supranational Communities should be resolved by strengthening these institutions, by a merger of their three executives in particular, rather than replacing them by new political bodies on an intergovernmental basis.[19]

During the fall of 1960, it became increasingly clear that the Dutch were not the only ones critical of De Gaulle's as yet informal propositions, as described in the French President's press conference on 5 September. Adenauer's initial full support for the Rambouillet-proposals, including their anti-NATO and anti-Communitarian overtones, had rather worried and puzzled the Dutch. How can we possibly explain, a high ranking policy maker wondered, that a couple of hours sufficed to convince the Chancellor that a policy he had pursued for years now suddenly was to go down the drain?[20] More reassuring for the Dutch were those diplomatic contacts which suggested that a considerable part of the German administration structurally disagreed with the Chancellor's policy of accommodating De Gaulle and was as critical of the perspective of French leadership of a continental block as the Dutch themselves.

By November, the German state secretary Carsten, in a discussion with the Dutch Ambassador in Bonn, Van Vredenburch, concluded that the debate on the Rambouillet-plan had become *ziemlich still* (rather silent) and he informed his interlocutor that the German federal government could well live with that situation and would certainly not come forward with new initiatives. The German Chancellor himself wrote Luns that he would wait for the opinion of the new US government before deciding on his position.[21]

---

19 Min. BZ, II, GS, 913.10, 1885, Luns circulaire 60, 1.9.1960.

20 NA, MR, Notulen Ministerraad 19.8.1960; Min. BZ, II, 913.10, 1888, Vredenburg aan Tuyll van Serooskerken, 13.2.1961.

21 Min. BZ, II, GS, 913.10, 1887, Van Ittersum to Spierenburg, 12.11.1960.

This positive news, however, did not mean that Luns felt certain that at the next move by De Gaulle they would find the Chancellor on their side. On the contrary, Adenauer's admiration for De Gaulle lent the Federal Republic's stance a degree of unpredictability and the Dutch remained anxious about a possible Franco-German agreement which would subsequently be presented as a would-be *fait accompli* to Italy and the Benelux-countries. When finally, in February 1961, De Gaulle's Rambouillet proposals were formally discussed by the Six in a conference of the Heads of State or Government in Paris, Dutch fears of *fait accompli* policies turned out to be well founded.

Diplomatic sources suggested, Luns told the Cabinet before the Paris meeting, that the conference would not approve institutionalizing meetings of the Heads of State or Government and that, for this and the other French proposals, the most probable outcome was a study group with a sufficiently vague mandate. De Gaulle's proposals constituted a threat to NATO as well as to the European Communities. On foreign policy, the Dutch stance was to be that the United Kingdom should participate if foreign and security policy was to be discussed between the Six on an institutionalized basis. British participation was to be considered necessary in order to avoid a political division of Western Europe and would equally facilitate the upkeeping of NATO interests. In fact, when preparing for the conference, Luns had secured a promise from British Foreign Minister Heath, that the UK would gladly join the talks if the Six invited her to do so. An alternative approach, aimed at initiating foreign policy cooperation among the Six within the Brussels framework of the European Communities and with participation of the European Commission, was suggested and briefly discussed. Luns agreed that he would table it in Paris, although he did not think that such a proposal would stand a chance, especially not with the French government.[22]

In fact, at the Paris conference, Luns and De Quay turned out to be the sole opponents to De Gaulle's proposals. At the occasion of another bilateral meeting on the eve of the conference, De Gaulle had secured Adenauer's support for institutionalized and periodical meetings of the Heads of State and Government, as well as of the Six Ministers of Foreign Affairs. For the preparation of such meetings and the implementation of decisions to be taken a permanent secretariat was to be established. Franco-German pressure and promises (e.g., Italy gained the seat of the projected European University for Florence) eventually made all but the Dutch delegates agree with a previously prepared draft communiqué along these lines. Luns expressed his objections to institutional-

[22] NA, MR, Notulen Ministerraad 27.1.1961 and 3.2.1961; Min. BZ, II, GS, 913.10 1888 "Conferentie op 10 februari 1961 te Parijs van Regeringsleiders en Ministers van Buitenlandse Zaken", 2.2.1961.

ized meetings leading to a political division of Western Europe in two separate blocks. If the other governments, in spite of these objections, preferred to proceed on this matter, UK participation in the negotiations would be a condition for Dutch approval. In lieu of arriving at decisions there and then, a study commission should be established, to report on what was possible and desirable in terms of extended cooperation between the Six and the provisos of British participation. The ensuing discussion between De Gaulle, Adenauer and Luns gained interesting dimensions. The French president qualified the Dutch point of view as illogical: how could The Hague combine the ideal of an integrated common foreign policy on a supranational basis, which thus would preclude British participation, with demanding British participation as a condition for foreign policy cooperation on an intergovernmental basis? Once more, Luns explained Dutch apprehensions concerning block formation within NATO and the undesirability of adding a political split to the economic one in Western Europe. "I was unable to convince De Gaulle", Luns reported to the Cabinet, "neither was the opposite the case, naturally". According to Luns' report of the conference, Adenauer's reaction to the Dutch blockade was downright aggressive. The German Chancellor commenting on the institutionalization issue regarded it a *reine Dummheit* (genuine stupidity) to spend more than three minutes on such a matter of course. The Dutch proposal to suffice with the creation of a study group to deal with the issue he deemed *lächerlich* (ridiculous). Eventually, the conference could do nothing but agree on the utmost the Dutch were willing to accept: the establishment of an official study group which would report to a second meeting of the Heads of State or Government.[23]

Back in The Netherlands, Luns showed himself pleased with the result but highly critical of the course of events and pressure exerted by France and Germany at the conference. Not only had Benelux cooperation cracked down completely, the proceedings elegantly demonstrated the fate lying ahead for the smaller nations in the kind of confederal structure which De Gaulle *cum suis* had in mind, boiling down to France and Germany calling the shots and expecting the smaller countries to play the cheerleaders' part. Dutch resistance to this kind of politics would toughen, Luns promised his colleagues in the Cabinet. Indeed, he summoned the five ambassadors and instructed them to tell their governments that The Hague was anything but pleased at the *fait accompli* the Netherlands, Belgium, Luxembourg and Italy had been confronted

---

23 Min. BZ, II, GS, 913.10, 1888, Luns circulaire 16 14.2.1961; NA, MR, Notulen Ministerraad 17.2.1961.

with and in this respect expected the forthcoming meeting to be distinctly different.[24]

This concerned as well as defensive reaction set the tone for the Dutch stance during the months to come. In the newly established study group, chaired by French Ambassador to Denmark, Fouchet, The Netherlands continued its policy of aiming at British participation and, more in general, procrastinating, meanwhile trying to minimise the damage for NATO and the Communities. As a possible Dutch concession, annual meetings of the EC Council of Ministers at Prime Ministers' level was contemplated, but not tabled.[25] At the first meeting of the study group the Dutch delegates reiterated The Hague's demand that the United Kingdom should be invited to participate in the negotiations. The other delegates refused, arguing that if the UK felt like participating in the political cooperation negotiations, she should apply for membership of the European Communities first. And, since Belgian Foreign Minister Wigny did not wish to team up against the French proposals, Benelux cooperation was powerless and the Dutch delegates found themselves isolated once again.[26] The Netherlands' delegation formally stated that The Hague no longer considered itself committed to the outcome of the deliberations. Even so, the Dutch stayed in Paris and continued negotiating, hitting back by proposing direct elections for the European Parliament, a merger of the executives of the three Communities and similar "supranational" measures, i.e. typically aimed at fostering the "Communitarian system" as laid down in the Rome treaties. Luns was pleased to see that four of the five partner countries responded positively and that on such issues, France and not the Netherlands, found itself standing alone. Likewise, as far as the institutionalization of the proposed foreign policy cooperation was concerned, the "other four" appeared to have second thoughts, in that regular meetings of the ministers of defence and an extensive organizational framework as desired by the French, were rejected. Finally, the proposals for regular meetings of the Heads of State or Government were now referring to "coordinating" foreign policies, instead of arriving at "common decisions" mentioned in earlier drafts. These were hopeful signs and constituted important arguments against walking out of the negotiations altogether, an option seriously considered in March 1961. EC founding father and former Foreign Minister Beyen strongly advised against such a course; delegation leader

---

24 Min. BZ, GS II, 913.10, 1888, Luns 14.2.1961; NA, MR, Notulen Ministerraad 17.2.1961.

25 Min. BZ, II, GS, 913.10, 1889, "Memorandum inzake Franse voorstellen betreffende Europese politieke samenwerking, voor de aanstaande Ministerraad (10 maart)", 7.3.1961 and "Studiecommissie Europees politiek overleg", 14.3.1961.

26 Min. BZ, II, GS 913.10, 1889, Luns to S, 20.3.1961 and De Vos van Steenwijk to M., 22.3.1961.

De Vos van Steenwijk on the other hand suggested that the other Five would not pursue without Dutch participation. During the Spring of 1961, both in the Paris study group and the Hague Cabinet, lengthy, though largely academic discussions were held about supranationalism and its suitability for foreign policy decision-making.[27] Some emphasized that the French proposals lacked supranational perspectives, like Agricultural Minister Marijnen in whose view France was attempting the establishment of a confederation rather than extending integration from economics to politics: "If the French aimed at political integration the way they agreed to economic integration in 1955, The Netherlands would not reject such a course".[28] Foreign Minister Luns clearly was of a different opinion; the time was neither ripe for political integration, nor for a common foreign policy among the Six. As he had pointed out in July 1959:

> Presently, policy consultations in general – as well as among the Six – can serve at the very most coordination of the policies of the participating countries. This is different from setting up a common foreign policy which can only emerge as a result of a previous integration process. An essential condition for political integration, however, is the development of a substantial community of interests over a wide range of topics, particularly as a consequence of economic integration. Thus, a realistic attempt at political integration needs to be directed at the development of such an internal community of interests and not at the creation of a common foreign policy that can only emerge as the coping stone of the integration process.[29]

In The Hague, a sizeable minority of Cabinet Ministers insisted on British participation as a *conditio sine qua non* for whichever Dutch commitment to foreign policy cooperation might evolve. Others preferred an "upgrading" of the Paris proposals by removing the latters' anti-NATO and anti-Communitarian features. The latter tendency prevailed. In Paris, the Dutch delegation tabled a compromise proposal, wherein meetings of the Heads of State or Government were feasible if subjects "concerning NATO structure and strategy" were excluded from the agenda and each meeting was accompanied by parallel consultations within the framework of the Western European Union (thus allowing for British participation). Since discussing NATO-related issues among the Six was the *raison d'être* of the French proposals, the first condition

---

27 Min. BZ, II, GS, 913.10, 1889, "Werkgroep van de Zes inzake politieke consultaties en ontwikkeling der gemeenschappen" (De Vos van Steenwijk to M.), 23.3.1961 and Luns 62 (to London embassy), 27.3.1961 and "Politieke samenwerking Zes" (Beyen to M), 21.3.1961.

28 NA, MR, Notulen Ministerraad 17.3.1961.

29 Min. BZ, II GS, 913.10, 1881 Luns circulaire 37, 10/11.7.59.

alone sufficed in making this proposal unacceptable for the Paris government.[30]

In order to avoid an embarrassing *échec*, the second meeting of the Heads of State or Government was postponed and when it eventually took place, resulted in nothing but a vaguely worded pseudo-compromise. In accepting the communiqué of the 18 July 1961 conference in Bonn, The Netherlands acquiesced in institutionalizing foreign policy cooperation, in return for explicit references stressing the importance of the Atlantic Alliance and the European Communities. The Foreign Ministers would meet "to compare their views, to concert their policies and to reach common positions in order to further the political union of Europe, thereby strengthening the Atlantic Alliance". The preparatory committee headed by Fouchet was instructed by the Six to draft concrete proposals "on the means by which a statutory form can be given (...) to the union of their peoples".[31]

Luns, though hardly pleased with this result, considered the Bonn declaration a statement of lofty intentions aimed at the long term, rather than a deal for practical purposes on the purpose and limits of foreign policy cooperation. Nothing of substance had been agreed upon and, in his minimalist view, he expected subsequent negotiations to result in institutionalizing the 1959 compromise on policy consultations among the Six. More important than the wordings of the Bonn Declaration, he considered the fact that, on issues of substance, France, rather than The Netherlands, had found itself in an isolated position. This fact reflected among other things, successful restoration of Benelux cooperation; now that Paul Henri Spaak took reluctant Wigny's place at the Brussels Foreign Ministry, at last the Netherlands' delegation found an ally on most arguments concerning NATO and the fate of the European Communities.[32]

An even further de-isolation of the Dutch stance came into view when at the end of July 1961 British Prime Minister Harold Macmillan at last announced what the Dutch had been hoping for: Britain now wished to join the European Economic Community. In view of the agreement among the Netherlands' five partners in which only Commu-

---

30 Min. BZ, II, GS, 913.10, 1890, "Stand van zaken Parijse Studiecommissie inz. plannen De Gaulle", 27.4.1961; Min. BZ, II, GS, 913.100, 1891, Vredeburch 240 (Luns to Foreign Ministry), 5.5.1961; NA, MR, Notulen Ministerraad 7.4.1961, 17.4.1961, 28.4.1961, 26.5.1961.

31 *Towards Political Union. A selection of Documents with a foreword by Mr. Emilio Battista*, s.l.: European Parliament, 1964, 9-10.

32 NA, MR, Notulen Ministerraad 21.7.1961; Min. BZ, II, GS, 913.10, 1892, Fack 333 from Bonn, 18.7.1961 and Luns circulaires 63 and 64, 21.7.1961 and Kymmell to Italianer, 31.7.1961.

nity members were to engage in political cooperation talks, the British membership application constituted "a godsend for the Dutch".[33] Denmark and Ireland followed suit and entry negotiations started in October. In Luns' analysis these developments profoundly changed Europe's political landscape. The United Kingdom's entry in the EEC should, according to him, coincide with British participation in the projected treaty on policy cooperation.

Precisely this later perspective was, according to Luns, what the French government wanted to preclude when Fouchet, only a few days after MacMillan's announcement, tabled a complete draft treaty for a Political Union between the Six. This French proposal, apparently based on De Gaulle's original proposals, suggested cooperation in the field of foreign policy, culture and defence. No reference was made to NATO, nor to the exclusion of NATO-related issues from the deliberations of the Heads of State or Government. As far as the European Communities were concerned, the draft prescribed a general review, with a view to "centralizing" the latter within the framework of the new Union of European Peoples, three years after the treaty had come into force.[34]

Clearly, as Luns had told his audience at the national ambassadors' conference in September 1961, De Gaulle attempted "to make hay while the sun shines"; once more essential concerns regarding the Communities and NATO were ignored, once more political cooperation without the UK was attempted.[35]

Spaak and Luns managed to delay negotiations on the Fouchet draft for a number of weeks, insisting on British participation in the talks. "Il n'est logique, ni correct, ni sage de tenir les Anglais à l'écart" Spaak argued.[36] This Belgian-Dutch *préalable anglais* proved effective in that a number of concessions containing safeguards for NATO and the Communities were agreed upon. On the main question, however, whether the Six should proceed without British participation, no agreement could be reached and in December 1961, Spaak broke the common Benelux front, bowed to the majority and agreed to negotiations be-

33 R. Dingemans and A.J. Boekestijn, "The Netherlands and the enlargement proposals 1957-1963", in: A. Deighton and A.S. Milward (eds.), *Widening, Deepening and Acceleration: the European Economic Community 1957-1963*, Baden-Baden: Nomos, 1999, pp. 215-241, (p. 235).

34 Towards Political Union. A selection of documents with a foreword by Mr. Emilio Battista, s.l.: European Parliament, 1964, 11-14; NA, MR, Notulen Ministerraad 27.10.1961.

35 Min. BZ, II, GS, 913.10, 1892, De Vos van Steenwijk to Luns, 1.9.1961; Min. BZ, II, GS, 913.10, 1893, De Vos van Steenwijk to Luns, 24.10.1961 and Chef DEU to Luns, 26.10.1961; NA, MR, Notulen Ministerrraad 27.10.1961.

36 Min. BZ, II, GS, 1894, De Vos van Steenwijk to Luns, 2.12.1961.

tween the Six on the basis of the Fouchet draft.[37] The Belgian minister's desertion came as a nasty shock to Luns, who had invested high hopes in renewed Benelux' cooperation as a policy instrument which could make crucial difference in Europe. Spaak had expressed himself in the same vein, shortly after retaking office, in June:

> Le maintien de l'unité des pays du Benelux est certainement l'un des points que nous devons nous efforcer d'atteindre [...]. Quand [...] nous pouvons trouver un point de vue commun et le défendre ensemble, je crois que nous sommes alors une puissance, je ne dirai pas avec laquelle it faut compter, ceci pourrait paraître excessif, mais dont certainement le potentiel ne peut être négligé dans les discussions.[38]

Such hopes were now turned into disillusion. Once more, the Netherlands found itself isolated. Luns stuck to the *préalable anglais*, reminding his colleagues in the Cabinet of the fact that The Hague had ratified the 1957 Rome Treaties, convinced that the free trade area negotiations with the UK would bear fruit. Since nothing had come of the latter, "this time we want to be sure".[39] In practical policy this meant that the Dutch delegation supported the substantial pro-Communitarian improvements to the Fouchet draft which Belgian, German and Italian co-pressure brought about, while insisting on British participation.[40]

Interestingly enough, it was De Gaulle who came to the rescue of the Dutch negotiators. In his second draft treaty proposal of 18 January 1962, nearly all French concessions agreed upon during the fall of 1961, were withdrawn. The Council of Heads of State or Government was to have intergovernmental preponderance over the supranational Brussels institutions. References that could be interpreted as acknowledging NATO's primacy in defence matters had been erased. As De Gaulle biographer Lacouture would argue afterwards, a few pencil strokes sufficed in making the French position entirely untenable:

> En quelques 'coups de crayon' le général avait ruiné les efforts de ces négociateurs qui savaient ne pouvoir aboutir qu'en ménageant à la fois Washing-

---

37 Min. BZ, II, GS, 1893, Van Baarda 209 to De Vos van Steenwijk, 6.11.1961 and "Resumee van Minsterieel Benelux gesprek op dinsdag 7 november 1961 te Brussel", 8.11.1961 and Beyen 528 to Min. BZ, 10.11.1961; Min. BZ, II, GS, 1894, Celer 162 to various embassies, 18/19.12.1961 and Celer circulaire 107, 18/19.12.1961 and Luns 64 to Brussels, 20.12.1961; G.H. Soutou, "Le général de Gaulle et le plan Fouchet", De Gaulle et son siècle, Vol. V., Paris: Institut Charles de Gaulle/Plon, 1992, pp. 126-143, p. 136.

38 Chr. Franck, "La politique européenne belge: une continuité de quarante ans", in: M. Dumoulin, G. Duchenne and A. van Laer (ed.), *La Belgique, les petits états et la construction européenne*, Brussel: P.I.E.-Peter Lang, 2003, pp. 261-277, p. 266.

39 Min. BZ, II, GS, 913.10, 1893, "Frans ontwerp-verdrag Europese Unie", Luns to Cabinet, 1.11.1961 and Celer to various embassies, 23.11.1961.

40 Min. BZ, GS, II, 913.10, 1894, Luns 3 to embassy Brussel, 22.12.1961.

ton et les organismes de Bruxelles... Ce soir-là, le négociateur français Jean-Marie Soutou nota tristement sur son carnet: 'C'est la fin de tout cela...'.[41]

What induced the French President to kill his own brainchild? Following Vanke, we can assume that it was done intentionally: De Gaulle had hoped to unite the Six behind French international positions. This unacknowledged intention was recognized by the Dutch, who tactically insisted on British membership since this would obstruct De Gaulle's undeclared purposes. As De Gaulle preferred his project's absolute failure to its dilution he let it run aground.[42]

II. Dutch Supranationalism and Atlanticism: Some Interpretative Comments

For all practical purposes De Gaulle's January 1962 interception killed the Fouchet negotiations. Be that as it may, in February 1961, the French President had been right in detecting a seemingly "illogical" element in Dutch European policy, in that two apparently irreconcilable aims, supranationality and British membership of the European Communities, were presented as mutually exchangeable.

Indeed, Dutch Foreign Minster Luns' supranationalism was not tarnished by a high federalism content. Supranationalism was deemed necessary to guarantee the carrying out of the Rome treaty obligations against policies and interests of individual member states. As such, the Foreign Minister's stance reflected – and should be understood against the background of Dutch institutional philosophy on European integration as it had developed since the early 1950s.

The Dutch view regarding the institutional form to be given to European organizations and frameworks had always been closely bound up with the objectives the government had set itself in its European policy. Initially, from the end of the Second World War, up to 1952, intergovernmentalism prevailed. Hence, during the negotiations that led to the creation of the ECSC, the Netherlands sought to limit the powers of the High Authority and worked successfully towards the setting up of a Council of Ministers to act as a 'watchdog' to ensure that the ECSC would adequately respect national interests. However, when Jan Willem Beyen took over the Foreign Ministry in 1952, a fundamental policy

41 J. Lacouture, *De Gaulle, 3. Le Souverain 1959-1970*, Paris: Ed. du Seuil, 1986, pp. 321-322; G.H. Soutou, "Le général de Gaulle et le plan Fouchet d'union politique européenne: un projet strategique", in: A. Deighton and A.S. Milward (eds.), *Widening, Deepening and Acceleration: the European Economic Community 1957-1963* (Baden-Baden: Nomos, 1999, pp. 55-71, *passim*.

42 J. Vanke, "An Impossible Union: Dutch Objections to the Fouchet Plan, 1959-1962", *Cold War History*, Vol. 2, No. 1 (October 2001), pp. 95-112.

change took place. Hesitantly at first, Dutch policy makers grasped that only transfers of national sovereignty could materialize the bigger-than-Benelux market they aimed at.

For Beyen himself, as we argued in Chapter 1, the rationale of negotiating in the limited context of the Group of Six, was precisely this possibility of arriving at horizontal integration on a supranational footing, something seen as impossible in wider bodies such as the OEEC.

In 1955, at the historical Messina conference, the Dutch reiterated their view that a supranational executive equipped with far-reaching powers was a necessary condition for the actual achievement of a customs union and, ultimately, a common market. During the ensuing EEC negotiations, the Dutch delegations advocated an institutional structure in which decision-making powers in the Community would lie with the Executive, that is, the European Commission, on all questions related to the achieving and the smooth running of the Common Market. This stress on the Commission's position as the pivot around which the other actors in the decision-making process were to turn, was in line with Dutch concepts on governmental responsibility for economic and social conditions within the Netherlands itself and was attributable to various factors. Firstly, the conviction among Dutch policy makers that an intergovernmental organisation would be insufficiently capable of circumventing important national interests where this was necessary to implement Treaty provisions played an important part. This applied in particular to the sought for Common Agricultural Policy (CAP), so important for Dutch exports. An intergovernmental set-up of such a policy, Agricultural Minister Mansholt argued, would lead to major influence by farm interest groups, particularly in Germany, France and Belgium, with the result that the CAP would either not come into being or else take on a heavily protectionist character. A second reason for placing the European Commission at the fore was constituted by the experience Dutch policy makers had accumulated in the Benelux context. The slow, difficult progress in developing Benelux from a customs union towards a full economic union was, in their view, the fault of its weak institutional structure. It was precisely because Benelux, as an intergovernmental organisation, had no supranational agencies with their own powers that it was so difficult to adjust the policy of the three participatory states to each other and bring about a genuine free market in farm products. If primacy in the decision-making process was not placed with the Commission, Treaty agreements would be torpedoed in the Council of Ministers because of the lack of unanimity[43] (see Chap-

43 A.G. Harryvan, "Tussen voorbeeld en schrikbeeld. De doorwerking van de Benelux-ervaringen in de Europese integratiepolitiek van Nederland en België, 1948-1958", in: E.S.A. Bloemen (ed.), *De Benelux-factor. België, Nederland en Luxemburg en de*

ter 3). In short: Benelux was taken as a countermodel for the administrative organisation of the EEC. A third factor was the consideration that the rights and interests of medium and small Member States would best be respected in a supranational context. Precisely this consideration testified to the Dutch fear of being locked into a protectionist block dominated by a Franco-German directorate. Failing British participation in the Communities, The Hague sought guarantees against such domination in the incorporation of Member States on as equal a footing as possible in Community decision-making. In this latter respect particularly, supranationalism embodied the defensive trait clearly recognisable during the Fouchet negotiations in Dutch policy makers' attacks on intergovernmental decision making structures in which smaller nations, though formally entitled to a veto, *de facto* found themselves forced to follow the lead of the larger ones and the *fait accomplis* with which the latter confronted them.[44]

This view towards the institutional base of European integration and supranationalism set the tone for the decades to come. From the establishment of the Community in 1958 onwards, The Netherlands attempted to defend the powers of the European Commission, advocated their extension, supported the principle of majority vote in EEC decision making, as well as stressing the basic equality of the EC Member States. Nevertheless, it should be pointed out that this stance generally reflected a functional or instrumental approach towards supranationalism rather than a federalist creed. Supranationalism, like European integration as a whole, was considered as a means rather than an end. Although among high-ranking civil servants, and in the Cabinet, supporters of European federalism could be detected, Foreign Ministers Luns and most policy makers in his wake were of a different persuasion and advocated, what

---

integratie van Europa 1948-1957, Amsterdam: NEHA, 1992, pp. 169-191; The transformation of Benelux itself into a supranational organisation was indeed proposed, but met with great objections in both Brussels and The Hague. It was completely inconceivable for a larger number of seats on the supranational executive to be held by either Dutch or Belgian representatives. But with an equal number of seats, in the event of conflict, Luxembourg would have the casting vote, something unacceptable to either government.

44 Penders and Kwast mention the need to integrate Germany in Western Europe as an additional argument for supranationalism, since only a supranational EC acting as a Community could perform this function. J. Penders and M. Kwast, "The Netherlands and Political Union", in: A. Pijpers (ed.), *The European Community at the Crossroads*, Dordrecht: Nijhoff, 1992, pp. 253-270, p. 254; For a more elaborated discussion of Dutch supranationalism during the EC's formative years see A.G. Harryvan, "The Netherlands and the administration of the EEC: Early principles and practices (1952-1965)", in: *Die Anfänge der Verwaltung der Europäischen Gemeinschaft/Les débuts de l'administration de la Communauté européenne* [Hrsg. Erk Volkmar Heyen] Baden-Baden: Nomos, 1992 (Jahrbuch für europäische Verwaltungsgeschichte; 4), pp. 239-254.

could be called, "instrumental supranationalism" as a vehicle for realising the Common Market and checking the Larger Powers. Of course, The Hague showed itself critical of the practical functioning of the European Commission. Neither did Luns expect to live and see the day that a communitarian foreign policy would be decided upon by majority voting among the EC member states. All the same, De Gaulle's aggression towards and policies concerning that assembly of "technocrates qui veulent diriger l'Europe", as the French President worded it, were deemed decidedly more dangerous and provocative than Hallstein *cum suis*. Thus, Luns' defence of the European executives was the heart and soul of his instrumental supranationalism, or, as he – significantly enough – preferred to call it, the "communitarian method".

Although instrumental supranationalism or "the communitarian method" rather than European federalism was the dominant approach among the Dutch foreign policy elite, during the late 1950s and most of the 1960s the *Tweede Kamer* (lower house of Parliament) was in the grip of an outspoken and vociferous majority of *Europeanen* (federalists), which, as we will argue in the next chapter, seriously influenced the tone and direction of the country's European policy.

The communitarian method and its underlying aims proved compatible, rather than contradictory, with traditional Dutch Atlanticist policies. For five out of the six partner countries, British membership of the Communities was to be welcomed. In The Hague, the primacy of Atlanticism was never seriously at stake. The "contradiction" De Gaulle was hinting at, was apparently not experienced as such. On the contrary, British accession to the EEC and a modest degree of supranationalism by means of the "communitarian method" were considered complementary conditions for realising the larger European Common Market, The Hague's ultimate aim.

When analysed at the level of the underlying motives, Dutch Atlanticism and supranationalism appear to be serving a common goal. During the Fouchet negotiations, Luns repeatedly stressed that "the establishment of a European block would endanger the basis of NATO, i.e. the equality of her members".[45] It can well be argued, indeed, that the prime motive for Dutch Atlanticism was (and is) political rather than military in nature: The Netherlands prefer leadership "at a distance" from the USA over bids for dominance from large neighbouring European states, especially Germany and France. Cultural and historical suspicion of these two countries, Van den Bos argues, constitute the main motive for the primacy of Atlanticism. By accepting the dominance of the USA, all European partners find themselves at the same, second level. Thus

[45] Min. BZ, PV-EEG Brussel, 996.0 EEG Plan De Gaulle II, Luns/Van de Vos van Steenwijk 13.5.1961.

American leadership of NATO underpins 'equality before the USA' and precludes hegemonic attempts of the larger European countries.[46] Viewed in this light, Luns' Atlanticism in general, and the *préalable anglais* in particular, served the same purpose as his defence of the EC-executives' powers.

Dutch fears of Franco-German hegemonic attempts reflected a tradition of anti-continentalism in The Hague's foreign policy. Since the end of the Second World War onwards, however, Dutch foreign policy appeared somewhat ambiguous in this respect. On the one hand Luns *cum suis* were convinced that Franco-German understanding was a condition for – as well as an important object of – Western European cooperation and integration. On the other hand, intensive bilateral contacts between these two countries were deemed dangerous, if and when they would lead to *fait accompli* understandings to the detriment of the other EC-member states and the European Communities.

During the 1959-1962 negotiations such fears of a Paris-Bonn axis appear to have been fostered by De Gaulle's apparent influence on German Chancellor Adenauer and, more in general, by the image in the Netherlands of the new French Republic and the policies of its president.

Public opinion and the press showed themselves concerned about the developments and institutional changes in France during the late 1950s, a concern shared by the Netherlands' foreign policy elite. De Gaulle's return to power in 1958 was received with mixed feelings. True, the crises of the Fourth Republic and its inherent political weakness, made some dramatic change appear inevitable in what was generally considered the 'sick man of Western Europe'.[47] Also, for the chances of carrying through the EEC and its Customs Union, De Gaulle's return to power and the relative political and economic stabilization in its wake, turned out to be crucial. A cause of alarm, however, were the accompanying authoritarian tendencies and crisis of democracy, indicated by the Dutch press. Commentators and politicians alike showed themselves unconvinced that De Gaulle and the new Fifth Republic were indeed a cure for, rather than an expression of, the ailments of France's political system. At the time of De Gaulle's assumption of power in May 1958, the major newspapers agreed that France's democracy was in danger. The leading *Handelsblad* described the situation as "suicide of a democracy". Although De Gaulle himself, as was generally underlined, was not to be considered a dictator or fascist, comparisons with the demise

---

[46] B. van den Bos, "Tussenstation Maastricht: op weg naar een Europese veiligheidsidentiteit", *Nieuw Europa*, December 1991, pp. 40-44.

[47] H. van Galen Last, "Frankrijk: een Nederlands probleem", *Intermediair*, 12.1.1979 pp. 7-13, p. 7.

of the German Weimar Republic in 1933 and Spanish dictator Franco's coming to power 1936 were made. After all, it was deemed, the principles of democracy were not firmly rooted in French political culture and De Gaulle – as well as the French in general – appeared to be "living in the past". One of best informed Catholic journalists noted "an unpleasant pre-fascist climate in France".[48] Such misgivings turned out to be exaggerated, and by September 1958, De Gaulle's effectivity at stabilising a country that had been at the brink of a civil war found the admiration it deserved. The democratic quality of the new regime, however, remained in doubt. The new Constitution expressed authoritarian traits by concentrating power at the executive level, while diminishing the role of parliament. The results of parliamentarian elections under the new electoral law in November 1958 were considered shocking. Dutch observers, used to proportional representation, pointed to the fact that the Gaullist party, with a number of votes roughly equal to that of the Communists, eventually obtained twenty times the latters' number of seats and an overwhelming majority in parliament.[49]

For the years to come, in the Netherlands, the image of the French Republic remained characterized by what could be called an ideologically one-sided set of negative judgements, expectations and prejudices. The new French Republic was considered potentially unstable and democratically not quite up to the mark, heir to and thus tarnished by collaboration, communism, corruption and *coups d'états*.[50]

Of course, and fortunately, such popular images played a limited role in foreign policy making and it should be stressed that large areas of Dutch-French bilateral relations remained untouched by this negative image. Luns himself went to lengths to stress that, in spite of differences of opinion, bilateral relations with France were blooming. In most EEC matters, indeed, the two cooperated smoothly. Likewise, in (post) colonial affairs mutual understanding and help was the norm. French support for The Hague during the Dutch New Guinea conflict was

48 H.L. Wesseling, "De terugkeer van De Gaulle. Nederlandse reacties op 1958", in: H.L. Wesseling, *Oorlog lost nooit iets op*, Amsterdam: Bakker, 1993), pp. 238-250.

49 *Ibidem.*

50 Van Galen Last, "Frankrijk"; Former State Secretary E.H. van der Beugel offered a fine example of Dutch consciousness on this matter in a contribution to "Le monde Diplomatique" in 1963: "Cet enthousiasme envers la politique de coopération et la chaleur des sentiments en faveur de l'Europe intégrée n'ont jamais été remis en cause, bien qu'étant parfois tempérés par une certaine crainte quant à la composition de l'Europe des Six. Les Pays-Bas sont une nation éprise de stabilité et pourvue d'une solide tradition démocratique. Les trois puissants partenaires des Pays-Bas dans le cadre de l'Europe des Six ont un passé différent sous ce rapport". E.H. van der Beugel, "De la nouvelle relance européenne?", in: *Ernst Hans van der Beugel 65 jaar*, s.l.: Brill, 1982, pp. 27-31, (p. 28).

reciprocated by Dutch support for Paris in the Algerian war.[51] In both Atlantic and European matters, however, in dealing with France, Dutch policy makers reputed for their composed and down to earth attitude, expressed and recorded in their files multitudinous indications of personal feelings of surprise, bewilderment, amusement and indignation *vis-à-vis* French demeanour and diplomacy.

Undoubtedly, these reactions partly reflect a wounded sense of pride of a former colonial Power trying to deal with its diminished importance, as well as the aforementioned concern for Franco-German leadership aspirations. "We have to make clear that we don't want to officiate as *decorfiguranten* for French or German performances or display of power, the way we are being treated during the last few months" an angry high-ranking civil servant wrote to Luns. "Pour qui nous prend-on?" an exasperated colleague had asked rhetorically during the preceding negotiations.[52] On several occasions, as will be recalled, the Foreign Minister himself saw signs of Franco-German attempts at domination in the way he was confronted with *fait accomplis* and raised his voice against them.

On top of this, however, the French Republic's poor image in the Netherlands played its part. As mentioned above, De Gaulle's September 1958 letter to Macmillan and Eisenhower, proposing a "triple directorate" of NATO consisting of the USA, the UK and France, left the Netherlands' government and public opinion flabbergasted. France's policy makers apparently had lost their sense of proportion, it was agreed. As the German negotiator Mueller Roschach aptly worded it a year later: "We are all smaller countries. The difficulty is that one of us is living with the illusion of being a Great Power".[53] Dutch delegation leader De Vos van Steenwijk, commenting on French European policy, did not mince his words either. "Due to the Algerian crisis and leadership by a defiant and chauvinistic individual, this country is in a condition of intoxication. Consequently, its political reflexes are primitive. In European affairs it aspires to hegemony".[54] Some of these compliments,

---

51 D. Bocquet, "France – Pays Bas, vers une meilleure comprehension?", *Nieuw Europa*, March 1992, pp. 18-22; Min. BZ, PV-EEG Brussel, 996.0 EEG, Plan De Gaulle III, Luns via Beyen to Min. BZ, 18.4.1962.

52 Min. BZ, II, GS, 1893, DIE to M., "Ministeriële bespreking 10 december over ontwerp-verdrag Europese Unie", 29.11.1961, p. 4; Min. BZ, PV-EEG Brussel; 996/0 EEG Plan De Gaulle II, Van de Vos van Steenwijk, via Beyen and Min. BZ to Brussel, Celer 13.11.1961.

53 Min. BZ, II, GS, 1883, Bonn (Fack) to Min. BZ, 27.7.1960.

54 Min. BZ, II, GS, 913.10, 1894, De Vos van Steenwijk to M., "Ministeriële conferentie 10 december over ontwerp-politiek statuut voor Europa", 2.12.1961, p. 6; Another example of De Vos van Steenwijk's "méfiance inquiète": 'the idea that this cooperation would result in the common denominator of the political stances of the Six

as well as "l'esprit des antigaullistes de La Haye et de Bruxelles", were returned:

> On ne peut pas forcer Spaak et Luns à adhérer à une Union des États. D'ailleurs, quels États représentent-ils? Et si ces deux ministres dressent tant de barrières devant la conclusion d'un accord, combien en dresseraient-ils devant son application? Je me demande si la Belgique et la Hollande n'ont pas peur de faire l'Europe, tout en prétendant que c'est leur plus cher désir. Elles se sentent toutes petites en face des plus grands. Elles espèrent que, si l'Angleterre se joint à la bande, les grands seront tellement opposés les uns aux autres que les petits pourront jouer de l'antagonisme des premiers.[55]

In the low countries themselves, however, Belgian-Dutch foreign policy cooperation was considered far from victorious. Rather, Benelux cooperation was and is looked upon, as, in fact, the major victim of the Fouchet episode. As Stelandre rightly points out, precisely the attempts among the Six to arrive at cooperation in foreign policy on a European level demonstrated to the Benelux governments the divergence of their views on the matter: whereas the Dutch were opposed to a restricted continental European framework, Luxembourg was inclined to support the Fouchet proposals while the Belgians "adoptent des attitudes variées qui ne manquent pas d'agacer leurs voisins du Nord".[56] To put it mildly. The Dutch-Belgian differences on Europe's political future might lead, De Vos van Steenwijk told his Belgian interlocutors in March 1961, to the political break-up of Benelux itself.[57]

III. Discussion

The Dutch "engineering" stance during the Fouchet negotiations was basically a conservative one. Luns' "instrumental supranationalism" was expressed in tenacious opposition against De Gaulle's attempts at disrobing the Communities of their powers and subjugating them to a structure of intergovernmental committees within the framework of a European Political Union. Thus, with Silj, we may conclude that the Fouchet plan was rejected because it represented a departure from the

---

seems illusionary. France will endeavour to impose its policy on the others. The ultimate reason why we cannot accept institutionalized cooperation as desired by De Gaulle, is the danger incorporated, in the Dutch view, in De Gaulle's policies and person.' Min. BZ, II, GS, 913.10, 1891, De Vos van Steenwijk to M, "Franse plannen inzake politieke samenwerking", 5.6.1961, p. 3.

55 Lacouture, *Le Souverain*, 323; Alain Peyrefitte, *C'était de Gaulle*, Paris: Éditions de Fallois/Fayard, 1994, p. 107; See also: Charles de Gaulle, *Lettres, notes et carnets. Janvier 1961-Décembre 1963*, s.l. [Paris]: Plon, 1986, p. 197.

56 Y. Stelandre, "Les pays du Benelux, l'Europe politique et les négociations Fouchet (26 juin 1959 – 17 avril 1962)", Journal of European Integration History, 2 (1996), pp. 21-38, p. 22.

57 *Ibidem*, 30.

Community system; that is from the existing European institutions. The French plans were considered by the Dutch as an attempt to cripple these institutions, by transferring their powers to a new political structure of an intergovernmental character.

The seeming incompatibility of supranationalism with pleas for enlargement and particularly British membership strikes the eye. Clearly, Atlanticism had been at the heart of Dutch reticence when responding to the Franco-Italian proposals of 1959 for political consultations among the Six. Throughout the 1960s UK membership was viewed as an insurance against French or Franco-German attempts at dominance on the European continent.

Nevertheless, considering the deeper motives behind Dutch Atlanticism and Dutch supranationalism (or "the community method"), these policies lose their seeming incompatibility. Dutch "instrumental supranationalism" was first and foremost a means to an economic and political end, namely the realization of a sizeable internal European market and the checking of the bigger members, if and where these pursued hegemonic policies. Likewise, British membership was considered useful because it would preclude hegemonic attempts by Germany or France.

As such, the gist of Dutch supranationalism was pragmatic-instrumental rather than federalist, in nature. UK membership was, to a considerable degree, interchangeable with "the community method" in that it equally held out prospects of realizing the same two policy goals.

CHAPTER V

A Successful Defence of the Communitarian Model?

The Netherlands and the Empty Chair Crisis

Introduction*

When De Gaulle's empty chair crisis hit the Netherlands, it hit a country with a mission. From the early 1950s onwards, the creation of a European common market had been the core objective of Dutch European policy. Free trade in Western Europe would bring the Netherlands the export markets, agricultural and otherwise, it so desperately needed for both its economic growth as well as the ambitious industrialisation schemes proposed by successive governments. Hence, "realising the Beyen Plan" was at the centre of The Hague's diplomacy from 1952 onward, when the Foreign Minister, Jan Willem Beyen proposed the gradual establishment of a customs union among the Six to be subsequently transformed in a fully fledged common market in a time-tabled process supervised by supranational institutions (see Chapter 1). After its initial demise, due to the shipwrecking of the European Political Community and European Defence Community, Beyen re-launched his plan at the 1955 Messina summit. Two years later he enjoyed the pleasure of witnessing the coming to life of his brainchild in the form of the Rome Treaty's European Economic Community (see Chapters 2 and 3). Since implementation of this Treaty, however, was far from certain, particularly after the breakdown of the Fourth French Republic in 1958 and the coming to power of De Gaulle, constructing the Common Market remained at the heart of Dutch European policy as a consummation devoutly to be wished and worked for. In this policy tradition, supranationalism was deemed a necessary means to further the Netherlands' European interests. A powerful and independent European Commission and decision-making based on majority voting in the Council, in

* An earlier version of this chapter was published as: Anjo G. Harryvan, 'A Succesful Defence of the Communitarian Model? The Netherlands and the Empty Chair Crisis', in: Jean-Marie Palayret, Helen Wallace & Pascaline Winand, *Visions, Votes and Vetoes. The Empty Chair Crisis and the Luxembourg Compromise Forty Years On*, Brussel: P.I.E.-Peter Lang, 2006, pp. 129-152.

particular, were considered indispensable for bringing about the Common Market. Both were rightly enshrined in the Rome Treaty, not for federalist sentiments, but to guarantee the effectiveness of the EEC's decision-making. Limited to European *economic* integration, such "functional supranationalism" or "instrumental supranationalism" was not at odds with the Hague-coveted primacy of Atlanticism in the realm of high politics

Nevertheless, The Hague's Atlanticism sometimes collided with the aspirations held by other European partners, as was the case in the early 1960s when the French government launched its Fouchet Plan with the aim of creating a forum for intergovernmental political cooperation on the European continent, outside of the EEC's institutional framework. As we argued in chapter 4, the Dutch government considered the creation of a European Political Union (EPU) without British participation to be detrimental in the longer run to Atlantic unity and American leadership thereof.

Furthermore, The Hague was shocked by President De Gaulle's unilateral decision in January 1963 to veto British membership of the EEC. On that occasion Foreign Minister Luns did not mince his words. The spirit of the Community had been "seriously compromised": "I do not exaggerate, Mr. Chairman, when I say that what has happened today has made it a black day for Europe". As we have seen, British entry was welcomed in the Netherlands for various reasons, among which the perceived importance of the UK as a counterweight to possible Franco-German attempts at dominating the Community. Luns also suspected that the creation of an EPU on an intergovernmental basis would have a negative – possibly contagious – impact on the forthcoming supranational development of the EEC (see Chapter 4).

In this chapter we analyse the Dutch handling of the empty chair crisis of 1965-1966 and the extent to which the Hague government managed to defend and further its European policy goals under the conditions brought about by the crisis.

I. Agriculture: the Motor behind Supranationalism?

At the outbreak of the crisis, the functional supranationalist approach to European integration was the dominant line in the Foreign Ministry as well as being supported by a majority in the *Ministerraad* (Dutch Cabinet), which had been chaired by Prime Minister Jo Cals since April 1965. Cals headed a coalition government (as was customary in the Netherlands) consisting of Labour (PvdA), the Catholic party (KVP) and the Protestant party (ARP), that had sound reasons to be satisfied with the integration process as it was developing in Brussels: the Common Market was well under way, thanks to a strong and active Commission and high economic growth, enabling trade liberalisation between the Six ahead of the EEC Treaty schedule. For the Netherlands, as the largest agricultural exporter of the Six, the proposed common agricultural policy (CAP) was of great importance as well. European Commissioner Sicco Mansholt, who was Dutch, had managed to successfully implement the rather loosely worded agricultural commitments of the Treaty of Rome. As qualified majority voting (QMV) was to be introduced only in the third Treaty phase, i.e. from 1966 onwards, until that year unanimity in the Council was a precondition for the adoption of legislation. Mansholt and his fellow Commissioners and staff devised ingenious package deals containing more or less equally distributed benefits for each of the member states. Thus, from 1962 onwards, agriculture gradually became the main engine of European integration. By the time the Cals government came to power "EEC" more or less equalled "agriculture", as 95% of the EEC budget, 90% of its regulations and 70% of the time spent on Council meetings was CAP-related.[1] In its government policy statement of April 1965, the Cals government stated its unwavering support for the Brussels integration process and emphasised "the speedy completion of the common market" as an "elementary economic interest of our country".[2] In this respect, QMV, to be introduced by January 1966, was more than welcome.

However, as we argued in chapter 4, in the Lower House of the Netherlands' Parliament, the *Tweede Kamer*, functional or instrumental supranationalism represented a minority position under constant and severe pressure from a rival approach. By 1965 a large majority in Parliament, as well as a sizeable minority in the Cabinet, were of an outspoken federalist persuasion. This is not the place for an in-depth analysis of the political and psychological origins of federalist convictions in Dutch politics and public opinion. The transformation is aptly characterized by De Bruin: from the late 1950s onwards, he quipped, "the Netherlands joined the European Communities the way other people join a religious order" ("*Les Pays-Bas sont entrés dans l'Europe communautaire comme d'autres entrent en religion*")[3]. Federalism as a "secular religion" went beyond the traditional left-right divide and found support among the rank and file of all the larger political parties. The resulting federalist pressure on the government was substantial: "The only foreign policy issue with clear roots in the population and thus in Parliament was Europe. (…) Parliament has functioned as an engine on

1 J.C.J.F. van Merriënboer, "Het avontuur van Sicco Mansholt", Centrum voor Parlementaire Geschiedenis, Politieke Opstellen, 15/16 (1995/1996), pp. 137-168, p. 156.

2 HTK 1964-65, 1309.

3 Robert de Bruin, "Les Pays-Bas et l'integration européenne, 1957-1967", Paris: Institut d'Études Politiques de Paris, 1978, p. 906.

the Europe issue", as Secretary of State for European Integration Ernst Van der Beugel (1957-58) phrased it.[4] The federalist majority in Parliament, pursuing a policy in which European unification, economically and politically, was an aim in its own right, going well beyond serving the Netherlands' economic interests, engaged in a permanent campaign for the construction, extension and empowerment of supranational European governmental institutions. Arguably, this pressure for supranationalisation was at its peak by the mid-1960s. From its inception, the Cals government showed an awareness that its diplomatic success in Europe, or its lack thereof, could well determine its longevity: "The government will continue (…) to insist on a substantial expansion of the powers of the European Parliament (EP). It shares the opinions expressed on this issue by the *Tweede Kamer*", it wrote in the aforementioned government policy statement of April 1965.[5]

Thus, when the crisis hit, the Cals government saw two of its vital interests at stake. Firstly, the unhampered completion of the Common Market, under threat from French unilateralism. Secondly, its own survival and the threat of being voted out of office at the hands of the multi-party federalist majority in the Hague parliament.

II. The Hague and the Commission's Package Proposal

Not surprisingly, in 1965, the Commission banked on the success of its earlier package proposals by again putting agriculture at the heart of its new initiative. The first element in the Commission's package, therefore, dealt with the issue of how to fund CAP in the future and how a uniform price system for all agricultural products should be implemented. The Commission's intention was to introduce such a common system by 1 July 1967. By early 1965 the member states still strongly disagreed on how to shape the CAP and in particular the French and German views on the financing of agriculture were strongly divergent. The Commission attempted to harmonize the various stances on the CAP by introducing a proposal on financial settlement that aimed at pleasing all the member states involved.

Secondly, the Commission insisted that it should have an independent source of revenu ("own resources" was the term used be the Commission) from which it could finance its future policies and activities. Until then the Commission had been entirely dependent on direct contributions by the member states from their national treasuries, but Presi-

4 Interview with Ernst van der Beugel in: A.G. Harryvan, J. van der Harst and S. van Voorst eds., *Voor Nederland en Europa. Politici en ambtenaren over het Nederlandse Europabeleid en de Europese integratie, 1945-1975*, Amsterdam: Boom, 2001, pp. 31-61, (pp. 54-55).

5 HTK, TK 1964-65, 1309.

dent Walter Hallstein wished to obtain more room for manoeuvre for his Commission from the tariffs and duties levied on imports – both agricultural and industrial – from third countries.

Thirdly, the European Parliament, until then a lame duck leading a rather anonymous existence, wished to acquire substantial powers for itself, especially in terms of control over the EEC budget. The low-key assembly aspired to become a parliament wielding genuine powers of control, and in that respect, the Commission proposal contained certain promising elements, in that Parliament would gain substantial authority to scrutinise the Commission's receipts and expenditure.

The latter two proposals were closely connected, because if the Commission were to gain an autonomous budgetary role, independent from the member states, then there would also be an obvious need for democratic control of its finances. National parliaments lacked authority over the Commission, so here an opportunity for extending the European Parliament's powers presented itself.

If adopted, the Commission proposal would certainly enhance the EEC's supranational character and standing and it was for this reason that the latter two elements of the package were strongly supported by the Dutch government. The Hague welcomed both the attribution of own resources to the Commission and, more in particular, the simultaneous extension of the Parliament's powers over the EEC budget. In this regard, the Dutch national Parliament had repeatedly spoken out in favour of equipping the EP not only with scrutiny functions but also with legislative authority. The federalist majority of MPs urged that the European Parliament should be in the position to amend or even veto European legislation and they put strong pressure on Joseph Luns, the Foreign Minister to raise and defend this *desideratum* in the EEC Council of Ministers. In Cabinet, this line of thinking was represented most significantly by the social democratic members Ivo Samkalden (Minister of Justice), Joop Den Uyl (Economic Affairs; future Prime Minister) and Anne Vondeling (Finance). In their pleas for furthering democracy in Europe, the Bureau of the six Socialist parties in the EEC member countries backed them.[6] The Christian Democrat Barend Biesheuvel (Minister of Agriculture) was more lukewarm about this proposal. During a Cabinet meeting in early June, he contended that a radical emphasis on the extension of the Parliament's powers risked adversely influencing European negotiations on the setting of agricultural prices, especially for cereals and dairy products. He feared that there would be no room for manoeuvre if the Cabinet proved overly receptive to the national Parliament's supranational demands. Foreign Minister Luns

6 NA, MR (784), Notulen Ministerraad 4.6.1965.

(Catholic Party) took up an intermediate position during the *Ministerraad* deliberations. He endorsed Biesheuvel's plea for progress in the CAP talks, but also sympathized with the MPs and the social-democratic insistence on granting more powers to the EP – perhaps not so much out of supranationalist enthusiasm, but rather as a tactical tool or counterweight to French attempts at curtailing the powers of the Commission and continuing to limit the Parliament's role to that of a harmless talking shop.

Hallstein's package met with a mixed response in the other member states. By early June 1965 it was clear that France largely supported the proposal concerning agriculture but vehemently opposed strengthening the position of Commission and Parliament. The French government made clear that it was prepared to pay a price – in terms of an additional payment for the CAP – if the provisions on the EP's budgetary control were withdrawn from the negotiating table. Belgium was rather undecided because at that stage – following the general elections of 23 May – it had to cope with the laborious task of forming a new government. Germany and Italy *grosso modo* agreed with the supranational contents of the package, but mistrusted the expected implications of the proposal on agriculture. Both countries complained about the course the CAP had taken since its inception in 1962 and felt that because of their relatively high contributions to the European budget, they indirectly helped to subsidize foreign farmers, without much compensation for themselves in other political or economic sectors.[7]

In this respect they differed from the Dutch position: although the Netherlands had initially preferred a system of free trade and free prices for agricultural commodities – because of its efficient and highly productive agricultural sector – in the early 1960s, The Hague had decided to go along with the French design for a more interventionist European agricultural policy, in view of the undeniable advantages for its national farmers. But the Dutch government had always maintained an ambivalent attitude towards the CAP, also because of the problems it created in worldwide trade negotiations. A consequence of the Commission's proposal was that the Netherlands would have a bigger share in the financing of the CAP than before. The government emphasized that it was only prepared to pay more for the CAP if this was accompanied by a corresponding increase in the EP's scrutinising and legislative powers. As before, France and the Netherlands found themselves taking up opposite positions: both were prepared to raise their contributions for agriculture, albeit for entirely different reasons. Once again, Dutch

[7] N.P. Ludlow, "Challenging French Leadership in Europe: Germany, Italy, the Netherlands and the Outbreak of the Empty Chair Crisis of 1965-1966", *Contemporary European History*, Vol. 8, No. 2, (1999), pp. 231-248, (pp. 236-238).

ambitions proved high, when, under pressure from their national parliament, the delegation at the negotiations on the Commission package advocated the introduction of some form of parliamentary veto over agricultural directives. It was obvious, however, that none of the other member states shared this ambition, although Italy came close to it. In the course of June, the Dutch Cabinet decided to drop the issue. From then on, it concentrated on the attribution of budgetary powers to the EP, to become effective simultaneously with the introduction of a common price system for agriculture, as proposed by the Commission.

Urged on by the Hague Parliament, the Dutch government insisted on the indivisibility of the three elements of the Commission package, but at the same time feared that its desire to link CAP financing with supranationalism was not shared by all the participants involved. During the Cabinet meeting of 25 June 1965, a possible scenario was sketched in which France would successfully insist on a quick solution for CAP financing and that it would then convince the Commission of the need for a more "flexible" strategy on the position of the Commission and the Parliament, thereby delaying progress on the other two elements.[8] The Hague suspected that the Commission – including the "own" Commissioner Sicco Mansholt – would be too vulnerable to French pressure and persuasiveness, without regard to the other members' preferences.[9] During the month of June, the Cabinet held its belief that any attempt at untying the package was simply unacceptable; as long as the Commission stood by its proposals, it could depend completely on support from the Netherlands.

III. First Phase: An Inevitable Clash?

Although the timing of De Gaulle's abrupt withdrawal from the Community's decision-making process unquestionably came as a surprise, in the longer run, many in The Hague considered a major conflict with France on the future of European integration inevitable. In early June, Foreign Minister Luns stated that at that stage it would be tactically foolish to give in to French demands on the Parliament's position, if Paris was planning to wage a battle on majority-voting in the Council later in 1965. "Whatever happens now", he argued, "it is almost certain that towards the end of the year we shall be in conflict with France, since the Treaty prescribes an end to unanimity rule by then". The Hague should therefore reserve its position for the time being, and avoid

8 NA, MR (784), Notulen Ministerraad 25.6.1965.

9 NA, MR (784), Notulen Ministerraad 4.6.1965.

being drawn into any discussion of possible compromises that might be acceptable to the Netherlands.[10]

Luns' colleagues in the Cabinet agreed that unity among the Five against possible French sabotage had to be the first priority, which justified backing the Hallstein package, even though its proposals for enlarging Parliament's powers were too modest for Dutch liking.[11]

As hoped for, in the course of 1965 the Five drew closer together. Unlike the initial stage of the Fouchet negotiations, when the Netherlands was seen as the most quarrelsome and obstructive member, now the Dutch government was elated to find ample support in yet another confrontation with France. This time, for a change, The Hague found a faithful ally in Germany, where Chancellor Erhard had clearly distanced himself from the "French-indulgent" policy of his predecessor Adenauer, with the German delegation sharing Dutch insistence on the indivisibility of the Commission package and on the expansion of the EP's powers of scrutiny. But Germany certainly had its own *desiderata* too: Bonn was no longer prepared to cough up the lion's share of EEC spending on agriculture if no further concessions were made to Germany in terms of political integration, fiscal harmonization and market liberalization for industrial products. Bonn put considerable pressure both on the Commission and on France to adapt the CAP part of the package to German preferences.[12] In response, the French delegation tabled a counter proposal in late June, seeking a continuation of EEC funding from national contributions until at least 1970, the year the Common Market was due to be introduced. This counter proposal met, however, with fierce criticism from the other member states, the Netherlands included. Italy, in particular, complained about its projected financial obligations to Brussels and urged a fundamental revision of the entire financing system.[13]

Consequently, by the end of June 1965 the national positions were strongly divided, with France finding itself more and more isolated from the other delegations. The night of 30 June-1 July, while the conclusive Council deliberations on the Commission package were taking place, French Foreign Minister Maurice Couve de Murville abruptly terminated the negotiations in the face of fierce objections by the other participants.[14] From then on, France refused to attend any further meetings

---

10 *Ibidem*.

11 *Ibidem*.

12 Ludlow, "Challenging French Leadership in Europe", pp. 236-241.

13 D.W. Urwin, *The Community of Europe. A history of European integration since 1945*, London: Longman, 1993, pp. 110-111.

14 Notwithstanding French declarations, aired at various occasions, that Paris considered June 30 the deadline for a deal on the Commissions's proposals. Given the

of the Council of Ministers; consequently, for a period of seven months, decision-making in the Council was to be stalled, because of the French empty chair.

At first, the French move was met with surprise, scorn and irony. The technical and political issues at stake did not justify the dramatic move Paris had indulged in. Apparently, (some of) the parties involved, Foreign Minister Luns quipped, needed some time off "on a political summer holiday" away from Brussels. There was no reason to doubt the member states' ability to arrive at some sort of compromise, serving the interests of all concerned.[15] Likewise, irrational motives were supposed to have played a role in making the French act as they did, as was illustrated by Franz Italianer, the then Director of the European Integration desk of the Dutch Foreign Ministry, and present at the Council meeting of 30 June-1 July. Italianer recounts that Couve de Murville was in a bad temper that day and that he expressed his displeasure in plain terms during the entire meeting. The frosty mood was not helped by a cold draught that caught him on the neck, attributable to the malfunctioning air-conditioning system in the conference room, rather than any of the difficulties in the discussions. Couve even decided to adjourn the meeting to have the air-conditioning repaired. When the meeting resumed he was entirely unwilling to search for a compromise, maintains Italianer. Italianer accuses Couve of an "abuse" of his chairmanship when he unexpectedly ended the session without setting a date for a new meeting.[16]

All in all, The Hague initially regarded the French outburst as a temporary inconvenience and no more than that. More disturbing, Luns argued in Cabinet, was the "peculiar capitulation" practised by the European Commission, which shortly after the infamous Council meeting had published its new proposals in which the French demands on the CAP were largely met.[17] In a memorandum of 22 July, the Commission suggested – consistent with initial Dutch suspicions – sticking to the contents and timetable of the agricultural section of its original package and delaying a decision on an independent source of revenu for the EEC and Parliament's budgetary control.

The Dutch government's response to the Commission's memorandum was negative at first but, faced with an isolated position on this issue and conscious of the importance of maintaining a united bloc of

---

Brussels' practise of "stopping the clock", however, none of the other delegations had taken these utterings seriously.

15 NA, MR (785), Notulen Ministerraad, 23.7.1965.

16 H.H.J. Labohm (ed.), *De waterdragers van het Nederlandse Europabeleid. Terugblik op 40 jaar DGES*, Den Haag: SDU, 1997, pp. 61-62.

17 NA, MR (785), Notulen Ministerraad 23.7.1965.

Five countries, it conceded that the attribution of own resources to the Commission and of budgetary powers to the Parliament could be postponed until 1970, more than two years after the establishment of a common price system in agriculture.[18] Following the previous concession in June – on the EP's legislative powers – the Cabinet must have felt rather uncomfortable to suffer another defeat on this matter, also considering the discontent in the national Parliament, the moving spirit behind the campaign for strengthening the EP's powers.

In retrospect and given the Commission's early white flag, the most remarkable feature of the empty chair crisis may well have been the fact that the five countries attempted and eventually succeeded in maintaining a united bloc *vis-à-vis* France. This was not a foregone conclusion. During the months of August and September, the Dutch government complained that its Benelux partner, Belgium, was leaning too closely to the French side. Immediately after the inauguration of the new Belgian government on 28 July, Foreign Minister Paul-Henri Spaak undertook to act as an intermediary between De Gaulle and the Five, but this self-appointed role was by no means appreciated in The Hague.[19] The Dutch felt much closer to the German delegation which had explained unequivocally that it was not prepared to make concessions to France, either on agriculture or on supranationalism. Foreign Minister Luns expressed his satisfaction about the constructive and persistent role German Foreign Minister Gerhard Schröder had played during the Council negotiations[20] and blamed his Benelux partners for being too vulnerable to pressure and advances by the French government. As pointed out by John Newhouse, with the Commission's original package superseded by its new July 22 memorandum, Luns was freed from the position of fully supporting the package proposed by the Commission, about which he had been dubious in the first place. Consequently, the Netherlands and Germany reached agreement on maintaining a common position. On the domestic front, Luns had to overcome pleas from Minister of Agriculture Biesheuvel to placate France in order to avoid jeopardizing the advantageous CAP. Luns' tactic, aimed at putting his government's full weight behind Schröder's position, appears to have been instrumental in encouraging and strengthening the latter's stance, both within Germany and among the Six. The chances were good that, with Belgium and Luxembourg concurring, Italy too would rally towards the common Dutch-German position. In spite of their disappointment, the *Tweede Kamer* and its Committee on Foreign Policy backed the Minister on this new, clearly more *defensive* approach.

---

[18] NA, MR (785), Notulen Ministerraad 17.9.1965.

[19] *Ibid.*

[20] NA, MR (785), Notulen Ministerraad 23.7.1965.

During the second half of 1965, the '*atmosphère de guerre sainte*' (holy war atmosphere) that had characterized the parliamentary debates in June gradually gave way to increasing political support for Luns and his tactics, centring on the German-Dutch common position. The five major parties reiterated their desire for "Democratisation of the Community" (i.e., strengthening the powers of the European Parliament), a subject that, during the Council's ill-fated June 30 meeting, had not been addressed at all. "Democratisation", however, had ceased to be the priority, for federalists and functional supranationalists alike. Above all, this was the time for all good men (of both genders) to come to the aid of the European Commission and its prerogatives. Luns agreed with the *Tweede Kamer*, stating that parliamentary control by the European Parliament had indeed been an important victim of the crisis. The Dutch government, however, he promised would continue to promote "democratisation". The annual Queen's Speech of 21 September 1965 underlined the basic creeds of the Dutch view on Europe: "The construction of the European Communities shall be continued on a supranational and democratic base and shall be inseparable from Atlantic co-operation". Thus, the empty chair crisis resulted in newly found unity between government and *Tweede Kamer*, effectively taking away the risk of the former being voted down due to lack of zest on the European front.[21]

IV. Phase two: Deteriorating Relations towards France and a Deepening Crisis

Spaak's favourable orientation regarding Paris did not last for long. The turning point was a press conference held by De Gaulle, early in September 1965, during which the French President fulminated against the EEC in general and particularly opposed the use *casu quo* extension of majority voting in the Council of Ministers. The Treaty of Rome specified that by 1 January 1966 policy issues on which majority voting was applicable would be extended to transport, agricultural prices, trade policy and capital movements. In his speech, full of invective against the Commission and the European Parliament, De Gaulle made clear that he considered such an alteration of the voting procedure wholly unacceptable. Spaak, fearing a serious violation of the EEC Treaty and the infringement of the working of the institutions, changed his mind and joined the group of member states in opposition to France. Before long, the Luxembourg government was to follow his example.

Even though a collision with France on the majority voting issue was deemed by many, including the Dutch government, as inevitable, the

---

21 John Newhouse, *Collision in Brussels. The Common Market Crisis of 30 June 1965*, New York: Norton 1967, 134-135. See also De Bruin, "Les Pays-Bas", pp. 716-745 (p. 716, p. 735).

timing of the next French move took The Hague by surprise. The then Deputy Permanent Representative with the EEC, Charles Rutten, recalls: "I remember as if it were yesterday that we were discussing the crisis with Luns and Mansholt in between one of those Council meetings, when Mansholt said: 'I have got news from Paris that it's no longer the financing of CAP alone that is at stake, it's about completely different issues too. Majority voting is also involved'". This was an issue that, until then, had not been tabled for discussion at all, but its disclosure did not come as a complete surprise, according to Rutten.

> Although the way in which it happened – the French drawing the conclusion at midnight that the discussion had run aground and that there was no sense in continuing and the French delegation's immediate *départ* from Brussels, not to return for a considerable time span – all that was quite a surprise and fairly shocking for all concerned. Indeed, such were the manners deemed applicable by some in those days, at least within the ranks of the Gaullist government.[22]

V. Third Phase: France out, Britain in?

By October 1965, the Dutch Cabinet openly started to worry that France, with its head-on approach, was seeking to torpedo the supranational foundations of the Community by insisting on a rigorous revision of the Treaty of Rome and on downgrading the Commission's position. After all, new intelligence suggested that from the early spring onwards France had been preparing for a showdown and that Couve de Murville had been acting under explicit orders to close the June negotiations *avec éclat* (with a bang).[23] Couve de Murville's address to the French parliament on 20 October expanded on his President's 9 September news conference: Paris required a *révision d'ensemble* (general revision) of the Community system and the establishment of a "political Europe", presumably along the intergovernmental lines of the Fouchet proposals.[24]

The polarizing strategy followed by De Gaulle and his government shocked the Cabinet, as appears from the unanimity in condemnatory judgment during the meeting of 22 October. Prime Minister Cals sug-

---

22 Interview with Charles Rutten, in: Harryvan, Van der Harst and Van Voorst, *Voor Nederland en Europa*, pp. 189-231, (p. 213). In the same vein: D. Thompson, "The European Economic Community After the 1965 Crisis", *International and Comparative Law Quarterly*, 16, 1967, pp. 1-28 (p. 1).

23 Min. BZ, III, 913.100, No. 5451 (Coördinatie Commissie 28), "Punten voor uiteenzetting in Coördinatie Commissie", 27.9.1965.

24 Min. BZ, III, 913.100, No. 5451 (Coördinatie Commissie 28), "Conclusies van de Coördinatie Commissie voor Europese Integratie- en Associatieproblemen van 21 oktober 1965", 22.10.1965; Notulen Raad voor Europese zaken, 22.10.1965.

gested taking France to court if it refused to comply with its treaty obligations concerning majority voting in the Council.[25] Minister Samkalden stated that the French government deliberately aimed to destroy the institutional mechanism of the European Communities while Minister of Social Affairs Jacob Suurhof added that the crisis should no longer be regarded as just another French ploy aimed at securing an advantageous CAP settlement: "The French government is determined to destroy the EEC", he claimed echoing Samkalden.[26] Under these circumstances, the Cabinet rejected a proposal by Spaak to convene a meeting of the six Ministers of Foreign Affairs outside the EEC framework, to pacify the French. The general feeling in The Hague, in government circles and *a fortiori* in Parliament, was that *au contraire* the blame for the crisis should be openly put on France.

During the Cabinet meetings, there was widespread speculation about the possibility of going ahead in the EEC without France. Immediately after the start of the empty chair crisis, a group of legal experts under Willem Riphagen from the Ministry of Foreign Affairs investigated the issue of whether the Treaty of Rome allowed the taking of binding decisions among the Five, without France participating. Unlike their colleagues in Germany, the group concluded that the relevant treaty articles were too ambiguous to permit an incontestable "go-it-alone" by the Five.[27] The Netherlands was prepared to convene so-called restrictive Council meetings, with the authority to deliberate on policy matters but *not* to decide on them.

Thus, with the legal aspect of the crisis being dealt with cautiously, Cals and his staff did not refrain from addressing the political issue at the heart of government policy-making. By November, Luns had repeatedly told his colleagues in the Cabinet that, if the efforts to make France resume cooperation within the EEC framework were to fail, the government would have to make a decision in principle in favour of continuing integration with the four remaining partner countries.[28] Likewise, State Secretary for European Affairs Anton de Block concluded that the Five's teaming up did not suffice; now that France was disengaging itself from the Rome Treaty, a more fundamental exchange of views was called for. A new common market among the Five, the future of Euro-

---

[25] NA, MR (879), Notulen Raad voor Europese Zaken (Council for European Affairs, a sub-committee of the Ministerraad) 22.10.1965.

[26] *Ibidem.*

[27] NA, MR (785), Notulen Ministerraad 23.7.1965.

[28] NA, MR (879), Notulen Raad voor Europese Zaken 22.10.1965; NA, MR (785), Notulen Ministerraad 22.11.1965.

pean cooperation within NATO and the evolution of Germany's position within the West were among the issues to be addressed.[29]

Contingency planning on alternatives to cooperation among the Six should, as Samkalden pointed out to his colleagues in the Cabinet, be on a multiple scenario basis: with or without French membership, the EEC could survive; an associate status might be offered to France as an alternative for full membership; and under the prevailing conditions entry negotiations with the United Kingdom might be embarked upon soon. The combined efforts of Luns, Biesheuvel and Den Uyl, however, brought about a postponement of policy preparations along these lines, partly because of the political impact such planning might have on the ongoing negotiations with the Five and France and, partly, because of doubts as to whether the partners, Italy in particular, were ready to discuss a Community without French membership.[30]

In a memorandum by the Foreign Ministry in November, the prospects of a continuation of an EEC of six countries were portrayed as gloomy, especially at a time when the French position in NATO was also considered troublesome. On various issues, among which the long-running debate on creating a Multilateral Nuclear Force, France had moved away, slowly but surely, from its Atlantic partners. The drafters of the memorandum were rather circumspect in their policy recommendations regarding the crisis. On the one hand, they found it hard to envisage an EEC of five countries, at least as long as cooperation with France in NATO – however fragile – would last. But if France's EEC membership were to end, the Foreign Ministry contended, Germany's economic weight would result in a position of predominance for that country, necessitating immediate entry negotiations with the United Kingdom and other European countries.[31]

In November, De Gaulle told his European partners that, in order to overcome the deadlock, he was prepared to discuss *political* issues with them, but, to the annoyance of the Dutch government, he refused to tackle urgent economic problems of the time. Minister of Agriculture Biesheuvel pointed to the adverse impact of the empty chair crisis on the agricultural sector in Europe and on the evolving trade negotiations with

---

29 Min. BZ, III, 913.100, No. 5490, "Verslag van de vergadering van de Coördinatie Commissie voor Europese Integratie- en Associatieproblemen gehouden op 21 oktober 1965".

30 NA, MR. (879), Notulen Raad voor Europese Zaken 22.10.1965.

31 Min. BZ, III, 913.100 F/12591/65a, "Mogelijkheden tot oplossing van de huidige crisis in de Europese Gemeenschappen", s.a. [16.11.1965]; NA, MR (785), Notulen Ministerraad 22.11.1965. The French-instigated NATO crisis, which started in late 1965, appears to have affected the empty chair problem in a number of ways which will not be dealt with in this chapter.

the US within the Kennedy Round. As before, Biesheuvel, in his position as representative of agricultural interests, was the minister most inclined to look for ways to stay in contact with the French, even if this implied making concessions in areas other than agriculture. He warned that the farming community in Europe would be in serious trouble if no agreement was reached on common prices for cereals, beef and dairy products. In November, he suggested a temporary "gentlemen's agreement" with France, in order to solve the most pressing agricultural problems.[32] He also urged a quick resumption of trade negotiations with the US, not least because after 30 June 1967 the US President's special negotiating authority on trade would expire, which was expected to hamper – temporarily, in any case – progress in transatlantic tariff reductions.

With hindsight, Biesheuvel's way of thinking was destined to carry the day. Deep down, there was always the feeling that, one way or another, the French delegation could not but return to the negotiating table. There were crucial interests at stake for all parties concerned. To reach a solution on agricultural questions concerning cereals and dairy products and for the continuation of the Kennedy Round on tariff reductions, full French participation was an absolute requirement. And, *vice versa*, France, with its enormous agricultural and industrial interests in Europe, could not abstain for too long from the Council meetings. At the end of the day, France's stakes in the Community could be protected only by its own presence. The mutual oath taking of the Five, as Newhouse describes it, "meant that before very long France would have to return to Brussels". Nevertheless, the general feeling was that it would be hard to find a mutually acceptable agreement until after the French presidential elections in early December.[33]

VI. Fourth Phase: Retaining Unity and Calling Bluff

Thus, from Spring 1965 onwards, by maintaining their united front, the Five were able to "call France's bluff", as Ludlow would have it.[34] In late October, in response to De Gaulle's demands for an overhaul of the Communitarian system, the Five issued a Council declaration asserting their common determination to stand by the principles of the Treaty and inviting France to take part in a special meeting of the Council, without the customary presence of members of the Commission. For once, as

32 NA, MR (785), Notulen Ministerraad 22.11.1965.

33 NA, MR (879), Notulen Raad voor Europese Zaken 22.10.1965; John Newhouse, *Collision in Brussels. The Common Market Crisis of 30 June 1965*, New York: Norton, 1967, p. 142.

34 Ludlow, "Challenging French Leadership in Europe". Ludlow, however, applies the term in a more restricted way, to the May/June negotiations alone.

Hayes-Renshaw and Wallace, in the most encompassing analysis of the Council's institutional development so far, criticise as far too simplistic the picture that until the 1987 Single European Act decisions in the Council were mostly subject to the unanimity rule and to the implicit acceptance of the right to veto.[48] They argue, firstly, that the heavy reliance on consensus, practised during the first half of the 1970s, was, above all, inspired by *functional* reasons. Consensus was sought with a view to encouraging compliance. The progressive strengthening of Community law began to provide an alternative guarantee for compliance and the implementing of Community decisions in domestic law. Second, votes started to be taken more often during the late 1970s, and with increasing frequency in the early 1980s. Budget appropriations, CAP rules and trade issues, in particular, frequently led to decisions being taken by QMV. Many decisions on internal market issues were taken in this same way well before the ratification of the Single European Act in 1987. Third, the Luxembourg "compromise" did affect the Council, but in a more nuanced way than has been widely assumed. Legally no more than an entry in a footnote to the minutes of a Council meeting, the views on its status as an operating norm differed widely. Generally speaking, its major effect may well have been psychological, in inducing delegates in the Council not to push their colleagues too far, when these were facing serious domestic constraints.

The Hayes-Renshaw/Wallace analysis is supported by the testimony of Charles Rutten, the Netherlands' Permanent Representative in Brussels from 1980 to 1986.[49] He, too, refers to "a widespread misunderstanding", needing correction:

> When the Treaty allows for QMV, QMV is almost always applied. The aim to arrive at a consensus, however, is always present. QMV is only applied when consensus cannot be attained and yet a decision has to be taken. But those occasions constitute an exception to the rule, in that – 'vital interests' or no 'vital interests' apart – it is in nobody's interest to outvote countries time after time. (…) I think that the number of cases decided upon by QMV after 'Luxembourg' is quite considerable. Almost all budget decisions were arrived at by QMV, because reaching consensus on the budget was always extremely difficult and yet decisions had to be taken. On matters of trade policy, as well as in some other areas, issues were decided upon by QMV'.[50]

---

48 Fiona Hayes-Renshaw and Helen Wallace, *The Council of Ministers*, Houndmills: Palgrave, 2nd edition, 2006, pp. 263-270.

49 In earlier years, from 1960 to 1969 Mr. Rutten was Deputy Permanent Representative. His long-term involvement in the Brussels' decision-making process provides him with an excellent overview on the impact of the Luxembourg "compromise".

50 Interview with Charles Rutten, in: Harryvan, Van der Harst and Van Voorst, *Voor Nederland en Europa*, pp. 189-231, (p. 214). Rutten's observation is fully in line with Ludlow's conclusion that what the Six did agree upon in Luxembourg was no more

These observations gain corrobation from Golub's quantitative analysis of 759 proposed Directives in the 1966-1981 period. To the extent that these years were marked by legislative paralysis, the latter was caused by formal unanimity rules and the diverging preferences of member-states. The "Luxembourg compromise" had little or no lasting effect and it did not render inoperative formal rules for QMV: legislative input and output under QMV grew steadily after 1966 and QMV consistently expedited EEC decision-making. Golubs' point is clear: the EEC member-states deliberately included QMV in the 1957 Rome Treaty in order to get things done and this original bargain survived De Gaulle's challenge.[51]

Andrew Moravcsik equally criticizes the importance traditionally attached to the Luxembourg "compromise", but on completely different grounds. Since all of the "rapid movements" of the 1960s, he argues, were decided upon with unanimity, before as well as after the empty chair crisis, the "compromise" did not make much difference. Nor did it add substantially to the Treaty guarantee that all new policies were to be decided upon unanimously. Approvingly, he quotes John Lambert's remark that "as regards the long-term issues of the federalist-nationalist conflict, the 1965-66 crisis changed nothing".[52]

On the issue of QMV *after* the Single European Act there appears to be a convergence of opinion (with Andrew Moravcsik possibly again as an important exception) on the growing importance of QMV in the EEC's and EU's decision-making practice.

We may thus conclude that the outcome of the empty chair crisis was possibly a short-term success for France – also in view of the opportunities it offered for domestic propaganda – but, that at a more substantial level and, in the longer run (as in the case of majority voting), developments were to take a turn not unfavourable to the Netherlands and its partners.

---

than reaffirming a generally accepted, if unwritten rule: "the basic reality that majority voting could not be used to steam-roll a partner state into accepting the unacceptable was recognized by all before the Luxembourg encounter had even begun". The fact that this rule needed explicit stating was "a reflection of how much trust between the Six had broken down". N.P. Ludlow, "The Eclipse of the Extremes. Demythologising the Luxembourg Compromise", in: W. Loth (ed.) *Crises and compromises: the European project 1963-1969*, Baden-Baden: Nomos, 2001, pp. 247-264, (pp. 248-249).

51 Jonathan Golub, "Did the Luxembourg Compromise have any consequences?", in: Jean-Marie Palayret, Helen Wallace & Pascaline Winand (eds.), *Visions, Votes and Vetoes. The Empty Chair Crisis and the Luxembourg Compromise Forty Years On*, Brussels: P.I.E.-Peter Lang, 2006, pp. 279-320, *passim*.

52 A. Moravcsik, *The Choice for Europe. Social Purpose and State Power from Messina to Maastricht*, London: UCL Press, 1998, p. 230.

In comparing the aftermaths of the empty chair crisis and the Fouchet negotiations, we are faced with an interesting mirror image of the two events. In contrast to the Luxembourg "compromise", the failure of "Fouchet" was generally considered a diplomatic victory for the Netherlands. With great skill, Luns had managed to block the creation of a continental European political body on an intergovernmental basis and had forestalled French attempts at undermining the supranational structure of the EEC. However, satisfaction with this diplomatic result was short-lived. During the 1970s, we witness the foundation of two new EEC-related bodies, the European Political Cooperation forum and the European Council of Heads of State and Government. Both encountered a rather sceptical reception in the Netherlands – mainly because of their intergovernmental purport – but were welcomed in France as late heirs of the original Fouchet design.

In contrast, early in 1966, France could well be considered the short-term winner of the empty chair crisis. However as stated above, subsequent developments proved that in the longer run the German-Dutch communitarian approach was to prevail over De Gaulle's short-term successes. Today's European Union, in which qualifying majorities and blocking minorities are the order of the day and the co-decision procedure has upgraded the European Parliament to a co-legislative role, *a fortiori* reflects the victory of communitarianism over De Gaulle's confederal ideas.

CHAPTER VI

Swan Song or Cock Crow?

The Netherlands and the Hague Conference of December 1969

Introduction*

During the 1960s, French-Dutch relations had deteriorated, mainly as a result of EC controversies, such as the French vetoes on British entry, the heated discussions on the Fouchet plans, the empty chair crisis and unwillingness by Paris to confer real powers to the embryonic European Parliament. Nevertheless, by the end of the decade Dutch European policy-makers would have a number of successes to look back upon. Riding the tide of economic prosperity the "Original Six" managed to establish the Customs Union as agreed on in the Rome Treaty by July 1968, well before it was due, thus realising the Netherlands' most important European policy goal since the launching of the Beyen plan in 1952. True, the French taste for high external tariffs was still looked upon with scorn, but the GATT's Kennedy Round had eased part of the pain.

Throughout the 1960s, however, fear of remaining "locked up" in a limited and protectionist continental block constituted a major motive for Dutch insistence on enlargement of the Communities, also known as the *préalable anglais*. The government's *political* motive for enlargement was poignantly worded by Prime Minister Piet de Jong during a Cabinet (*Ministerraad*) meeting late in 1967: he deemed it

> irresponsible to lead the Netherlands towards a European satellite state under French, and after De Gaulle's death, under German hegemony. History teaches us that French or German hegemony does not leave democratic principles in safe hands. British and Scandinavian accession is of the highest importance for maintaining democracy in Europe.[1]

---

* An earlier version of this chapter was published as: A.G. Harryvan and J. van der Harst, "Swan Song or Cock Crow? The Netherlands and The Hague Summit Conference of December 1969", *Journal of European Integration History*, Vol. 9, 2003, No. 2, pp. 27-40.

1 NA, MR (845), Notulen Ministerraad 27.10.1967.

Of equally high importance as British accession was, in the government's view, the establishment of the Community's common agricultural policy (CAP). On this issue, France and the Netherlands saw eye to eye, at least to a considerably larger degree than on institutional matters and enlargement. Benelux had taught the government the hard way that under no condition was this sector to be exempted from the general process of economic integration. As the largest agricultural exporter among the Six, the Netherlands needed European outlets for its agricultural surplus production as offered by the EEC's common agricultural market. The resulting Dutch-French coalition had managed to dominate the Community's agricultural decision-making process during the CAP's formative years (1958-1963).[2] Such positive results, however, did not conceal the fact, that by the end of the decade disagreement between France and the other five member states on a number of institutional, financial and foreign policy issues had led to a virtual standstill of the Community's integrative momentum.

The Hague summit of heads of state and government of December 1969 is generally regarded as the diplomatic breakthrough that ended this stagnation. This chapter analyses Dutch European policy and resulting engineering influence with regard to the Hague summit and the extent to which this summit was deemed instrumental for re-launching European integration.

I. Signs of Hope and Reappraisals

De Gaulle's resignation as French president in April 1969 raised new expectations among advocates of European integration and co-operation, both in the Netherlands and abroad. De Gaulle's successor Georges Pompidou clarified his intentions to re-launch Europe soon after his inauguration in mid-June. On 29 June, exactly two weeks after Pompidou's coming to power, the Dutch Cabinet referred to the announcement of a French plan for a European summit to be held in the autumn of 1969. Although the plan obviously needed further elaboration and clarification, the Netherlands welcomed it as the first signal of a chang-

---

2 It is interesting to note that the Dutch-French agricultural coalition reached its peak simultaneously with the clash between Paris and The Hague over De Gaulle's proposals for a European Political Union, in the framework of the so-called Fouchet-negotiations. J.H. Molegraaf, *Boeren in Brussel. Nederland en het Gemeenschappelijk Europees Landbouwbeleid 1958-1971*, Utrecht: 1999, pp. 291-292. Mansholt's vision on Europe and his brainchild the CAP are dealt with in: J.C.J.F. van Merriënboer, *Mansholt. Een biografie*, Amsterdam: Boom, 2006. For a detailed analysis of the Dutch and French impact on the CAP negotiations in the early years of the EC, see also A.C. Lauring-Knudsen, "Defining the Politics of the Common Agricultural Policy. A Historical Study", PhD thesis EUI, Florence, 2001.

ing climate in France.[3] Apparently, Pompidou realised the importance of keeping the European integration process alive and attractive for West Germany. In this respect, Chancellor Willy Brandt's *Ostpolitik* constituted an obvious success for the Federal Republic as well as a challenge for France. Fear of a German *Alleingang* appeared to make palatable what had been unacceptable for Pompidou's predecessor. The degree to which France would be willing to commit itself to enlargement and British membership, however, remained to be seen.[4]

At an earlier stage, at the Rome conference of 1967, Foreign Minister Joseph Luns had raised objections to summit conferences in general. In the Dutch political system he and not the Prime Minister was to be responsible for the country's foreign policy. Traditionally, the Dutch Prime Minister is a *primus inter pares* rather than the government's political boss. Consequently, Luns rather than De Jong represented the country at international conferences. Also, summitry smacked of undermining – *à la Fouchet* – the communitarian system. Thus, the fact that Luns did eventually acquiesce in the Hague summit is an indication of the value he attached to a breakthrough from the integrative impasse. Institutionalisation of summitry, however, was a phenomenon to be guarded against. Dutch and, for that matter, Benelux agreement necessitated a Council resolution stating that "cette conférence des chefs d'Etat et de gouvernement ne doit pas être considérée comme la première d'une série".[5] In the context of the Hague conference, the joint editing of this text proved one of the few occasions of successful collaboration between Luns and his Benelux colleagues. Personal and political convergences hampered combined action of Belgium and the Netherlands in the framework of the Six. Brussels tended to criticise Luns for self-willed and tactless behaviour, whereas the Netherlands blamed its southern neighbour for being over-sensitive to French views on enlargement and agriculture.

On 4 July, during an extensive Cabinet discussion on European integration issues, Foreign Minister Luns noticed an internal struggle within the new French government – headed by Prime Minister Jacques Chaban-Delmas – between the so-called "European" group (represented by Minister of Agriculture Duhamel, Minister of Finance Giscard

---

3 NA, MR (952), Notulen Ministerraad 27.6.1969.

4 Molegraaf, *Boeren in Brussel*, p. 261.

5 "'U moet het genuanceerd zien', vraaggesprek met D.P. Spierenburg", in: A.G. Harryvan, J. van der Harst and S. van Voorst (eds.), *Voor Nederland en Europa. Politici en ambtenaren over het Nederlandse Europabeleid en de Europese integratie, 1945-1975*, Amsterdam: Boom, 2001, pp. 261-283 (pp. 277-279), and M.T. Bitsch, "Le sommet de la Haye. La mise en route de la relance de 1969", in: W. Loth (ed.), *Crises and Compromises: the European Project, 1963-1969*, Baden-Baden: Nomos 2001, pp. 539-565, (pp. 544-547; quote: 547).

d'Estaing, Minister of Foreign Affairs Schumann and State Secretary for Foreign Affairs De Lipkovsky), other moderate Gaullists and orthodox Gaullists. On 1 July, the Netherlands had begun its six-month chairmanship of the EC Council of Ministers and the government sought to use this period and position to launch new initiatives, particularly regarding the Community's enlargement. Since the early 1960s, the Netherlands had developed into a fervent advocate of UK membership, but during the entire decade De Gaulle successfully managed to thwart Dutch ambitions by blocking enlargement unilaterally.

De Gaulle's departure opened new avenues. Luns urged the *Ministerraad* to approach the new French government with caution – in order to spare sensitivities – and suggested developing a carefully worded declaration of intention regarding EC enlargement, including a proposal on starting accession negotiations with the UK as of 1 January 1970. The Cabinet supported Luns in drafting such a declaration, to be presented to the European partners. The Foreign Minister further hoped that France would retake – without loss of face – its seat in the West European Union (WEU), after having abandoned this seat in the spring of 1969. To pacify the French government, the WEU Council should draft a list of sensitive issues that should not be raised, Luns suggested.

A more controversial topic discussed at the *Ministerraad* meeting was agriculture. France urged the speeding up of EC talks on finding a definite arrangement for the financing of common agricultural policy, but the Dutch Cabinet feared that too much progress in this area would endanger the prospect of British entry, for two reasons. Firstly, there was the risk that the Pompidou government would relapse and revive its resistance against British entry, once the financial arrangement had been agreed upon. Secondly, it was felt that the latter would entail further price-increases for farm products on the continent. This would be disadvantageous for Britain with its tradition of low agricultural prices. Consequently, even though the interests of France and the Netherlands, as two major agricultural producers and exporters which would both profit from a generously financed CAP showed considerable overlap, no EEC agreement could be reached on the matter, due to the differences on British accession. A few Cabinet members suggested some way of British involvement – "in the wings" – in the ongoing discussions on finding a definite solution for CAP financing, but Minister of Agriculture Lardinois disagreed. Rather than having the British involved, he thought it sufficient to "inform" London of progress in the CAP talks. In all circumstances, Lardinois expected a long transitional period for British agriculture to adapt itself to European standards, so there was no need of a special treatment of Britain at this stage.

The Cabinet meeting of early July also discussed a monetary integration plan put forward by European Commissioner Raymond Barre and supported by the French government. The plan provided for some form of mutual credit support between the six EC member states. The Hague's view was that integration in this area was only open to discussion *after* British entry into the Community, in line with the wording of a recent Benelux memorandum on this issue. Likewise, the government made progress in political integration conditional on the results booked at the enlargement negotiations.[6]

Luns' declaration of intention regarding EC enlargement met with a striking lack of interest abroad. In particular, France was unwilling to accept the date of 1 January 1970 to open membership negotiations with Britain. It seemed that The Hague's cautious diplomacy vis-à-vis France had failed to produce the desired effect. Instead, the French government reconfirmed its preference for convening a summit of the heads of state and Prime Ministers of the six EC countries, to be held in the month of November. State Secretary for Foreign Affairs Hans de Koster warned the Cabinet for a further delay of EC enlargement "with at least four months" if the French got what they wanted.[7]

II. Towards a European Summit: Passing the Buck and a Triptych Emerging

Late in July, the government came to realise that there was no credible alternative to dropping the declaration of intention and accepting the plan for holding a European summit. In an attempt to justify this early concession, De Koster said that French Foreign Minister Schumann had proved to be much more co-operative than his two predecessors, and that France thus deserved a fair chance to demonstrate its European intentions. As chairman of the Council, the government therefore proposed to organise the conference in The Hague. At the Cabinet meeting of 24 July, the discussion centred on the preferred location for the summit: either the historic buildings of the *Binnenhof* in the centre of town or the more modern and spacious but lesser charming *Congresgebouw* (Conference hall). For security reasons, the eventual decision turned out in favour of the *Ridderzaal* (Knights' Hall) located on the *Binnenhof*. The government emphasised that the meeting should be held in mid-November at the latest and, that in the meantime the European Commission should not waste time, but continue its work on updating the 1967 advice on enlargement. The government also stipulated a proper and equal Commission representation at the summit meeting.

6 NA, MR (953), Notulen Ministerraad 4.7.1969.

7 NA, MR (953), Notulen Ministerraad 18.7.1969.

This was another bone of contention with Paris, the latter preferring a much lower Commission profile during the conference.[8]

Concerning agriculture, the Cabinet supported minister Lardinois in his resistance to a coupling of agricultural financing and enlargement; a parallel treatment of the two issues was to be preferred. This seemed to confirm both the importance of CAP's implementation to the national economy and the prominent position the Minister of Agriculture held in the Cabinet.[9] As Lardinois worded it, linking CAP financing and enlargement "(…) would not constitute a problem for a country like Italy. The Netherlands' interest in a common agricultural policy, however, [was] way too large for such a course of action".[10] After all, he argued, the country topped the bill of intra-EEC agricultural exports, making a speedy CAP arrangement of vital importance. Issue linkage would, at the very least, lead to adverse effects on the level of national contribution to CAP. In spite of Lardinois' protestations, it was agreed that for tactical and diplomatic reasons, minister Luns would be allowed to use the word "coupling" during the negotiations with France and the other European partners.[11] Lardinois felt uneasy about this, and urged Luns continuously to be very reticent in using the term.[12]

In August 1969, the "honeymoon" in the Dutch approach of the new French government was suddenly over, when Paris announced a devaluation of the French franc, without prior consultation with the European partners. Apart from irritations about French unilateralism, the Netherlands feared a substantial increase in farm prices, particularly of dairy products as a result of the French decision. In the context of enlargement, this was seen as unpropitious. Eventually, the pain was eased by the introduction of an intricate system of import subsidies and export levies for France during a period of three months (lasting till December) which succeeded in keeping prices under control. Despite this quick solution, the government's suspicions regarding French intentions started to become more evident and contributed to a hardening of tone regarding EC matters.

At the same time, the political situation in Italy was a matter of concern. In August, Mariano Rumor was appointed Prime Minister of a Christian Democratic minority government, dependent on parliamentary support of the Socialist and Republican parties. The Hague feared

8 NA, MR (953), Notulen Ministerraad 24.7.1969.

9 This had also been the case with Lardinois' predecessor Biesheuvel, who had a dominant impact on EC discussions within the Cabinet, for example during the Empty Chair crisis of 1965; see Chapter 5.

10 NA, MR (953), Notulen Ministerraad 4.7.1969.

11 NA, MR (953), Notulen Ministerraad 4.7.1969 and 24.7.1969.

12 NA, MR (953), Notulen Ministerraad 24.10.1969.

political instability in Italy, not so much because of the abundant size of the Rumor government (consisting of 33 ministers and 55 state-secretaries, as Luns could not resist telling his colleagues) but mainly because of the seemingly unstoppable rise of the Communist party. Communist presence in a future government was no longer to be excluded.[13] In spite of these misgivings, Italian support for British membership was deemed as important as ever.

In September, the government discovered that France was not prepared to co-operate on any European issue (including enlargement), as long as a definite agreement on agricultural financing was not secure. However, Luns thought that the *Ministerraad* should allow the summit to take place – in mid-November – on the strict condition that, during the meeting, a positive decision would be taken on British entry. It was still unclear then when the negotiations on UK membership would begin. In July, France had rejected the date of 1 January 1970, and March 1970 was also considered as too early. The Cabinet deliberated on the minimum conditions to be fulfilled before it could agree on holding the conference. Most members wondered whether a rigid approach was realistic, given that the Netherlands, being the host of the meeting, should "not incur the odium of torpedoing the negotiations". Luns remarked that Italy's stance on enlargement was similar to that of the Netherlands and he therefore preferred to "pass the buck" (for criticising the French position and promoting enlargement) to the Italian Foreign Minister Moro.[14] This is what eventually happened.

New developments broadened the projected summit's agenda. The Cabinet meeting of 3 October centred on the expected revaluation of the German mark, as the fluctuating exchange rate of the Mark caused great anxiety in the Netherlands.[15] A couple of weeks later, at the end of October, the Cabinet proved apprehensive of rumours concerning a revaluation of the Belgian franc.[16] Monetary problems in Europe proved persistent and eventually induced the Belgian government to develop a plan for monetary co-operation to be presented at the conference in the Hague.

In mid-October, the Council of Ministers convened in Luxembourg and agreed on a common trade policy, implying that after 1 October 1970 bilateral trade arrangements with third countries were no longer to be allowed. Although the *Ministerraad* was pleased with this important result, it also worried about the exceptional provision accepted in Lux-

13 NA, MR (953), Notulen Ministerrad 22.8.1969.

14 NA, MR (953), Notulen Ministerraad 12.9.1969.

15 NA, MR (953), Notulen Ministerraad 3.10.1969.

16 NA, MR (953), Notulen Ministerraad 31.10.1969.

embourg that for a period of three years and under certain conditions, bilateral agreements were still possible, particularly with Eastern European countries. Luns said that on this point France, initially claiming an exception for five years, had made a concession, and added that his French colleague wanted to "prevent this issue from becoming contentious" during the summit in the Hague.[17] It was clear that, in the short run, Paris had other, more pressing problems that needed to be solved in a European context.

Early in November, it was decided to postpone the European summit – originally scheduled for 17 and 18 November – to 1 and 2 December 1969. The official reason given was a serious illness of Italian Foreign Minister Moro, but the *Ministerraad* also pointed to internal political problems in Italy as another important cause for the delay. The Cabinet anticipated that the conference would be characterized by general observations, rather than thorough discussions on technical issues. The *Ministerraad* meeting of 7 November used, for the first time, the terms "completion, widening and deepening" (*voltooiing, verbreding en verdieping*), the so-called triptych, to describe the objectives of the forthcoming Hague summit. As for enlargement (widening), the *Ministerraad* was rather pessimistic about the results of preliminary talks with the French government. As has been said above, the fixing of a concrete starting date for the negotiations with Britain was rejected, and the Cabinet now felt itself forced to accept "an indication for the start of the negotiations". This position was far from the original preference to begin the enlargement talks on 1 January 1970. Another point of contention with France concerned the degree of Commission representation at the summit. The *Ministerraad* noticed that Paris was now prepared to accept Commission attendance at the second day of the conference, but not on the first day. For the government, preferring unrestricted Commission participation, this was at least something, after France's initial point-blank refusal.[18]

Concerning political integration (deepening), Luns refused to make concessions. He reiterated his stance of 4 July that the Netherlands was not prepared to allow progress on this issue, unless the other delegations accepted the *quid pro quo* of British membership.[19]

However, another aspect of "deepening", monetary integration, gave more room for discussion in the *Ministerraad*. Belgium had just

---

17 NA, MR (953), Notulen Ministerraad 24.10.1969.

18 NA, MR (954), Notulen Ministerraad 7.11.1969. For a more detailed analysis of the Commission's position and its representation at the summit, see N.P. Ludlow, "An Opportunity or Threat? The European Commission and the Hague Council of December 1969", *Journal of European Integration History*, Vol. 9 (2003), pp. 11-25.

19 NA, MR, (954), Notulen Ministerraad 21.11.1969.

launched the Snoy plan[20], which advocated further steps in this area, motivated by European exchange rate problems in the autumn. Likewise, in July, Jean Monnet's Action Committee for the United States of Europe had called for a fully-fledged Economic and Monetary Union.[21] The Hague was confronted with a difficult dilemma. It had always regarded monetary integration as a potential copingstone, i.e. final phase, of the economic integration process rather than an issue of *immediate* political concern. Moreover, Finance Minister Witteveen was anxious not to throw good money after bad and, with some justification, suspected France of attempts to make Germany and the Netherlands foot the bill for its own financial and monetary problems. At the same time, the government realised that a flat refusal of the Snoy plan was tactically inexpedient. It therefore decided to a "forward escape", announcing that the plan was acceptable if accompanied by closer co-operation on economic and financial policies and real parliamentary control; "if this was accepted, one should also add the social and income policies".[22] As we have argued elsewhere[23], the prospect of the Hague summit did have an important impact, in that it brought traditional Dutch reluctance to monetary cooperation outside the Bretton Woods institutions (including the Bank for International Settlements and the Group of Ten) to a close. Monetary co-operation within a European framework was no longer considered an issue for some distant future but from now on a valid topic for present-day political discussion and an acceptable mid-range policy goal. As before, sound economic and fiscal policies by all countries involved were deemed an essential precondition for Dutch co-operation on this issue. Under no circumstances should intra-European solidarity foot the bill resulting from a lack of financial discipline by national governments. Thus, Witteveen viewed mutual credit mechanisms as proposed in the Barre plan with caution. Emphasis on preceding harmonisation of economic and fiscal policies characterized Witteveen's policy at The Hague, as well as during the subsequent negotiations leading to the Werner report.

---

20 The Snoy plan comprised the gradual establishment of a European monetary community and the introduction of a single currency in three stages.

21 "Resolutions et déclarations communes adoptées par le Comité. Quinzième Session, 15 et 16 juillet, Bruxelles", Private collection Max Kohnstamm.

22 NA, MR (883), Notulen Ministerraad 28.11.1968. For a more elaborate discussion of Dutch European policy with regard to the monetary integration issue: J.W. Brouwer and A.G. Harryvan, *Les Pays-Bas et la coopération monétaire européenne, 1968-1972*, in: *Le rôle des ministères des Finances et de l'Economie dans la construction européenne (1957-1978)*, Paris: Comité pour l'histoire économique et financière de la France, 2002, pp. 85-108.

23 *Ibidem*.

III. Meeting in The Hague: Completion, Widening and Deepening

On 1 and 2 December 1969 the long awaited conference took place on the *Binnenhof* in The Hague. Although the Foreign Ministry had to cope with a number of logistical problems and setbacks, most of them could be solved in time. The efforts of the French embassy to convince the owner of the local pub *Chez Pompidou* to change the name of his establishment were, however, to no avail.[24] While the background noise of demonstrations by ardent federalists and their clashes with the police heightened the spirits, deliberations in the *Ridderzaal* commenced. The Dutch delegation consisted of Prime Minister De Jong and Foreign Minister Luns, assisted by the top civil servants Hartogh, Italianer, De Ranitz, Ringnalda and Spierenburg. Contrary to Dutch preferences and expectations, the various proposals for monetary co-operation as well as suggestions for revitalising Euratom, in fact attracted considerable attention during the plenary meeting. De Jong had intended to start the conference by discussing the enlargement issue, arguing that the other two subjects were to be dealt with in the presence of the European Commission, i.e. on the second day of the conference. The French delegation, however, supported by Belgium and eventually Germany, successfully argued in favour of prioritising the EC's "completion", in the form of finding a definitive arrangement for the financing of agriculture first.[25] According to some analysts, this order was adhered to so as not to endanger a previously prepared compromise between Pompidou and Brandt.[26] It is questionable, however, that such a pre-conference compromise ever saw the light of day. True, an exchange of letters between Brandt and Pompidou and a series of preparatory bilateral talks among all participating governments, cleared the air substantially and – at least with hindsight – foreshadowed possible compromises. Perhaps equally important, these confidence-building interactions led Brandt to the conviction that this time the French veto could indeed be lifted. But agreement had not been reached yet, as the disappointing lack of progress on the first conference day would show. In his memoirs, Brandt indicates that decisive agreement was reached only after the state ban-

24 F. Italianer, "Terugblik op een ambtelijke loopbaan", in: H.J. Labohm (ed.), *De waterdragers van het Nederlandse Europabeleid. Terugblik op 40 jaar DGES*, Den Haag: SDU, 1997, pp. 53-81, 66.

25 Min. BZ, III, 999.0 Europese Gemeenschap, Europese topconferentie 's Gravenhage, 1-2 december 1969, deel II, dec. 1969 t/m 1970, "Tekst van communiqué uitgegeven na afloop van Franse Ministerraadsvergadering, 5 December 1969".

26 M.E. Guasconi, "Italy and the Hague Conference of 1969", *Journal of European Integration History*, Vol. 9 (2003), pp. 101-116. J.W. Brouwer and J. Van Merriënboer, *Van buitengaats naar Binnenhof, P.J.S. de Jong, een biografie*, Den Haag: SDU, 2001, p. 199.

quet at the end of the first day.[27] All in all, it appears safe to conclude with Marie-Thérèse Bitsch that up to the start of the summit, the governments had "assoupli leurs positions mais rien n'est acquis lorsque la conférence s'ouvre le 1er décembre".[28]

With French, German and Dutch support the issue of CAP finances was resolved quickly, providing for a financial regulation by 31 December 1969. On this issue, like many others, the final communiqué was cautiously worded and did not go beyond stating the participants' intention of arriving at a definitive arrangement before the end of the year. Analysts do point, however, to the *geest van Den Haag* ("spirit of The Hague") when explaining how the hoped-for agreement did actually materialise. The debate on how to finance CAP was relieved of the strongly ideological overtones it had carried in 1965, which had hitherto made compromise impossible. Indeed, on 22 December, the Council would reach agreement on CAP finance as well as the own resources issue. No longer burdened by the accession conflict, overlapping interests and converging stances could at last prevail. At least in this respect, the positive "spirit of The Hague" appears to have been of overriding importance.[29]

The Belgian plan for monetary union was taken up, somewhat transformed and strongly supported by the West German government. Federal Chancellor Brandt considered an Economic and Monetary Union imperative: EMU, as previously proposed by the Action Committee for the United States of Europe, to which Brandt adhered, would meet concerns caused by FRG's *Ostpolitik* in linking the country to Western Europe "in such a way it could no longer cut loose", as Pompidou worded it. Likewise, EMU and the ultimate introduction of a common European currency served as an indication that Germany did not intend to use its economic and financial strength to gain economic and possibly political supremacy in Europe. Lastly, a European monetary agreement would facilitate the establishment of a common monetary policy *vis-à-*

---

27 N. P. Ludlow, "Chronicle of an Enlargement Foretold? Pompidou, The Hague Summit and the lifting of the French Veto" [draft paper presented in the context of Breakthrough Project, Barcelona, in November 2002]; Brandt: "Pompidou und ich hatten die Angelegenheit im Schriftwechsel und mit Hilfe tüchtiger Mitarbeiter vorgeklärt. Am Abend des ersten Sitzungstages, nach dem Essen, zu dem die Königin geladen hatte, setzten wir im Zweiergespräch den Punkt auf i". W. Brandt, *Erinnerungen*, Frankfurt am Main: Siedler, 1989, p. 454.

28 Bitsch, "Le sommet de la Haye", p. 558. On the monetary issue, in particular, the conference outcome would go well beyond the scope of the preparatory communications between Brandt and Pompidou.

29 Molegraaf, *Boeren in Brussel*, p. 261.

vis the United States.[30] Thus, the conference agreed upon designing a plan for creating an Economic and Monetary Union in stages. This did not imply that Brandt's support for monetary integration was unqualified. On German, Dutch and Luxembourg insistence, the communiqué prioritised the harmonisation of economic to monetary policies and the European Reserve Fund was scheduled to emerge only at the end of the transition to economic and monetary union. Therefore, as Dyson and Featherstone observe, the EMU paragraph of the communiqué was by no means a clear victory for Pompidou. The French, strongly supported by the Belgian delegation, did succeed in getting monetary integration on the EEC's negotiation table, but the issue was to be dealt with along the lines of a German/Dutch agenda.[31] Franco-German preparatory talks on this issue had remained limited in scope. Brandt had shown himself willing to go along with the creation of a European reserve fund, as an expression of monetary solidarity among the Six. At the conference, however, he presented this fund in the much broader context of a general development towards EMU, which came as a surprise to Pompidou as well as, presumably, the other delegations.[32] Pompidou, however, gave the German proposals his full support.

Dutch Finance Minister Witteveen was only partly convinced. He deemed the EMU set-up too far-reaching, advocating informal exchanges of opinion among the EEC finance ministers instead. Luns' view that France being *demandeur* on the monetary issue was "convenient" and should be put to good bargaining use won the day.[33] As late as June 1970 Witteveen complained about the pressure the Foreign Minis-

---

30 A. Szász, *The Road to European Monetary Union*, Houndmills: MacMillan, 1999, p. 28.

31 K. Dyson and K. Featherstone, *The Road to Maastricht. Negotiating Economic and Monetary Union*, Oxford: OUP, 1999, pp. 106-107. G. Eyskens, "De topconferentie van Den Haag en de Monetaire Unie", in: O. de Raeymaker, *Belgisch buitenlands beleid en internationale betrekkingen* (liber amicorum), Leuven: s.n., 1978, pp. 295-307.

32 A. Wilkens, "Westpolitik, Ostpolitik and the project of the Economic and Monetary Union. Germany's European policy in the Brandt era (1969-1974)", *Journal of European Integration History*, Vol. 5, 1999, pp. 73-102, (pp. 80-81). More generally, Wilkens argues, "[t]he program Brandt finally presented in The Hague [...] was much more extensive than his former communication to Pompidou". For a more detailed treatment of the Franco-German bilateral contacts and preparations for the Hague summit see Claudia Hiepel, "In Search of the Greatest Common Denominator. Germany and the Hague Summit Conference 1969", *Journal of European Integration History*, Vol. 9, 2003, pp. 63-81.

33 Brouwer and Harryvan, "Les Pays-Bas et la coopération monétaire européenne", p. 98; NA, MR (954), Notulen Ministerraad 7.11.1969 and NA, MR (987), Notulen Ministerraad 5.6.1970.

try had exerted on him to accept the EMU compromise at the Hague summit, six months previously.[34]

Thus, at the Hague, the EMU decision laid the foundation for the subsequent heated discussions its corollary, the October 1970 Werner report, would give rise to. In prescribing communitarisation of economic and fiscal policies, the report would go well beyond what was acceptable for the rank and file Gaullists, led by Michel Debré, necessitating Pompidou and his finance minister Giscard d'Estaing to distance themselves hastily from its contents. This made *The Economist* cast doubt on the sagacity of Pompidou's earlier stance at the Hague summit:

> Then, in what can only be regarded as a political fluke, the French president at the now famous summit meeting at The Hague a year ago picked up the ball of monetary union and ran like a bull with it for the line. There is good reason to believe that President Pompidou would not have done what he did if he had realised where it might lead.[35]

Further talks on "the best way of achieving progress in the matter of political unification" were to take place "within the context of enlargement", as worded in the communiqué. This formula was reassuring for – and indeed insisted upon by – the Dutch government as far as the struggle for British membership and against a continental "Third Way" was concerned. But its vagueness made this formula utterly unsatisfactory in terms of the hoped-for strengthening of Community institutions, the Commission and European Parliament (EP) in particular. Much like Commission president Jean Rey, the Hague government regretted that there had been "hardly any mention of political union and no discussion on strengthening the Community institutions", such strengthening deemed "crucial to the progress of the Communities".[36] The subsequent success of the Davignon Committee and its proposal for European Political Co-operation (EPC, see also chapter 7) were far from evident at the time of the summit. Actually, the lines that were to give birth to EPC were tucked away as the penultimate paragraph in the final communiqué. As Hill and Smith rightly comment: "Even the interested ob-

---

34 Brouwer and Harryvan, "Les Pays-Bas et la coopération monétaire européenne", p. 98; NA, MR (954), Notulen Ministerraad 7.11.1969 and NA, MR (987), Notulen Ministerraad 5.6.1970; At the first *Ministerraad* meeting following the Hague summit, Witteveen blamed Luns and De Koster for the allegedly "unbalanced composition" of the national delegation at the conference: Foreign Affairs had been over-represented, while the departments with more specialised know-how had not been allowed to attend sufficiently. NA, MR (954), Notulen Ministerraad 5.12.1969.

35 *The Economist*, 21 November 1970.

36 W.F.V. Vanthoor, *A Chronological History of the European Union 1946-1998*, Cheltenham: Elgar, 1999, p. 39.

server might have been forgiven for failing to notice"[37], and George argues that the paragraph was generally considered a sop for Pompidou's Gaullist supporters and few observers thought it would amount to anything.[38] The clause "within the context of enlargement" was inserted on Dutch insistence, expressing the thought that political co-operation concerned a wider circle than the Six alone.[39] Nevertheless, on at least two occasions, Luns had to remind fellow Cabinet ministers that European political co-operation, once Britain were to join the Community, was not a bad thing.

At first sight the Dutch delegation appeared to have been left short-changed as far as enlargement was concerned. Pompidou refused to commit himself to mentioning a concrete starting date in the final communiqué. Although in a private conversation with Prime Minister De Jong, he pledged himself to enlargement – by giving his word of honour[40] – an official written statement, even an indication, was considered impossible at that stage. At the suggestion of the Belgian delegation De Jong proposed to use Pompidou's own wordings on the matter, as registered on tape, to which the latter could scarcely object.[41] Thus the conference communiqué stated that the states "agreed that the essential preparatory work for establishing a basis of negotiation [with the applicant countries] could be undertaken as soon as practically possible".[42] Moreover, De Jong secured permission for issuing a press statement, saying that all delegations were of the opinion that "preparations of the Six for negotiations with Great Britain will have to be finished by 30 June 1970 at the latest and the negotiations were to start immediately afterwards".[43] Which is how things turned out eventually.

---

37 Chr. Hill and K.E. Smith, *European Foreign Policy. Key Documents*, London: Routledge, 2000, p. 72.

38 S. George, *Politics and Policy in the European Union*, Oxford: OUP, 3rd ed., 1996, p. 261.

39 J.K. de Vree and M. Jansen, *The Ordeal of Unity. Integration and Disintegration in Modern Europe*, Amsterdam: Blackwall Publishing, 1988, p. 291.

40 Studies by Hiepel (C. Hiepel, "In Search of the Greatest Common Denominator. Germany and the Hague Summit Conference 1969", *Journal of European Integration History*, Vol. 9 (2003), pp. 63-81) and Guasconi (M.E. Guasconi, "Italy and the Hague Conference of 1969", *Journal of European Integration History*, Vol. 9 (2003), pp. 101-116) provide evidence that Pompidou's word of honour was also given to the other Prime Ministers present at the meeting.

41 UK Public Record Office London, PRO, Telegram Sir P. Garran No. 619 to Foreign and Commonwealth Office London, 2-12-1969 (with thanks to prof. Alan Milward).

42 "Final Communiqué of the meeting of heads of state or government of the EC Countries", *Bulletin of the European Communities*, 1970, No. 1, pp. 11-16.

43 Italianer, "Terugblik", p. 66; De Vree and Jansen, *The Ordeal of Unity*, p. 308.

But in December 1969, these ideas still had to take shape. Hence, reviewing the conference a couple of days afterwards, the *Ministerraad* felt rather uncomfortable about the outcome, not only regarding enlargement, but also in view of its initial desire to reinforce the position of the European Parliament. The Dutch delegation had pleaded for both EP control over CAP financing and the Community's own resources, as well as direct elections for the Parliament, but these *desiderata* had remained largely unfulfilled. Likewise, the summit had failed to widen the possibilities for majority voting in the Council of Ministers, as the government had hoped for. De Jong diagnosed that the conference "had been neither a resounding success, nor a failure". State Secretary for European Integration De Koster blamed the French president for having shown lack of commitment, deeming the latter's European debut "disappointing". On the other hand, he gave high praise to the Federal Chancellor, complimenting Brandt for having "saved the meeting".[44]

In Kersten's analysis, "only at the Hague summit of December 1969 did Luns become convinced that Bonn dared to confront Paris. Thus his long-time perception of the Federal Republic as a hesitant supporter of further European integration finally fell apart".[45]

In other European capitals Dutch summit diplomacy was looked back upon with equally mixed feelings. The Belgian government felt that Luns had overreacted against the negative attitude of Pompidou, with the lamentable result that on the first evening the conference was in disarray. On the other hand there was general praise for Prime Minister De Jong and the way he had presided over the conference.[46]

IV. Discussion

"How should the summit be typified: as a swan song or cock crow?"[47] In an effort to assess the results of the meeting, State Secretary De Koster brought up this question during a parliamentary debate at the end of December. It was another sign of the government's initial ambivalence

---

44 NA, MR, (954), Notulen Ministerraad 5.12.1969.

45 A. Kersten, "De langste. Joseph Antoine Marie Hubert Luns (1952-1971)", in: D. Hellema, B. Zeeman and B. van der Zwan (eds.), *De Nederlandse ministers van Buitenlandse Zaken in de twintigste eeuw*, Den Haag: SDU, 1999, pp. 211-227, p. 224.

46 UK Public Record Office, PRO, Telegram Sir J. Beith No. 408 to Foreign and Commonwealth Office London, 3-12-1969 (with thanks to Prof. Alan Milward); Brouwer and Van Merriënboer, *Van buitengaats naar binnenhof*, pp. 199-200. Possibly, some of the Belgian irritation was aggravated by the bleak picture offered by Benelux foreign policy cooperation before and during the summit. Attempts at Belgian-Dutch co-operation were scarce and unsuccessful.

47 Handelingen Staten Generaal Tweede Kamer (HTK) 1969-1970, 36e vergadering, 23 December 1969, 1751.

regarding the outcomes. To what extent did the *Ridderzaal* event constitute a real breakthrough in European integration or "had [it] all been rather more like a normal council meeting than a summit", as Foreign Affairs delegate Hartogh lamented.[48] In the immediate aftermath of the conference, this was far from clear.

The Netherlands' original condition for agreeing to a summit of the Six turned out to be eventually, from the government's perspective, its most important outcome: the French promise to go along with enlargement negotiations with Britain in the near future. At least, that was what the French president had acceded privately. Otherwise, in the short run, the Hague results were to be considered rather disappointing: little or nothing of substance had been agreed upon in terms of progress towards European economic and monetary union on a communitarian footing. The empowerment of the European Parliament fell short of Dutch wishes and further intergovernmentalisation of the decision-making process was looming.

In the greater scheme of things, however, "The Hague" would turn out to be the summit that initiated both – the first attempt at – EMU as well as EPC, plus the actual beginning of the first enlargement, all three to become of the greatest importance in the Communities' development during the 1970s and later decades to come. Moreover, at the Brussels conference of 21 and 22 December, agreement was reached to give some budgetary powers to the European Parliament.

Thus, in terms of engineering influence, the historical importance of the Hague summit is by and large to be attributed to the subsequent implementation and follow-up of the conclusions it arrived at. Had the Brussels conference, the Werner and Davignon committees and the enlargement negotiations been unsuccessful, the by now famous triptych "completion, widening and deepening" would have remained null and void. In this respect the "spirit of the Hague" appears to have been of more importance than the actual wording of the compromises arrived at in the *Ridderzaal*.

What is fundamentally new about The Hague summit was the decisive role played by the West-German government, led by Chancellor Brandt. The German contribution went well beyond its advocacy of EMU. As worded by Kersten: "Die Regierung Brandt hatte sich zugunsten der Erweiterung und Vertiefung entschieden und nicht versucht, die Gegensätze innerhalb der EWG durch einen vagen Kompromisz zu

48 UK Public Record Office London, PRO, Telegram Sir P. Garran No. 626 to Foreign and Commonwealth Office London, 3-12-1969 (with thanks to Prof. Alan Milward).

vertuschen, der den Anschein eines französischen Sieges gehabt hätte".[49] As such, the German performance heralded a new era in European integration. The *Bundesrepublik* definitely freed itself of its historically determined reticence in post-war European affairs and, thus emancipated, was ready and willing to lead the Community towards further integration and against future attempts at dominance. It had excellent reasons to embark upon this course since international support for its *Ostpolitik* was both required and on offer. In this respect, one can agree with Urwin's statement that with "the exception perhaps of De Gaulle's dramatic press conference vetoes of British entry, the Hague summit was the most significant event within the Community since its inception".[50] For the Netherlands, now that the *préalable anglais* was about to be fulfilled, such further European propositions were again open for consideration.

Both the 1965-1966 empty chair crisis and the outcome of the Hague summit conference of 1969 underline the fundamental importance of German Chancellor Adenauer's departure from active politics in 1963. Until then, room for manoeuvre for the Netherlands and its Benelux partners was by and large determined by the ongoing relationship between France and Germany. Konrad Adenauer had been the key figure in determining the leeway for the Netherlands and its Benelux partners. If and when the German Chancellor decided to prioritize on a Franco-German understanding – and this was generally the case – Benelux' chances at effectively promoting diverging negotiation outcomes were slender, at least on major issues. Adenauer's successors in Bonn, by prioritizing a European understanding amongst the Six, considerably broadened The Hague's room for manoeuvre. Likewise, France's president De Gaulle's unilateral policy choices contributed to a new power constellation within the EEC, in which it was France, rather than the Netherlands that painted itself into a corner and lost out against the new reality in which a basic understanding between Germany, Italy and the Benelux countries (The Five) on the communitarian destiny of the Community and its open character prevailed. The emancipation of Germany's European policy, effective cooperation between the Five and a new dawn in France collectively triumphed in the Hague summit of December 1969.

In this way, The Hague demonstrated that within the framework of the international organizational framework of the European Communi-

---

49 A.E. Kersten, "Das Europäische Gipfeltreffen in Den Haag 1969", in: J.W.F. Wielenga (ed.), *Nachbarn. Niederländer und Deutsche und die Europäische Einigung*, Bonn: s.n., 1997, pp. 45-49, p. 49.

50 D.W. Urwin, *The Community of Europe. A History of European Integration since 1945*, London: Longman, 1993, p. 138.

ties, Smaller Powers like the Netherlands by being part of an effective coalition could bridge the power and influence gap with larger states and achieve their policy aims.

Part III

Externalizing Europe

CHAPTER VII

Learning Interdependence the Hard Way

The Netherlands, European Political Co-operation and the First Oil Crisis

Introduction*

Today, co-operation on foreign policy, as well as its gradual upgrading into a common foreign and security policy constitute long-standing ideals of European integration. Towards the end of the 1960s the foundations for a far-reaching integrative framework were laid, eventually resulting in the EU's present-day Foreign and Security Policy (CFSP). For the Netherlands, a former colonial Power with global presence and strongly 'atlanticist' foreign policy traditions, a European identity in the area of high politics was far from self-evident. Singled out for an oil boycott by Arab OPEC-countries due to The Hague's policies on Israel and the Palestine issue, the Netherlands learned to appreciate European Political Co-operation (EPC) as a significant and occasionally important foreign policy instrument.

This chapter deals with the question of the extent to which the establishment of EPC reflected a cleavage in Dutch policy on European integration, as compared with the period of the 1960s. To which extent did the European Community, in lieu of a threat to Dutch Atlanticism, grow into an actively pursued policy forum for engineering influence in the area of high politics? The research is based on primary source material, the minutes of the *Ministerraad* (Cabinet) meetings in particular, a number of recently published monographs on Dutch foreign policy, as well as interviews with some of the protagonists.

---

* An earlier version of this chapter was published as: Anjo G. Harryvan and Jan van der Harst, "Learning Interdependence the Hard Way. The Netherlands, European Political Co-operation and the Oil Crisis, 1967-1977", in: F. Knipping & M. Schönwald (eds.), *Aufbruch zum Europa der zweiten Generation. Die europäische Einigung 1969-1984*, Trier: Wissenschaftlichter Verlag Trier, 2004, pp. 150-164.

I. Finding New Bearings. The Hague's Views on EPC during the 1960s

The Hague's approach towards European Political Co-operation was first and foremost a cautious one. Since the foundation of NATO in 1949, the Netherlands prioritised the Atlantic security alliance with the United States and feared that developing European alternatives for or within NATO, would damage transatlantic cohesion and therefore provoke Washington into weakening the security link, deemed necessary to defend the country against communist aggression. The government also suspected that, within a strictly European framework, France would attempt to become the political leader of Europe, possibly in an alliance with the Federal Republic of Germany. This was also the reason why, during the 1960s, the Netherlands strongly favoured British entry into the EC. In The Hague's reasoning, UK membership would not only boost Atlantic partnership, but would also neutralise tendencies directed towards Franco-German leadership of the Community. The government did not hide its irritation when in the 1960s French President De Gaulle unilaterally blocked British entry to the Community.

As pointed out in chapter four the Dutch stance on the Fouchet negotiations, in the early 1960s, had been of an equally conservative nature. The Gaullist version of the Fouchet plan was rejected because it represented a departure from the Community system, that is from the existing European institutions. The French plans were considered by the Dutch as an attempt to cripple these institutions, by transferring their powers to a new political structure of an intergovernmental character. In tenacious opposition to De Gaulle's attempts at subjugating the Communities' powers to a structure of intergovernmental committees within the framework of a European Political Union, Minister of Foreign Affairs Luns advocated the concept of "instrumental supranationalism". Pragmatic rather than federalist in nature, instrumental supranationalism was first and foremost a means to an economic and political end, namely the realisation of a sizeable internal European market and the checking of the stronger members, if and where the latter pursued hegemonic policies.[1] Likewise, British membership, although difficult to relate to supranationalism, held out prospects of realising the same two policy goals.

---

1 See Chapters 4 and 5, as well as: A.G. Harryvan "Supranationality or Britain? The Netherlands and the Fouchet negotiations, 1959-1962", conference paper to be published in a volume on European integration in the 1960s, edited by Prof. G. Trausch of the Robert Schuman center in Luxembourg, at press; A.G. Harryvan and J. van der Harst, "For once a united front. The Netherlands and the empty chair crisis of the mid-1960s", in: W. Loth (ed.), *Crises and compromises: the European project 1963-1969*, Baden-Baden: Nomos, 2001, pp. 173-191.

European political co-operation resurfaced on the agenda during the late 1960s in a radically different setting: "It now became possible, as it had not been at the time of the Fouchet Plans (...) to envisage an increased political role for Europe in the world without at the same time subordinating the Community principle to an overarching union of states".[2] Due to the French Republic's Atlantic and European policies, this perspective had been effectively torpedoed during the 1960s.

True, as early as June 1967 Prime Minister De Jong stated at the EC Rome summit conference that foreign policy consultations were "to be considered" if (and when) Britain was to participate in them from the outset. At the same conference, however, De Jong and his Benelux colleagues rejected a Franco-German proposal to institutionalize consultations among the Six and provide them with a secretariat. Clearly, for De Jong such arrangements smacked too much of "Fouchet" and were considered premature.[3] The second French veto later that year would prove him right.

By the end of 1967, indeed, French foreign policy – only moderately popular with the Dutch since the 16th century anyway – reached an all-time low in The Hague's appreciation. Apart from the second veto, fundamental disagreements on NATO and WEU reduced the opportunities for fruitful foreign policy co-operation to something close to nil. In Cabinet meetings Prime Minister De Jong drew a sombre picture of the situation: democracy in Europe was at stake. He refused to accept a future for the Netherlands as a satellite state of France or – after De Gaulle's demise – of Germany. "History teaches us that democratic principles are not compatible with French or German hegemony. The accession of Britain and the Scandinavian countries is of the greatest importance for maintaining democracy in Europe".[4] Long-standing Foreign Minister Joseph Luns agreed that De Gaulle's attempts at leadership were not in the best of taste. France, however, was in an isolated position and he warned against retaliation policies as proposed by De Jong: these ran the risk of overshooting their aim, unless London agreed on such a "show down policy". There were numerous other possibilities to show Paris the error of her ways. Luns' arguments won the day, with support from the Minister of Agriculture, who feared that the Prime Minister's boldness would backfire on the common agricul-

---

2 Chr. Hill and K.E. Smith (eds.), *European Foreign Policy. Key Documents*, London: Routledge, 2000, p. 71.

3 NA, MR (844), Notulen Ministerraad 2-6-1967. Much to Foreign Minister Luns' dismay Belgian Foreign Minister Harmel at the conference did toy with the idea of a secretariat for policy consultations among the Six, i.e. without UK participation.

4 See Chapter 6 and NA, MR (845), Notulen Ministerraad 27.10.1967.

tural policy, with concomitant risks for the income situation of Dutch farmers.[5]

In January 1968 Benelux views on the desired course of European integration were expressed in a common Benelux memorandum. The three governments did not mince their words. They expressed their loyalty towards the supranational or "communitarian" model as laid down in the Rome Treaty on the one hand and called for policy consultation with Great Britain and other non-members for those policy areas not covered by the Treaty – foreign policy included – on the other. As far as foreign policy co-operation was concerned the Benelux message to Bonn and Paris was clear: policy consultations without British participation were a non-starter.[6]

From April 1969 onwards, the diplomatic climate in Europe improved substantially following De Gaulle's departure and his succession by Georges Pompidou, who, almost immediately, abandoned the dogmatic rejection of EC enlargement. The end of the 1960s witnessed the accomplishment of two long-standing aims of the Hague's European policy: the completion of the EEC Customs Union in July 1968 – ever since the early 1950s, the primary aim of Dutch European policy had been the liberalisation of trade among the Original Six – and, the reopening of the negotiations on enlargement.

In The Hague, the prospect of forthcoming British EEC membership appears to have made all the difference. Within a few months foreign policy co-operation gained acceptance as a negotiable issue. Nevertheless, preparations for the political dimension of the Hague December 1969 summit conference were far from elaborate. Policy papers on the subject remained confined to the view that the Netherlands was in favour of policy co-operation on an intergovernmental basis between the Six plus the UK and, that, revitalising the WEU framework and expanding its membership with the three other applicant states, was the way to do so. France, boycotting the WEU meetings since 1968, would have to change her ways. Luns, in the relative secrecy of *Ministerraad* meetings, indicated that eventually – following British accession – a more ambitious approach along the lines of the so-called second Fouchet draft

---

5 NA, MR (845), Notulen Ministerraad 27.10.1967, 1.12.1967.

6 NA, MR (880), Notulen Ministerraad 16.2.1968; J.J.C. Voorhoeve, *Peace Profits and Principles. A Study of Dutch Foreign Policy*, Leiden: Martinus Nijhoff, 1985, p. 171. The memorandum gave rise to intricate but unsuccessful negotiations between the Five and the Four (the applicant states) on a technical co-operation agreement. By November 1968 this confrontational Benelux approach had run out of steam: Belgium grew increasingly hesitant to support Dutch policy proposals against French wishes, whereas Britain entertained – and voiced – doubts on the sense of multilateral co-operation arrangements without French participation. NA, MR (883), Notulen Ministerraad, 15.11.1968 and NA, MR (954), Notulen Ministerraad, 29.11.1969.

might be called for. In arguing so, he was referring to the draft treaty that the Six had found agreement upon in January 1962 – proposing an intergovernmental framework for foreign policy co-operation that would gradually develop into a communitarian-based and eventually supranationally-driven common foreign policy framework – and which was subsequently torpedoed by De Gaulle's unwillingness to underwrite the (rather vague) communitarian perspective it embodied (see Chapter 4).[7]

II. The Hague Summit, the Davignon Report and Dutch Views on the EPC Machinery

Foreign policy co-operation was generally recognised as a moot point at the Hague summit of December 1969 and received relatively little attention. Without much ado, German Chancellor Brandt's suggestion to request the Ministers of Foreign Affairs to look into the matter and report on what was possible "within the context of enlargement" found its way into the penultimate paragraph of the conference communiqué: "They agreed to instruct the Ministers of Foreign Affairs to study the best way of achieving progress in the matter of political unification, within the context of enlargement. The Ministers would be expected to report before the end of July 1970". Thus, in a few lines tucked away in the final communiqué, European Political Co-operation was born. As we quoted Hill and Smith previously: "Even the interested observer might have been forgiven for failing to notice".[8] Fascinated by the short-term prospect of British accession, and eagerly participating in the debate on the long-term issues of economic and monetary union (see Chapter 6), Dutch policy-makers generally qualified for this category.[9] In this they were not alone; the paragraph was generally considered a sop for Pompidou's Gaullist supporters and few observers thought it would amount to anything.[10] In the months following the Hague summit, political co-

---

7 NA, MR (845), Notulen Ministerraad 1.12.1967, NA, MR (881), Notulen Ministerraad 11.4.1968, NA, MR (953), Notulen Ministerraad 4.7.1969, and 10.7.1969 and NA, MR (954), Notulen Ministerraad 12.9.1969; Min. BZ, III, 913.100, No. 5463, "Nederlandse doelstellingen voor de topconferentie", with accompanying letter 11.11.1969.

8 Min. BZ, EEG 1965-1974, 17 (996.0), codetelegram 5-12-1969 "Volgt verslag topconferentie, gehouden te Den Haag op 1 en 2 december 1969"; "Communiqué of the Conference of the Heads of State and Government of the Member States of the European Community (The Hague Summit Declaration), The Hague, 2 December 1969", in: Hill and Smith, *op. cit.*, 71-74.

9 J.W. Brouwer and A.G. Harryvan, "Les Pays-Bas et la coopération monétaire européenne, 1968-1972", in: *Le rôle des ministères des Finances et de l'Economie dans la construction européenne (1957-1978)*, Paris: Comité pour l'histoire économique et financière de la France, 2002, pp. 85-108.

10 Stephen George, *Politics and Policy in the European Union*, Oxford: OUP, 3rd edition, 1996, p. 261.

operation and integration were discussed in the Cabinet as necessary conditions for economic and monetary unification and as a prerequisite for a future Political Union. *Foreign* policy co-operation rarely featured in these talks.

The intergovernmental set-up elaborated in the Davignon report on European Political Co-operation, presented in October 1970, met with disappointment and profound criticism in the Dutch Cabinet, where it was labelled "a capitulation to French opinions". From a communitarian perspective the Davignon machinery was totally insufficient: the lightly structured decision-making process was projected parallel to and separate from that of the Community, with only a minor role for the Commission and the European Parliament and none for COREPER, the latter being substituted by the Political Committee of the political directors of the Foreign Ministries. As several ministers pointed out, the apparatus depended totally on the building up of consensus and did not constitute anything in terms of progress towards political unification of Europe. Nevertheless, withholding Dutch consensus to the report, state secretary for Foreign Affairs De Koster pointed out, would plunge the Community into a political crisis that could easily backfire on the entrance negotiations with Denmark, Ireland, Norway and the UK. Grudgingly, the Cabinet approved the Davignon proposals.[11]

This critical attitude with regard to the EPC set-up was to remain a dominant feature of Dutch European policy. Luns' successor in the Biesheuvel government (1971-1973), Schmelzer, stressed the artificiality of the institutional separation between the Community and EPC. A quarter of a century later, looking back on the early 1970s, he stated: "We emphasised perpetually that the European Commission ought to play an integral role in all European policy, on account of the cohesion and indivisibility between socio-economic and financial (and related) events on the one hand and external policies on the other. The two could not be disconnected".[12] To the extent that a tension existed between "those who hoped that EPC would transcend its own limitations and carry the whole integrationist project forward and those (...) who saw it as a pragmatic form of assistance to national foreign policy", as Hill and Smith word it, the Netherlands clearly was on the former side.[13] This stance reflected the reinforced communitarianism typical of

---

11 NA, MR (987), Notulen Ministerraad 18.9.1970. Luns did not attend the meeting, hence state secretary De Koster voiced the opinion of the Foreign Ministry.

12 Interview with drs. W.K.N. Schmelzer, in: A.G. Harryvan, J. van der Harst en S. van Voorst (eds.) *Voor Nederland en Europa. Politici en ambtenaren over het Nederlandse Europabeleid en de Europese integratie, 1945-1975*, Amsterdam: Boom, 2001, pp. 233-259 (p. 247).

13 Hill and Smith, op. cit., 83.

Mr. Schmelzer. Successor to Joseph Luns, who had served the country as Foreign Minister for over 19 uninterrupted years, Schmelzer would turn out to be the most outspoken *federalist* Foreign Minister of the post-war period.[14] He advocated a European federation along the lines of the Federal Republic of Germany in which the Netherlands' position in the European Community would be comparable to a *Land* in the *Bundesrepublik.* This was a highly idealistic but, in the context of the 1970s, also somewhat parochial approach, in that the trend in European co-operation at the time was distinctly of an intergovernmental rather than a federalist or supranational nature. Ironically, this intergovernmentalist trend was clearly reinforced by British entry, so vigorously advocated by the Dutch.

Apart from being fundamentally artificial, the institutional separation between the Community and EPC was deemed dangerous, in that the intergovernmental EPC could potentially "contaminate" the Community's supranational and communitarian character. The establishment, proposed by France, of a distinct and high-powered political EPC secretariat to be located in Paris was deemed particularly detrimental to the Community and the policy-initiating role of the Commission. In this respect, the Netherlands suspected the Pompidou government of trying to reproduce the old Fouchet plan in a new format. At the European summit conference in Paris in October 1972 Schmelzer successfully blocked proposals of this nature.[15]

Such strictures regarding EPCs institutional insufficiency did not prevent the Dutch foreign policy making elite from appreciating its potential added value for Dutch foreign policy as a whole. In January 1972, an evaluative Cabinet paper arrived at the conclusion that EPC foreign policy consultations could be judged favourably, as long as one kept in mind that their intergovernmental set-up seriously limited their scope and that the talks should not be to the detriment of NATO unity.[16]

---

[14] Mr. Schmelzer was supported in this by state secretary Westerterp, who was of an equally federalist persuasion.

[15] NA, MR (1160), Notulen Ministerraad 17.3.1972, NA, MR (1161), Notulen Ministerraad 9.6.1972 and NA, MR (1162), Notulen Ministerraad 21.10.1972; Harryvan, Van der Harst en Van Voorst, *op. cit.*, p. 249. The 1986 Single European Act would eventually provide EPC with a (small) secretariat based in Brussels.

[16] BZ, III, 913.100, No. 5469, "Discussienota over de Europese eenwording", with accompanying letter 4.1.1972.

III. A Rude Awakening. The Netherlands, EPC and the 1973 Oil Boycott

Misgivings that EPC, by intensifying foreign-policy co-operation in Europe, would adversely affect the relationship with the US in NATO proved not unwarranted. In the early 1970s, in the US, the Nixon-Kissinger government became increasingly worried about European assertiveness in the international arena; to counter this tendency and to intensify the Atlantic ties, Kissinger proclaimed 1973 as "The Year of Europe". This failed to produce the desired result, however, and American-European tensions increased further following the start of the Yom Kippur War in the Middle East, on 6 October 1973. In the Netherlands, the centre-right Biesheuvel Cabinet was succeeded by a centre-left coalition (under Prime Minister Den Uyl), which was less inclined to consider Arab sensitivities than its predecessor, particularly Foreign Minister Schmelzer, had done. Three days after the start of the war, the new government issued a declaration, stating that Syria and Egypt had taken the initiative to the hostilities, and had thereby unilaterally violated the regional truce in force since 1967. The aggressors were summoned to withdraw behind the pre-6-October-1973 demarcation lines. In the declaration, the government seemed to interpret UN resolution 242 along the following lines: Israel was entitled to have safe borders, and therefore border adjustments were not to be excluded beforehand. This interpretation left no room for endorsement by all the contending parties, as – previously – pleaded for by Schmelzer.[17]

The government's pro-Israel policy by and large followed the American strategy in the conflict, and was thus in line with the country's atlanticist traditions. The other eight EPC countries – France in particular – were more inclined to pacify the Arab countries, and urged the start of a so-called Euro-Arab dialogue which would also take into account the rights of the Palestinian people.

Not for the first time, the Middle East became a bone of contention among the EPC countries. From the start of EPC co-operation onwards, of all the issues discussed in the Political Committee, Middle Eastern affairs were the most difficult on which to reach common positions. This was above all due to the Dutch government's prioritising of Israeli

[17] D. Hellema, *Buitenlandse politiek van Nederland*, Utrecht: Het Spectrum, 1995, p. 259. Due to his so-called "evenhanded" Middle East policy, Schmelzer had encountered heavy criticism on the part of the Israeli government (see also: H.A. Schaper, "Nederland en het Midden-Oostenconflict", in: *Internationale Spectator* 29 (1975) 4, pp. 235-238). It seems that by choosing this position, Schmelzer was an exception among postwar Dutch foreign policy-makers, while the Den Uyl government (1973-1977), taking an undiluted pro-Israel stance, returned to a more traditional policy on the Middle East conflict.

security and its emphasis on the Netherlands' special relationship with Israel, resulting in highly diluted and thus ineffectual compromise texts in EPC.[18] Political director Van Lynden warned his Foreign Affairs Ministry against idiosyncrasy on the Middle East file.[19] However, the government's persistence clashed with the partners and effectively blocked a common EPC position. While meeting with his fellow Political Directors in the Political Committee in Copenhagen, Van Lynden was instructed by the Foreign Office: "This is not the moment for a declaration of the Nine". On at least two occasions during October and November the Netherlands torpedoed a mandate for France and the UK to act on behalf of the Nine in the UN Security Council. Dutch reticence incapacitated EPC, and caused political damage by undermining the country's goodwill in the European capitals and thus the European solidarity the Netherlands would need urgently and soon.[20] Both Foreign Minister Van der Stoel and Van Lynden found themselves wedged between Arab demands and EPC incentives on the one hand and the strong pro-Israel sentiments in Dutch public opinion and Parliament on the other. Prime Minister Den Uyl himself (1973-1977) and some departments within the Foreign Office were inclined to keep the EPC profile on the matter as low as possible.[21]

The pro-Israel views of both government and public did not fail to attract the attention of the oil-producing countries' policy-makers. Defence Minister Vredeling's participation in a pro-Israel demonstration in Amsterdam had not remained unnoticed either. About the same time, Vredeling secretly started delivering ammunition, artillery shells and reserve parts to the Israeli army.[22]

---

18 Interview with Dr. Charles Rutten in: Harryvan, Van der Harst and Van Voorst, *Voor Nederland en Europa*, pp. 189-231 (pp. 224-225).

19 Whereas Van Lynden advocated cautious policies on the Middle East his colleague Meijer, the director-general for development aid distinctly practiced a pro-Israel line. Early in 1973, Meijer instructed the Dutch delegation to vote against a proposed WHO resolution together with – solely – Israel and the USA. Alarmed by this isolated stance Van Lynden argued that – as a rule of thumb – such deviant (voting) behaviour should be supported by at least one other EPC country and preferably more. W. van Eekelen, *Sporen trekken door strategische jaren*, Meppel: Ten Brink, 2000, p. 75.

20 NA, MR (1237), Notulen Ministerraad 9.11.1973.

21 Van Eekelen, Sporen trekken, pp. 76-81.

22 P. Bootsma en W. Breedveld, *De verbeelding aan de macht. Het kabinet Den Uyl, 1973-1977*, Den Haag: SDU, 1999, p. 124. Whether Prime Minister Den Uyl and Foreign Minister Van der Stoel were left as unacquainted with Vredeling's secret arms deals as they later claimed, is a moot point. In his memoirs, state-secretary for Defence Bram Stemerdink states he and Vredeling acted on their own. When Stemerdink visited Den Uyl shortly before the latter's death in 1987, Den Uyl recollected his surprise when, while visiting Israel in 1974, Golda Meir showered

When in October 1973 OPEC proclaimed an oil embargo, the Netherlands – together with the United States – was the country most seriously affected by this measure. The reason why the Netherlands and – in Europe – the Netherlands alone, was singled out for a fully-fledged boycott can be only partly attributed to the country's Israel-mindedness and its isolated stance in EPC. It seems that tactical considerations on the part of OPEC played an important part as well. The position of the port of Rotterdam as the home base of one of the world's biggest oil companies (Shell) made the Netherlands an obvious target for Arab repercussions. Moreover, the hub position of Rotterdam for German and Belgian oil supplies contributed to the latter countries' circumspect stance in the conflict, and enhanced Dutch isolation.[23] In retrospect, Van der Stoel assumed that these tactical considerations had motivated the Arab countries to start preparing the embargo against the Netherlands months before the actual outbreak of the October War.[24]

Apart from the United States, the government received little help from the partner countries and complained about the lack of solidarity in EPC. Irritations grew when the British Foreign Minister Douglas-Home confided to Van der Stoel that "the supply of crude oil to Britain has to

---

him with kisses, thanking him for the help offered by the Netherlands during the Yom Kippur War. A help Den Uyl himself had considered to be of an extremely limited nature: The Netherlands' official Government stance was that only when Israeli territory itself would be in danger arms procurements for Israel were to be considered. B. Stermerdink, *Tussen dromen, daden en twijfels. Dagboekaantekeningen over de sociaal-democratie in Nederland en daarbuiten 1986-1993*, Amsterdam: Van Gennep, 1993, pp. 249-250 and P. Rusman, "Dilemma's bij de wapenleveranties aan Israel, 1956-1977", in: Ph. Everts (ed.), *Dilemma's in de buitenlandse politiek van Nederland*, Leiden: DSWO Press, 1996, pp. 143-180. Bootsma and Breedveld in their book on the Den Uyl government (1972-1976) deem it likely that Van der Stoel was uninformed about the arms deals, but argue that Den Uyl – although possibly unaware of what was going on at the time – was filled in about the arms deliveries shortly afterwards. Bootsma and Breedveld, *De verbeelding*, pp. 124-125. Hellema, Wiebes and Witte carry this argument further in their book on "Nederland en de oliecrisis": Van der Stoel's evasive answers to the *Tweede Kamer*, testimony by Israel's ambassador to the Netherlands Bar-On and American sources appear to suggest that both Prime Minister Den Uyl and Foreign Minister Van der Stoel were perfectly aware of the Netherlands' support for the Israeli war effort. Duco Hellema, Cees Wiebes and Toby Witte, *Doelwit Rotterdam. Nederland en de oliecrisis 1973-1974*, Den Haag: SDU, 1998, pp. 32-37.

23 J. van Ginkel, *Het Westen en de oliecrisis 1973-1974*, 's Gravenhage: Nederlands Instituut voor Vredesvraagstukken, 1978, pp. 69-70; NA, MR (1237), Notulen Ministerraad 9.11.1973 and Bootsma and Breedveld, *De verbeelding*, pp. 124-125; NA, MR (1237), Notulen Ministerraad (9.11.1973 and 16.11.1973).

24 Hellema, Wiebes and Witte, *Doelwit Rotterdam*, p. 260.

be assured" and when French president Pompidou "consoled" the Dutch that they 'would not die of hunger and thirst' because of the embargo.[25]

Early in November, Arab pressure increased with a boycott of the Royal Dutch airline, KLM, and the threat of a further cut in the production and supply of oil from the Middle East. Despite public professions implying the contrary, Van der Stoel eventually decided to give in and to support the "neutral" EPC line towards the crisis, by signing the EPC resolution of 6 November – a French initiative – in which for the first time the rights of the Palestinian people were formally recognised.[26] Although the resolution was not the appropriate vehicle for removing away all Euro-Arab and intra-European divergences, it certainly helped to improve the Dutch diplomatic position, all the more so when in 1974 – in reaction to the oil embargo – the United States instigated the creation of an International Energy Agency (IEA) of the oil-consuming countries, an institution which all the EC countries joined except France. From that time on, France – instead of the Netherlands – became the isolated party in the conflict. Diplomatic pressure by the US on the OPEC countries, the prospect of a Euro-Arab dialogue, as well as OPEC's awareness that the boycott had largely missed its mark, eventually resulted in the lifting of the oil embargo in July 1974. Furthermore, to Dutch relief, the US successfully stipulated mutual consultation between the Atlantic partners in cases where EPC dealt with issues directly affecting NATO. This substantially reduced the possibilities of EPC acting as a divisive force within NATO.[27]

The crisis in the Middle East was an obvious example of the difficulty in aligning the EPC countries in times of emergency. Despite the improvements it brought in communication between the ministries of foreign affairs of the Nine, EPC was still not seen as the proper policy instrument to make Europe a credible and forceful player in the international arena. Nevertheless, despite these limitations, the 1973/74 oil crisis also pointed out an EPC *potential*. In future, Mr. Rutten, the director-general for political affairs at the Foreign Ministry (1974-1980) noted, EPC could and should be used to avoid the Netherlands being singled out as a target for wrath and retaliation by third countries. This

---

25 Hans H.J. Labohm (ed.), *De waterdragers van het Nederlandse Europabeleid. Terugblik op 40 jaar DGES*, Den Haag: SDU, 1997, pp. 108-109. Although The Hague was gravely hurt by Pompidou's lack of sympathy, the French president hardly vitiated the truth. In fact, thanks to the distribution policy of the domestic company Shell, the Netherlands – despite the oil embargo – was one of the best-supplied European countries during the crisis; Hellema, Wiebes and Witte, *Doelwit Rotterdam*, pp. 114-118.

26 Hellema, Wiebes and Witte, *Doelwit Rotterdam*, p. 261.

27 Voorhoeve, *Peace, Profits and Principles*, pp. 235-246.

is the so-called "umbrella-function" of EPC.[28] Moreover, EPC proved a useful tool in domestic politics. In the wake of the oil embargo, successive Dutch governments made use of EPC to gradually amend the country's formerly unmitigated pro-Israel policy (again, with the exception of Schmelzer's brief tenure). The Hague's agreement with a series of EPC declarations, in which with increasing clarity the rights of the Palestinian people found recognition, steered the country's Middle East policy in European mainstream direction. Such policy convergence proved beneficial for EPC. The second half of the 1970s witnessed a constructive Euro-Arab dialogue resulting in the Community's 1980 Venice Declaration, recognising the right of the Palestinians to a Palestine homeland. But before this was to take place, the Netherlands had experienced a long and difficult way of learning interdependence.

IV. The Netherlands and EPC in the 1970s. A Godsend for Dutch Cabaret?

Clearly, most of the EPC's policies were highly declaratory and the stream of communiqués it issued during the 1970s gave the forum the image of a "paper tiger". Foreign Office political director Rutten would sometimes compare EPC to the choir in a Greek tragedy: standing next to the scene EPC furthered comments and opinions on what was happening on the stage: it would sing praise, denounce, state goals and preferences, but all this without taking part in the action itself.[29] Such impotence was not confined to Middle East policies. A joint strategy was also lacking in the European response to the *apartheid* regime in South Africa, with on the one hand the "moralists" (Denmark, Ireland and the Netherlands), pleading for a tough stance towards Pretoria in the form of a weapon embargo and economic sanctions and, on the other side, the "realists" (Germany, France and the UK), advocating less drastic steps. Likewise, the EPC was unable to play a role in mitigating the problems resulting from the economic recession of the 1970s, simply because it lacked due powers in economic areas.

Nevertheless, on a number of other foreign policy issues, EPC *did* function and it can well be argued that the *overall* picture of EPC in the 1970s was a successful one: European foreign policy co-operation constituted a noticeable exception to the rampant eurosclerosis of the time.[30] The Euro-Arab dialogue after 1975, the common positions adopted at the Conference on Security and Co-operation in Europe

---

[28] Interview with Dr. Charles Rutten in: Harryvan, Van der Harst and Van Voorst, *Voor Nederland en Europa*, pp. 189-231, (p. 224).

[29] *Ibidem*, pp. 189-231 (pp. 224-225).

[30] Voorhoeve, *Peace, Profits and Principles*, p. 182.

(CSCE), as well as their parallel voting patterns in the UN and its specialised agencies testified to the coherence-enhancing quality of EPC policy co-ordination.

EPC's influence in stimulating and operating the CSCE was welcomed in the Netherlands, first and foremost because of the opportunities the conference offered to highlight the human rights situation in Eastern Europe. Whereas until then the Netherlands' emphasis on human rights as a foreign policy objective had been treated with scepticism by friend and foe alike, the Helsinki negotiations provided the country with a forum. The Netherlands actively advocated the human rights issue and the free movement of people and information, to the extent that Soviet leader Brezhnev would scornfully refer to these issues as "Dutch cabaret".[31]

Such a distinct European role in the CSCE process was possible at that time also, because the US administration showed little interest in this European initiative – initially, at least. The American attitude would change after the Helsinki declaration of 1975, with the consequence of a decreasing EPC profile in CSCE affairs from then on.

European policy co-operation had eventually enabled the Netherlands to play a role both in the Middle East crisis and in mooting the human rights situation in Middle and Eastern Europe, Foreign Minister Van der Stoel concluded in 1977 – a role, at least a larger role, than the realm's own diplomatic means would have provided for.

National bureaucratic politics, argues George, may have contributed to this achievement. By 1970, the integration process had blurred the lines between foreign and domestic politics and in all Community member states the Foreign Office was engaged in a power struggle with various domestic ministries, including Agriculture and – above all – Economic Affairs, for control of Community affairs. For the challenged foreign ministries, George observes, "EPC was a godsend", enabling them to re-conquer their traditional positions of primacy within national foreign policy making.[32]

To which extent is the George thesis applicable to the Netherlands? As the Middle East crisis showed, EPC profiling was opposed by political forces outside of as well as *within*, the Foreign Ministry (see also Van Lynden's policy advise earlier in this chapter). One can expect that EPC was institutionally welcomed, apparently not so much by the Ministry in its entirety, but rather by the leading policymakers in the directorate-general for Political Affairs, who during the 1960s, had

---

[31] Voorhoeve, *Peace, Profits and Principles*, pp. 223-224, p. 134.

[32] S. George, *Politics and Policy in the European Union*, Oxford: OUP, 3rd edition, 1996, p. 264.

witnessed the relative political and financial clout of their department decline due to drastic expansion, both in terms of staff and budgets, of the rivalling directorates-general for European Co-operation and Development Aid, as well as of other domestic ministries. This helps to explain why, in the early 1970s, Political Affairs seized the moment of the oil crisis as an opportunity to provide EPC *and* the directorate itself with a higher profile. The George thesis, therefore, is applicable to the Netherlands, albeit only in part.

V. Discussion

The Hague's ardent support for British EC-membership throughout the 1960s originated in a defensive line of thinking: the government feared that within a purely continental framework, France would seek political dominance, possibly in an alliance with the Federal Republic of Germany. The Hague's reasoning, by contrast, was that UK membership would not only strengthen Atlantic partnership, but also neutralise the aforementioned tendencies towards Franco-German attempts at leadership of the Community. The government continued focussing on the Atlantic alliance as the decisive forum for discussing foreign policy and security issues. At the same time, in the areas of trade and welfare, The Hague opted for integration in a European context, by advocating supranationalism and furthering a strong European Commission.

As a result of this, the government's approach of European Political Co-operation was lukewarm. EPC was seen as potentially dangerous in that it could be used as a Trojan Horse for weakening the Atlantic link, sidelining the Commission and corrupting the community's supranational calling. Nevertheless, EPC foreign policy consultations were to be judged favourably as long as one kept in mind that their intergovernmental set-up seriously limited their scope and that the talks should not be to the detriment of NATO unity. From a communitarian perspective, EPC was considered of little importance: the creation of a foreign-political roof over the Customs Union and later the Common Market was deemed less urgent, especially if this roof lacked a connection with the EC's supranational foundation. This policy line was to remain unaltered, at least until the end of the Cold War in 1990.

At times, European policy co-ordination and group diplomacy was not an option, but a necessity. Especially the country's isolated position during the 1973/74 Middle Eastern crisis and oil boycott was instructive in teaching interdependence the hard way. At this point, it seemed that, for the first time since the Second World War – perhaps with the exception of the de-colonisation of the Dutch Indies and New Guinea – the Atlantic bond failed to give the Netherlands the desired protection and coverage against external threats. Despite the existence of a strong sense of solidarity between the US and the Netherlands, OPEC's oil policy hurt the Netherlands and manoeuvred the country into a vulnerable and diplomatically isolated position. It took some time before the government realised that going a *Sonderweg* and ignoring EPC harmed the country's national interest. For a change, the Atlantic framework did not suffice.

The Atlantic factor – though different in character – also played a role in the CSCE process. In this case, initial American *absence* gave the Netherlands leeway to participate in the discussions and develop a high profile on the human rights dossier. It was discovered that EPC convergence and joint action sometimes provided a Smaller Power like the Netherlands with political leverage enabling it to play a role that its national diplomatic means could not have provided for. Later, however, when Washington changed its mind and became involved in the Helsinki negotiations, Dutch enthusiasm for CSCE seemed to wither simultaneously.

On the national bureaucratic level, EPC provided the directorate of Political Affairs with a useful instrument to improve its status and influence within the Foreign Ministry. The other directorates – European Co-operation and Development Aid – were downright sceptical regarding the new phenomenon, and would not hesitate to ventilate this in intra-ministerial discussions. George's observation that the EPC constituted a "godsend" for the Foreign Offices of the members-states is therefore only partially true for the situation in the Netherlands.

To what extent is EPC a cleavage in Dutch policy on European integration, as compared to the 1960s? In conclusion to this chapter, we may certainly speak of a *change* in the country's appreciation of political co-operation in a European framework. When the UK entered the Community, the Dutch "Fouchet syndrome" faded into the background, making the country ripe for acceptance of EPC membership. While initially the government hoped that EPC would transcend its own limitations and carry the whole integrationist project forward, it gradually came to value the co-operation as a pragmatic form of assistance to national foreign policy. It would be inaccurate, though, to call this a *cleavage* because, together with support for EPC's development, Atlantic unity continued to be sacrosanct in Dutch foreign policy.

CHAPTER VIII

A Bumpy Road To Lomé

The Netherlands' Policy on Association and the Yaoundé Treaties, 1956-1969

Introduction*

North-South development efforts were not among the common policies foreseen for the European Economic Community (EEC) in its formative years. Therefore, the association of 18 African countries and Madagascar (AASM) with the EEC during the 1960s was considered by many as an "historical accident". An accident, however, which resulted in a unique framework of co-operation between industrialized and developing countries, as well as constituting the starting point of the fully-fledged Development Policy of the present-day European Union.[1]

"Voluntary silence" on behalf of the editors of the Spaak Report, the blueprint for the 1957 EEC Treaty, on the issue of the relationship between the future Community and the overseas territories of its member-states, forced France – far and away the largest colonial Power of the Original Six – to come forward on this issue with a proposal of its own. In the ensuing multilateral negotiations France, finding itself in the position of *demandeur*, spared neither effort nor argument to convince and coerce its reluctant partners, the most reluctant of which may well have been the Netherlands.[2]

---

* An earlier version of this chapter was published as: A.G. Harryvan and J. van der Harst, "A Bumpy Road to Lomé. The Netherlands, Association and the Yaoundé Treaties, 1956-1969", in: M.-Th. Bitsch and G. Bossuat (eds.), *L'Europe unie et l'Afrique. De l'idée d'Eurafrique à la convention de Lome I*, Brussel: Bruylant, 2005, pp. 319-343.

1 J. Westhoff, "Het associatiebeleid van de Europese Gemeenschappen", *Internationale Spectator* 27 (1973), pp. 149-155 (p. 129) and "Verslag van een gesprek met mr. J. Westhoff", *Handelingen van de Tweede Kamer*, (HTK) zitting 1970-1971, 10900 V 8, 13 October 1970.

2 E. Deschamps, "La Belgique et l'association des pays et territoires d'outre-mer (PTOM) au marché commun (1955-1957)", in: M. Dumoulin, G. Duchenne and A. van Laer (eds.), *La Belgique, les petits États et la construction européenne*, Brussels: P.I.E.-Peter Lang, 2003, pp. 119-145, (p. 123).

This chapter on the Netherlands' policy regarding association with the Common Market by overseas territories, dependencies and former dependencies is divided into two parts, dealing with the issue in a chronological order. The first section covers the period 1956-1962, from the Venice conference till the signing of the first Yaoundé convention, with the second part focusing on the period stretching from Yaoundé I until the signing of the second Yaoundé Convention in 1969. The central question is to what extent successive Dutch governments were willing to endorse overseas EC involvement, particularly in Africa and, to what degree, did they attempt to influence multilateral negotiations and policy outcomes on this matter.

I. From Venice to Yaoundé I: Association as a Price Tag on the Common Market

When, in October 1956, the French and Belgian delegations in the EEC negotiations finally tabled their common *Eurafrique* proposals, the latter proved an unpleasant surprise for the Dutch policy-makers. The *Eurafrique* concept, raised at the Venice ministers conference in May of that year, after several postponements, was now emerging, highly contrary to a plethora of Dutch interests and desiderata. As such, it was considered a direct threat to the central aim of Dutch European policy since 1953, to wit realizing the Beyen Plan, or in other words, the establishment of a common market between the six ECSC countries.

The Hague's inter-ministerial Co-ordination Committee (CoCo) advocated a partial, gradual, temporary and differentiated association of the overseas territories, allowing for specific treatment in each case. The Belgian/French proposal, however, demanded permanent, full and immediate association of these territories with the European Common Market, in that their exports to the EEC market would receive the same preferential treatment, as the Six were to establish amongst themselves. Thus the Belgian and French overseas territories would benefit from the progressive liberalization of intra-European trade. In return, the overseas dependencies would have to gradually enlarge the preferential trade regimes applied for imports from their respective colonial powers to all six EEC member-states. In the Dutch view, this proposal was GATT-incompatible, as well as seriously lacking in balance. Chief-negotiator J. Linthorst Homan and his delegates pointed out the discrepancy between full market access for the French and Belgian dependencies in Europe on the one hand and no more than limited non-discrimination for European exporters overseas on the other. "A problematic export increase in exchange for total liberalization", was their damning conclusion.[3] Likewise, the Chambers of Commerce of Amsterdam and Rotterdam spoke out against the proposals: a slackening of trade with the non-participating African countries, with the Middle East, with Latin-America as well as with Asia was to be feared, they argued.[4]

France and Belgium, moreover, proposed the establishment of an investment fund to facilitate economic development in the overseas territories, thus enabling the eventual creation of a fully fledged common market between Europe and the French and Belgian colonial possessions in Africa: *Eurafrique*. In The Hague, the suggestion of Dutch financial responsibility for economic development in Belgian and French colonial territories did not go down well at all. The establishment of a regional common market in Europe was not to be confused with solving each other's colonial predicaments, was the general opinion among Dutch foreign policy makers, as well as their German colleagues. Apart from financial considerations, Dutch reticence was based on political misgivings. At the time, neither France nor Belgium showed any inclination towards granting independence to their colonial possessions, largely ignoring African aspirations to national independence. Therefore, a distinct risk that the projected preferential and financial arrangements would involve EEC in future tension, political strife and military conflict in Africa was undeniable. For the Netherlands, bearing the traumatic decolonization of the Dutch East Indies fresh in mind, such adventures were deemed utterly unattractive.[5]

The Belgian-French proposals hit The Hague, by their sweeping nature as well as their timing. At a very late moment in the negotiating process they added to the already substantial problems on the way to a successful closure of the negotiations. Hence, observations by Küsters and others to the effect "Wie unvorbereitet der französische Vorstosz die Niederländische Regierung traf".[6] In particular, the proposed investment fund constituted a nasty surprise: Clearly, France intended EEC mem-

---

3 Min. BZ, II, 913.100, No. 66 "De Europese Gemeenschappelijke Markt en de overzeese gebieden der leden-landen" FotoBtz: 145874.

4 G. van Benthem van den Bergh, *De associatie van Afrikaanse staten met de Europese Economische Gemeenschap*, Leiden: Sijthoff, 1962, p. 49.

5 *Ibidem* and J. Linthorst Homan, *Wat zijt ghij voor een vent*, Assen: Van Gorcum, 1974, pp. 221-223 and Ch. Rutten, *Aan de wieg van Europa en andere buitenlandse zaken. Herinneringen van een diplomaat*, Amsterdam: Boom, 2005, pp. 54-56. Full association of the Netherlands' remaining overseas territories (Surinam, The Dutch Antilles and New Guinea) with the European Common Market was postponed for constitutional as well as economic reasons (see 8.2).

6 "How the French initiative hit the unprepared Netherlands' government" Min. BZ, II, 913.100, Weekbericht 16, Periode 19-22 november 1956; H.J. Küsters, Die Gründung der Europäische Wirschaftsgemeinschaft, Baden-Baden: Nomos, 1982, p. 384 (footnote 299) and Linthorst Homan, *Wat zijt Ghij*, pp. 221-222.

bership to bring Paris extra-leverage and a re-strengthening of its weakened political position in Africa. As *The Economist* argued, explaining the "remarkable" fact that African deputies to the French parliament so far had not spoken out in favour of full independence for their home countries: "African leaders are acutely aware that France provides nearly 200 million dollars a year of immediately profitable investment *and that the common market could double this figure*"[7] (emphasis mine, AGH).

In the ensuing international negotiations, the Netherlands and Germany set out to detonate the explosive *Eurafrique* package, fiercely defended by France. Belgium, Italy and Luxemburg took a more passive stance. Linthorst Homan accentuated the GATT-incompatibility of the proposals and the discrepancy between the trade regimes, a discrepancy in turn defended by France as a perfectly legitimate means of protection for the underdeveloped economies involved. Paris remained adamant that it deemed association and a public investment fund conditions *sine qua non* for France's EEC membership. It was willing, however, to concede on the magnitude of the Fund and its management.[8]

Gradually, the terms of a compromise emerged. *Eurafrique* was sidelined, but France obtained the association agreement, albeit a temporary one; its successor after five years would have to be agreed upon with unanimity.[9] A European Development Fund was to be established, although not as large as originally proposed and with a greater influence by the European Commission in its decision-making than France had considered desirable. The negotiations were extremely tough until the last moment. As late as 18 January 1957, Prime Minister Drees voiced his worst-case scenario in which France would obtain preferential treatment but the Common Market would *not* materialize and in which improvement of intra-Six trade would be outweighed by losing business with the rest of the world. For achieving agreement on the financing of the Fund and its policies an unprecedented summit conference of government leaders was set up at *Hotel Matignon*, the seat of the French Prime Minister, on 19 February 1957. Drees' willingness to compromise on the financial contribution by The Netherlands was stretched to the limit. Nevertheless, the government leaders reached a compromise at 21.40h, wrote Luns in his diary. According to Spaak's memoires more

7 *The Economist* 1957, 479; as quoted in: Van Benthem van den Bergh, *De associatie van Afrikaanse staten*, p. 47.

8 NA, MR (405), Notulen ministerraad 18.1.1957.

9 A result largely undermined by articles 14 and 15 of the Implementing Convention, stipulating the terms of a fall-back arrangement in case the new association agreement was not agreed upon after the expiration of its predecessor. P. Olijslager, *De associatie van de overzeese gebieden met de Europese Ekonomische Gemeenschap*, Leuven: Katholieke Universiteit Leuven, 1958), pp. 22-23.

time was needed: he states that the talks lasted till four o'clock the following morning. German Chancellor Adenauer, then at the vast age of 81, expressed his satisfaction by calling Drees, ten years his junior, "ein kluger junger Mann".[10]

All in all, the Dutch government did not particularly welcome the association agreement laid down in articles 131-136 of the Rome Treaty. The Hague also realized, however, that in the given circumstances they had no other choice than to go along with it. Political realities – notably the conditions *sine qua non* put forward by France – could not be denied.

The Treaty of Rome was by now a reality, but the political practice of association would give rise to a number of problems. Early in 1961, the Dutch Foreign Ministry noted the following:

Firstly, preferential facilities and the discrimination they entailed tended to reinforce unwelcome tendencies towards group formation amongst African countries, with the EEC committing itself one-sidedly to the French-speaking African countries.

Secondly, the economic and political links between the associated countries and EEC were subject to criticism of neo-colonialism by third countries.

Thirdly, preferential treatment proved detrimental to the economic and political links of the EEC countries, Germany and the Netherlands in particular, with a number of other African countries and countries in Latin America. Mentioned were Ghana, Nigeria, Brazil and others which were deemed economically – and presumably politically too – far more important than the associated countries of the French *Communauté*. Hence this state of affairs provided the Dutch with yet another motive for EEC enlargement and association of the (former) British dependencies.[11]

From July 1961 onwards, when the United Kingdom, together with Denmark and Ireland, applied for EEC membership these considerations were reinforced by one of overriding importance: the UK wished to associate the lesser developed Commonwealth countries and overseas British territories with the EEC according to the Rome Treaty arrangement laid down in articles 131 through 136. Such a pooling of prefer-

10 John Jansen van Galen, Herman Vuijsje, *Drees. Wethouder van Nederland*, Alphen aan de Rijn: Sijthoff, 1980, p. 147; Rutten, *Buitenlandse Zaken*, pp. 42-44; Linthorst Homan, *Wat zijt Ghij*, p. 223. Nationaal Archief, The Hague, collectie J.M.A.H. Luns, invnr. 2329, diary J.M.A.H. Luns, 19.2.57; Paul-Henri Spaak, *Combats inachevés*; *II De l'espoir au déceptions*, Paris: Plon, 1969, p. 96.

11 Rijksgeschiedkundige publicatiën (henceforth: RGP), kleine serie No. 97, *Nederlandse ontwikkelingssamenwerking I, 1945-1963* (Den Haag 2002), Chef DIE, DGES (Kymmell), 2 2.1961.

ences would deprive the currently associated French dependencies in Africa of their competitive preferential edge. Fierce resistance on their side was to be expected, possibly making France block British entry altogether.[12]

Precisely for these reasons, the Netherlands was originally against continued preferential treatment and financial support for the now rapidly growing number of former French colonies in Africa, which were gaining independence. Not surprisingly, The Hague arrived at the conclusion that "a privileged preferential regime for a small number of formerly French and Belgian countries" was not in the interest of the realm. A broader oriented Aid and Development Program for Africa as a whole, open to all African states, was to be preferred. Now that the separation between the Six and the Seven in Europe was about to be overcome, the *raison d'être* for a specific arrangement for former French dependencies did not make sense any more.[13]

The French plea for exactly such an agreement was deprecated by many in the Dutch policy-making elite. There was no automatic right, Minister of Foreign Affairs Luns reasoned, to continued preferences for former colonies. Jelle Zijlstra, the influential Finance Minister did not mince his words either. He did not approve of EEC funding of French colonies at all. "It has been done once, to bring the French around to accepting EEC but [he] was not prepared to do it again".[14] Other policy-makers in the foreign and economic ministries were less outspoken and viewed the issue as a complicated one: one did not want to insult the former colonies and maintain their ties with Europe on the one hand; one did not want to alienate the other African countries from Europe by denying them privileged treatment.[15] Legal evidence for the French claim, supported by the Belgians, may have been slight; their political and practical ammunition was extremely convincing: the abolishment of the association regime would be considered as a form of punishment for accepting independence. Abruptly ending their trading preferences would, Luns warned his colleagues in government, occasion rancour and encouragement to seek alternative contacts with the Communist bloc. For these reasons utmost caution was called for. It was the latter argument that won the day. Caught between a rock and a hard place, the

12 RGP, *Nederlandse ontwikkelingssamenwerking I*, Directie Integratie Europa, DGES, to minister van Buitenlandse Zaken, 28.11.1961.

13 RGP, *Nederlandse ontwikkelingssamenwerking I*, Min. BZ to minister-president, 4.7.1960; *Idem*, Chef Directie Integratie Europa, DGES, Kymmell, 2.2.1961; *Idem*, Raad voor Economische Aangelegenheden (henceforth: REA), 23.6.1961.

14 RGP, *Nederlandse ontwikkelingssamenwerking I*, Min. BZ to Minister-President, 4.7.1960; *Idem*, REA, 23.6.1961.

15 RGP, *Nederlandse ontwikkelingssamenwerking I*, Attachment to No. 228: DG BEB, Van Oorschot aan De Pous (economics minister), 14.12.1960.

government decided that the argument for continuation was to prevail, thereby accepting the basic logic behind the draft Yaoundé Treaty as drafted by the European Commission. By May 1962 the Netherlands was aiming, as Luns worded it, for an association regime for former colonies more or less similar to the Rome Treaty arrangement.[16]

So The Hague accepted continuation of association, within the Yaoundé framework, first and foremost for *political* considerations. A second factor, however, appears to have played a part: since 1957 mainstream Dutch society as well as the Hague policy elite had gradually adopted a more positive stance towards development policy in general and financial and preferential support for third world countries in particular. In 1963 Cabinet was enhanced with a state-secretary and, subsequently, (1965) a full Minister for Development Co-operation. Due to this evolution in the Netherlands' domestic political attitude towards the North-South issue, the option of torpedoing a preferential scheme beneficial for developing countries – even one of the Yaoundé variety – was politically contestable and hence unattractive. Thirdly, although the United Nations remained the preferred international institution for such multilateral aid and development efforts, the absence of progress on its SUNFED program had contributed to bringing "Yaoundé" to the fore as an alternative multilateral framework for Dutch development financing.[17]

Acceptance in principle facilitated a relatively smooth course of the EEC- AASM (Associated African States and Madagascar) negotiations. Compared with the latter phases of the Treaty of Rome talks, no agonizing reappraisals or last minute conferences of heads of state or government were called for. In the Dutch Cabinet such aloofness was further promoted by The Hague's own colonial concerns. Throughout 1962, with the Papua New Guinea crisis at its height, resulting in this last colonial outpost in Asia being ceded to Indonesia, the Cabinet had time for little else and in June even instructed the Dutch delegates at the EEC-AASM negotiations to act as they deemed fit.[18] Difficulties did arise, however, concerning a number of topics, resulting in tough negotiations.

Firstly, Germany and the Netherlands rejected the proposal to incorporate the projected tariff preferences in 18 separate free trade areas, one

16 Van Benthem van den Bergh, *De associatie van Afrikaanse staten*, p. 92; RGP, *Nederlandse ontwikkelingssamenwerking I*, Min. BZ to minister-president, 4.7.1960; NA, MR (675), Notulen Ministerraad 18.5.1962.

17 A point of view advocated by Foreign Minister Luns as early as January 1957, NA, MR (405), Notulen Ministerraad 18.1.1957. SUNFED stands for Special UN Fund for Economic Development.

18 NA, MR (675), Notulen Ministerraad 15.6.1962.

with each AASM country. "The fundamental significance of GATT", Economics Minister De Pous argued, was at stake and "would be undermined" by these free trade areas which would liberate trade only one way while discriminating against other tropical commodity producers. The issue, though valid enough, was sidelined, when in March 1962, the German delegation rather suddenly withdrew its objections and the Netherlands grudgingly followed suit.[19] As Dutch delegates did not fail to notice, their African interlocutors were not particularly keen on the free trade concept as such and would prefer more direct benefits, export volume and minimum price guarantees for their specific export products in particular. Such direct product arrangements were opposed by all EEC member-states but France and thus barred from the Convention. Notwithstanding that, in later years, they would emerge in the Lomé agreements.[20]

Secondly, difficult negotiations were conducted on the yet to be established new Fund for capital aid to the AASM countries. The Netherlands delegation aimed at diminishing both the magnitude of the Fund and the Netherlands' contribution to it. Finance Minister Zijlstra harvested a limited but precious success on the second issue. Such, for that matter, in spite of fierce opposition from his Belgian colleague Fayat, amply demonstrating the complete absence of Benelux foreign policy cooperation on this subject of EEC decision-making.[21]

Thirdly and most importantly, the Netherlands did their utmost to guarantee easy future access for the British territories and former dependencies in Africa to the Yaoundé Convention. In the course of the negotiations the two issues, British entry and Yaoundé, grew increasingly intertwined.[22] In this respect the Netherlands delegation managed to block a right to veto on new accessions to the Convention for the AASM countries. More importantly, a declaration of intent, indicating that the Yaoundé co-operation framework was open to countries with a comparable economic structure (to wit: Anglophone African countries and British and Dutch dependencies), was agreed upon.[23]

---

19 NA, MR (675), Notulen Ministerraad 30.3.1962; Van Benthem van den Bergh, *De associatie van Afrikaanse staten*, p. 132.

20 NA, MR (675), Notulen Ministerraad 6.4.1962.

21 NA, MR (675), Notulen Ministerraad 18.5.1962 and 22.6.1962; NA, MR (676), Notulen Ministerraad 6.7.1962.

22 As Economics Minister De Pous worded the issue in May 1962: 'If France is not prepared to accept the same trade policy regime for the Anglophone African countries as for the Francophone African countries it will be difficult for the Netherlands' delegation to co-operate on the further completion of an arrangement for the Francophone African countries.' NA, MR (675), Notulen Ministerraad, 11.5.1962.

23 See 8.2 for details.

The second and third issues were to remain on the negotiation table for subsequent years. For the details of the arrangement agreed upon in the Yaoundé Convention, as agreed upon in the course of December 1962, we refer to the next section.

Given the multiple links between the two policy issues, it is hardly surprising that French President De Gaulle's veto of British EEC membership on 14 January 1963 did not remain without consequences for the Yaoundé treaty. As a means to express their disapproval of the unilateralist French move, the Netherlands, in collaboration with the other EEC member-states, postponed signing the Yaoundé treaty for six months until July 1963.[24]

II. From Yaoundé I till Yaoundé II: The Netherlands as an Ambivalent Partner

Thus the first Yaoundé Convention was signed in the capital of Cameroon on 20 July 1963. As president of the Council of Ministers, Foreign Minister Joseph Luns added his signature on behalf of the EEC and its member-states. Yaoundé created a free trade area between the Six and 18 newly independent African states (former French, Italian and Belgian colonies). The latter continued to have the benefit of the EEC's internal tariff reductions, duty free entry for a certain number of tropical products and application of the common external tariff towards third countries. The AASM (Associated African States and Madagascar), in return, promised to reduce tariffs on industrial products coming from the EEC and granted all EEC members equal treatment. At the same time, they were allowed to impose duties or import quota's to protect infant industries, as well as to make trade arrangements with third countries.

Compared to the previous association period, the EEC member states increased the amount of financial aid under EDF. They agreed to make available over the next five years (1964-1969) a total of \$730 million (excluding EIB loans amounting to \$70 million), divided into \$500 million in development capital and \$230 million for the diversification of the African economies and promotion of efficiency in tropical agriculture. Of this Community Fund, France and Germany each supplied \$246.5 million, Italy 100 million, Belgium/Luxembourg 71 million and the Netherlands 66 million.

On the instigation of the Netherlands, a declaration of intent was added to the Convention, implying that EEC policies towards Africa should not be restricted to the French-speaking part of the continent only but extended to other countries with "comparable economic and produc-

[24] NA, MR (753), Notulen Ministerraad 21.1.1963, 25.1.1963, 15/18.2.1963, and 22.2.1963.

tion structures".[25] More in particular, Yaoundé gave African nations of the Commonwealth a perspective on future membership of the Convention or another form of association with the EEC. The latter was also considered for Surinam and the Dutch Antilles, two Dutch colonies in the Caribbean.

After its signing, the Convention did not come into operation until July 1964, mainly as a result of the protracted process of ratification in 24 national parliaments with different procedures. But it was not only the procedural problem that mattered, also content-related issues were at stake. The Netherlands was one of the last countries to file the ratification document, due to last-minute discussions on the – desired – involvement of Commonwealth African countries in the Yaoundé framework. Nigeria had filed a request for association with the EEC, a move which was strongly supported by the Dutch government but rejected by France. Paris feared that at such early stage Nigerian association would have adverse effects on the position of the "established" group of 18 AASM countries. At the time, it entertained strained diplomatic relations with Lagos, as a consequence of Nigerian protests against French nuclear tests in the Sahara. The Hague accused France of "certain sabotage" and of disrespect towards the letter of intent concerning association of other (third) African states. Nevertheless, eventually, the government decided to push aside its indignation and support ratification, because further delays "would not in the first place hit France, but the 18 African countries". The Hague also felt that the Yaoundé agreement left sufficient room for further interpretation and elaboration, as well as possibilities to exert diplomatic pressure on the French delegation.[26] Despite this, the tone was set. The disagreement on Nigeria heralded a long period of conflict and diplomatic tensions between France and the Netherlands on the contents and scope of the Convention. It appeared that there were only very few Convention- and association-related issues on which the two countries could agree.

The Dutch government's policy in the period until the signing of the second Yaoundé convention in 1969 was characterized by the following elements: extending the Yaoundé facilities to the non-French-speaking African countries; avoiding or reducing trade discrimination against (former) Dutch colonies; limiting national financial payments to EDF and supporting domestic firms in the francophone area.

---

25 Ministerie van Economische Zaken te Den Haag, (Ministry of Economic Affairs, The Hague), (henceforth: Min. EZ), Archief BEB (henceforth: BEB), No. 402, "Associatie-onderhandelingen Oost-Afrika", 19.7.1965. NA, MR, 948 Raad voor Europese Zaken (Council for European Affairs, a sub-council of the Ministerraad), (henceforth: REZ), "Conclusie Coördinatie Commissie van 10 juli 1968", 11.7.1968.

26 NA, MR 751, REZ, "Associatieverzoek van Nigeria", 15.5.1964.

A. Extending the Yaoundé Preferences to Other, Non-French-Speaking, African Countries

The EEC countries traded almost as much with the non-associated states in Africa as with the AASM. Although France naturally had most commercial links with the latter group, the opposite was true for the other five, including the Netherlands. During the membership negotiations with the United Kingdom (1961-1963), the EEC had discussed several options for dealing with the British Commonwealth countries in Africa, ranging from full association to separate commodity agreements. But, as written above, until mid-1964, France successfully blocked negotiations on the inclusion of English-speaking countries in any association framework. French resistance stopped at the moment of ratification of the Yaoundé treaty: in June 1964 the EEC Commission was given a mandate to open negotiations with Nigeria. Somewhat later, in March 1965, Kenya, Tanzania and Uganda were added to the list of potential *associés*.

This satisfied the Dutch government, which welcomed involvement of the Anglophone countries for many reasons, not only because of the expected economic benefits – as implicated above, the trade links with the Anglophone countries considerably exceeded those with the Francophone countries[27] – but, also and especially, because of the potential opening it offered to the desired British entry in the Community. The Hague had been abhorred by president De Gaulle's veto of British EEC membership in January 1963 and strongly felt that the European division between the Six and the Seven was not to be copied on the African continent. On the contrary, pan-African integration was seen as a laudable and realistic perspective.[28] The government also looked for possibilities to increase bilateral co-operation with Great Britain regarding African affairs.

However, concrete results were still remote. The candidate countries were not easy to deal with and, once again, France was unwilling to extend co-operation beyond the existing Group of 18. In December 1967, more than three years after the start of the talks, a senior Dutch official complained that France "consistently sabotaged the negotiations" with the non-AASM countries. He advised the government to give the French a taste of their own medicine, by coupling the coming negotiations on prolongation of the Yaoundé treaty (Yaoundé I was

---

27 An illustration is provided by the Unilever Company, which in 1960 invested some £23 million in the associated state of Congo and £48.5 million in non-associated Nigeria. C. Cosgrove Twitchett, *Europe and Africa: from Association to Partnership*, Westmead: Saxon House, 1978, p. 93.

28 Min. BZ, Code 996, (EEG), 1965-1974/4569 (96/431), "Financiële steun aan Afrika", 13.5.1968.

going to expire in 1969) with the association talks with Nigeria and the East-African states. The government should make it "absolutely clear that approval of Yaoundé II was impossible, so long as a satisfactory solution on new associations remained forthcoming".[29]

In reality, the Dutch negotiating position was far from unassailable. There were two particularly weak points in this position, which Paris and the other capitals regularly managed to exploit. Firstly, the Commonwealth African states were unwilling to apply the principle of reciprocity to their trade relations with the EEC. Although Nigeria was prepared to make limited concessions for a certain number of products, Kenya and Uganda initially refused to grant *any* preferences to the EEC, claiming that only a small part of their foreign trade (one-fifth) was conducted with the Community, implying that – in case of full association – the remaining part would be adversely affected. The EEC countries felt that conceding these claims would produce only a limited free-trade zone with unilateral preferences. It would also set an undesirable precedent (new African candidates looking for association would not refrain from demanding similar or even more exclusive privileges) and erode the relevant provisions of the GATT treaty regarding free trade zones. All this was clearly unacceptable to France, the AASM countries, Nigeria *and*, eventually, to the Netherlands itself, which emphasized the importance of respecting existing GATT rules and creating a uniform association structure for all African countries.[30]

The final result was still unsatisfactory. The treaties of Lagos (1966) and Arusha (1968) brought Nigeria respectively the three East-African states under a special relationship with the EEC, but on unequal terms. The Arusha treaty included serious derogations from the free-trade area principle and amounted to a disguised, discriminatory trade agreement in favour of the East African countries.[31] All this hampering certainly contributed to a weakening of the Dutch position during the negotiations.

The Hague further demanded that the negotiations on the prolongation of Yaoundé I should run parallel with the association talks with the Anglophone countries. This time, the Dutch wish was granted. Yaoundé II and the Arusha treaty came into force at exactly the same moment, on 1 January 1971. The treaty of Lagos was never ratified, due to insurmountable political conflicts between the EC and the military regime in Nigeria, predominantly concerning the secession of Biafra.[32]

---

29 Min. BZ, code 996 (EEG) 1965-1974, No. 4423, Hoogwater to Hartogh, 5.12.1967.

30 Min. EZ, BEB, No. 402, "Associatieonderhandelingen Oost-Afrika", 19.7.1965.

31 Cosgrove Twitchett, *Europe and Africa*, p. 146.

32 *Ibidem*.

A second problem concerned the Dutch position towards associating the Maghreb countries of Morocco and Tunisia. The Hague rejected such a construction for commercial reasons, but this was incompatible with the declaration of intent attached to the EEC treaty, entitling the two countries to negotiate an economic association with the Community. France sought to link the association negotiations with Nigeria to talks with the Maghreb countries, but this was unacceptable to The Hague, which pointed to the advanced stage of the negotiations with Nigeria, while Commission talks with Morocco and Tunisia had not even commenced. To solve this problem, the Commission suggested creating a free trade zone with the two North-African countries, based on article XXIV of the GATT treaty. The Dutch government agreed on the condition that the export of citrus fruits from Israel and Spain (both major suppliers of oranges to the Netherlands) would not suffer from a preferential treatment given to Morocco and Tunisia.[33] Although a formal association with the two Maghreb countries was indeed avoided, the French "coupling" tactics for a while delayed the negotiations with Nigeria.[34]

With regard to extending the association agreements, the government was rather reticent in giving the European Commission an important role in the negotiations. During the 1960s, the Netherlands had become well known for its outright support of a strong and autonomous position for the European Commission, but this was less the case with regard to the association issue. The Hague suspected the Commission of damaging Dutch interests by taking sides with France and the eldest group of associated countries, at the expense of the non-associated Anglophone countries.[35] In the Dutch view, the DG Associated Countries in Brussels was basically a French-dominated bulwark, with few possibilities for influence by other countries and nationalities. This image was confirmed by Jaap van der Lee, General Director General Affairs from 1958 till 1966, who – as a Dutchman – regularly felt himself "sandwiched" between Paris, The Hague and the intimidating French dominance at the DG in Brussels.[36]

With the benefit of hindsight we know that during the 1960s DG VIII was entangled in a existential fight with, ironically enough, the main initiator of EEC development policy, the French government. As demonstrated with verve by Dimier and McGeever, this disagreement

---

33 Min. EZ, BEB, No. 402, "Associatieonderhandelingen Oost-Afrika", 19.7.1965.

34 NA, MR (881), Notulen Ministerraad, 31.5.1968; NA, MR 948, REZ, "Conclusies Coördinatie Commissie van 10 juli 1968", 11.7.1968.

35 Min. EZ, BEB, nr. 400, M01912, Heronderhandelingen Yaoundé-Conventie", 23.4.1968.

36 Harryvan, van der Harst and van Voorst, *Voor Nederland en Europa*, p. 178.

was of an institutional nature, to wit DG VIII's struggle for autonomy *vis-à-vis* Paris, particularly with regard to controlling the impementation of the projects of the European Development Fund. EDF director Jacques Ferrandi (1963-1975) set up a system based on personal relationships, dependence and loyalty. In this campaign he was extending on his previous carreer as a French colonial administrator, using personal friendships, negotiaton and compromises with African heads of state:

> Individual projects were presented and adopted on an *ad hoc* basis, according to vague criteria, which at that time were linked less to the possible social and economic efficiency of the project proposed than to Ferrandi's personal relationships with his 'African friends' and political considerations (sometimes dictated by French priorities in Africa).[37]

When decolonization became imminent, however, France wanted to leave the control on development projects with local French companies or the consultancy firms linked to these companies. This was a direct threat to Ferrandi's network. Hence he got involved in a struggle for control with French Foreign Minister Couve de Murville, who accused him of behaving "like a governement". Eventually, the battle between the Commission and the French Government was solved "pragmatically, and in a provisional way". Thus, German and Dutch criticism on French policies that insofar as French companies were predominant on the spot, it was not difficult to see how the system could be prejudicial to other Member States' interest remained as valid as ever.[38] In this respect too, the perspective of British entry offered a window of opportunity.

Nevertheless, Dutch misgivings and the Ferrandi-Couve de Murville fight for control for once made France and the Netherlands adopt a common stance: both countries strove for a limited Commission role in African affairs.

Despite all this, the Dutch government was pleased to see that during the 1960s trade with the AASM had increased with almost 5% per year.[39] This was considerably less than the trade increase with the non-associated Commonwealth countries, but it was certainly better than the original doom scenarios had predicted. It confirmed the image of the Netherlands as an ambivalent partner in the Yaoundé process.

---

37 V. Dimier and M. McGeever, "Diplomats Without a Flag: The Institutionalization of the Delegations of the Commission in African, Caribbean and Pacific Countries", JCMS 44 (2006), pp. 483-505 (p. 488).

38 *Ibidem*, p. 488.

39 Cosgrove Twitchett, *Europe and Africa*, p. 63.

B. *Avoiding or Reducing Discrimination* vis-à-vis *(Former) Dutch Colonies*

In 1964, the Dutch Antilles and Surinam were brought into a special relationship with the EEC. This was at a rather late moment. In the 1957 Rome Treaty, the Six had made provision for association of the two colonies, without specifying the type of association regime.[40] It would take seven more years before agreement on further specification was reached. The main cause for the delay concerned constitutional constraints, in that the 1954 *Statuut van het Koninkrijk der Nederlanden* (Statute of the Kingdom of the Netherlands) forbade the Dutch government to sign international treaties for Surinam and the Dutch Antilles.[41] Explicit consent of the two colonies was required. In 1960, however, the two countries expressed their desires to start negotiations with the EEC and, four years later, the Council of Ministers gave its blessing to the association agreement.[42]

Although not falling under the formal regulations of the Yaoundé Convention, the two colonies hoped to benefit from the preferential partnership with the EEC. Like the AASM countries, they were allowed to impose duties or import quota's to protect infant industries, as well as to make trade arrangements with third countries. The Dutch Antilles were particularly interested in expanding their exports of natural and refined oil products to the European market. At the time, the country's refinery capacity amounted to no less than 40% of the EEC total. This dominant market position made France and the other member states protest against preferential treatment of non-EEC refineries. Eventually, the EEC countries gained some concessions in the form of safeguards against overabundant oil imports from the Caribbean, but all in all, the Dutch Antilles were happy with the outcome of the negotiations, the more so as the island economy had been in serious recession for several years and was in need of a boost.[43] Surinam was a less controversial candidate for association, which made the negotiations run more smoothly. Paramaribo hoped to promote the exports of raw materials (mainly bauxite and wood) and agricultural products (rice and citrus fruits). Apart from the commercial advantages, the association provided the colonies with development funds (at $35 million for the period

[40] Declaration of intention with a view to associating Surinam and the Netherlands Antilles with the EEC, attached to the Rome Treaty.

[41] R.A. Ferrier, *Suriname en de Europese Economische Gemeenschap*, Den Haag: Kabinet van de vice minister-president, 1962, p. 1.

[42] P.H.J.M. Houben, *De Associatie van Suriname en de Nederlandse Antillen met de Europese Economische Gemeenschap*, Leiden: Sijthoff, 1965, p. 104.

[43] *Ibidem*, pp. 18-20.

1964-1969) which were primarily used for improving infrastructure and training skilled labour.[44]

The association was appreciated to such an extent that in 1969, the two countries emerged as ardent supporters of continuation of the special relationship with the EEC and feared that the then on-going negotiations on the introduction of global preferences for developing countries would have a negative impact on the existing regional arrangements. On this score, the colonies clashed with the government in The Hague, the latter being in full support of general global trade arrangements (see also next paragraph).[45] Likewise, Surinam protested against the possibility of associating the Commonwealth countries in the Caribbean with the EEC market. Surinam argued that it would be unwise to associate countries which were already involved in a fairly closed trade system (in the Caribbean area),[46] but the deeper reason lay in their fear of increasing competition for Surinam products on the European market. On this issue, the government reassured the governing board in Paramaribo that association with the Caribbean area was not going to be discussed before full British membership of the EC.[47] Surinam further pushed the Dutch government to ensure that its associated position would not be affected in the event Surinam became independent (which would materialize in 1975[48]).[49]

Moreover, during the entire period, the Dutch government sought to limit possible adverse effects of the Yaoundé Convention on the export position of its former colony Indonesia. Dutch economic interests in Indonesia (independent since 1949) were still substantial and – to boost bilateral relations – the government supported Djakarta in gaining access to the EEC market.[50] As a consequence of the high external tariff and the preferences given to AASM countries, Indonesia experienced difficulties in exporting palm oil and tapioca to the European market. The Dutch government consistently sought a reduction or even abolition of the EEC external tariff raised against tropical products coming from

44 *Ibidem*, 103-105. The amount of $35 million had originally been destined for Papua New-Guinea, but in 1963 the Netherlands relinquished control over this dependency.

45 NA, MR (883), Notulen Ministerraad 11.10.1968.

46 NA, MR (866), "Nota inzake de verlenging en vernieuwing van de associatie-overeenkomst met de Afrikaanse staten", 24.10.1968.

47 Min. BZ, code 996 (EEG) 1965-1974, 4410, "Departementale bespreking Yaoundé III", 27.7.1972.

48 By mid-1977 Suriname acceded to the Lomé Convention. The Netherlands Antilles decided not to participate in Lomé.

49 Min. BZ, code 996.430, EEG 1965-1974, Memorandum 569, "Toekomstige relaties van Suriname en de Nederlandse Antillen", 3.7.1973.

50 NA, MR 948, REZ, "Conclusies Coördinatie Commissie van 10 juli 1968", 11.7.1968.

third countries. It thereby re-emphasized the impact of simultaneously running GATT negotiations on global trade liberalization. Global agreements should, in the Dutch view, gain precedence over regional schemes like Yaoundé. Similarly, the UNCTAD-instigated process of introducing general tariff preferences for developing countries was not to be hampered by so-called "reverse preferences" agreed upon within the Yaoundé framework. The Netherlands fiercely protested against the latter's damaging effects on the position of the developing countries. It was calculated that, as a consequence of "reverse preferences", a country like Gabon lost more in terms of customs revenues than that it gained from EEC financial support.[51]

C. Reducing the National Financial Contribution to the European Development Fund (EDF) and Providing a Level Playing Field for Dutch Firms Operating in Africa

When Yaoundé I started, the Dutch government was aware that domestic firms would have severe difficulties in penetrating the AASM-markets, given the traditionally advantageous position of French companies operating in the area. The government complained that even after granting independence to its African colonies, France protected the privileged position by concluding bilateral agreements with the associates.[52] Despite this, The Hague hoped that in the longer run Dutch entrepreneurs would acquire better facilities to do business with and invest in the countries of French-speaking Africa. In practice, this was difficult to accomplish. In July 1968, the national employers' organization informed the government that the distribution of projects financed from EDF monies still discriminated against Dutch firms. The European Commission had made several attempts to spread orders more evenly over the member states, but to no avail. The greatest proportion of EDF aid was given to infrastructural projects virtually excluding development of the industrial sector. As such, EDF mirrored the practices of former colonial donor states.[53] To remedy this situation, the employers suggested modifying EDF policies along the following lines: a) to extend the group of beneficiaries of the Fund to countries with better market access for Dutch businesses like Nigeria and the East African countries, as well as (former) overseas territories, above all Indonesia;[54] b) to stop

51 *Ibidem*.

52 Min. EZ, BEB, nr. 400, Note DGIH "inzake voortzetting van de associatie-overeenkomst met de G.A.S.M.", 27.9.1968.

53 M. Holland, *The European Union and the Third World*, Houndmills: Palgrave, 2002, p. 32.

54 The suggestion to include Indonesia fitted in with The Netherlands' plans to establish an international group of lenders to coordinate multilateral aid to Indonesia. Indeed,

prioritizing the financing of infrastructural works and, instead, concentrate on industrial and agrarian projects in the private sector; c) to counter the privileged position of French business by rewarding joint tenders handed in by firms of different nationalities, preferably including a firm based in a smaller country (which would stimulate also the formation of joint ventures by Dutch firms and their French counterparts); d) to give the European Investment Bank a more substantial role in the management of the Fund; and e) to make sure that a minimum percentage of orders would be allocated to domestic firms, related to the size of the national contribution to the Fund. For example, the Dutch EDF contribution amounted to 9% of total contributions; the employers thought it reasonable that a minimum of 4.5% of EDF-financed orders should be awarded to Dutch firms.[55] At that stage, it was calculated that the Netherlands acquired only 2.16% of total orders deriving from EDF (see Table 3).[56]

From Table 3 it appears that France was not only the main contributor to EDF (together with Germany), but also by far the greatest beneficiary from EDF-financed orders, both in absolute and relative terms. As for order-acquisitions in francophone Africa, the Netherlands was the least privileged partner, both absolutely and relatively. The fears government and business had expressed at the start of the association agreement in 1957 had proven justified. In the developing world, Dutch firms had acquired wide experience in doing business with their own (former) colonies and – to a lesser extent – with (former) British colonies, but they encountered continuous difficulties in entering the markets of French-Africa. For the government this was a major reason to plead against ever increasing national financial contributions to EDF.[57] This plea found some support: under Yaoundé II (1969-1974) EDF was – only modestly – raised to a total of $918 million, as compared with $581 million for the first five-year period (1958-1963) and $730 million under Yaoundé I. Such an absolute increase was not dramatic if seen over time, and the Dutch contribution in relative terms, remained fixed

in 1967, the Inter-Governmental Group on Indonesia (IGGI) was founded. The other members included Australia, Belgium, Britain, Canada, France, Germany, Italy, Japan, New Zealand, Switzerland, the United States, as well as the Asian Development Bank, International Monetary Fund, United Nations Development Programme and World Bank.

55 Min. BZ, Code 996 (EEG) 1965-1974, No. 4424, "Verlenging Conventie van Yaoundé", 9.7.1968.

56 Min. EZ, BEB, nr. 400, MO 1915, Note DGIH "inzake voortzetting van de associatie-overeenkomst met de G.A.S.M.", 27.9.1968.

57 NA, MR 948, REZ, "Voortzetting van de financiële steun aan de GASM en de LGO", 20.11.1968.

at 9%.[58] Dutch worries were further qualified by the fact that also under Yaoundé II Surinam and the Dutch Antilles kept benefiting from subsidies and other privileges resulting from their association with the EEC. For the period 1969-1974, the two colonies received $32 million in the form of gifts and $9 million in loans.[59]

Table 3. Distribution of EDF (Orders) in the Period 1964-1969

	Contribution in million $	Contribution %	Orders received	Orders received %
	Absolute	Relative	Absolute	Relative
Total	730	100%	126	100%
Netherlands	66	9%	3	2.16%
Germany	246.5	34%	25	19.88%
France	246.5	34%	58	46.13%
Italy	100	14%	10	7.7%
AASM/third countries	-.-	-.-	23	18.4%

Source: Min. EZ, BEB, No. 400, MO1915, Note DGIH "inzake voortzetting van de associatie-overeenkomst met de G.A.S.M", 27.9.1968.

III. Discussion

During the entire negotiation period, running from the Venice conference until the signing of the Yaoundé II convention, France and the Netherlands found each other at the two extremes of the political spectrum. Whereas France continuously pushed for preferential treatment and a privileged position of the francophone part of the African continent, the Dutch government proved reluctant, fearing that EC involvement in Africa would merely benefit French economic interests, at the expense of the other participants. Dutch firms found it hard to compete with their French counterparts on what they considered an extension of the French home market. From the beginning, the Dutch negotiating position was weak. The Benelux framework offered no solace, because Belgium, with its colonial interests in Africa (Congo), strongly leaned towards the French position. At times, the Netherlands received diplomatic support from Germany, but the German opposition to French plans and policies proved rather lukewarm. As a matter of fact, the Dutch government, with its explicit stance, found itself rather isolated at the negotiating table. The only supposedly reliable ally on this issue, the United Kingdom, had not yet entered the EEC. The government came to realize that approval of French Africa policies was the diplomatic price it had to pay for latter's acceptance of the European Common Market.

58 Dutch expenditure amounted to $80 million dollar, compared to $66 million in the previous period.

59 NA, MR 930, Memorandum Directie Integratie Europa, 2.7.1969.

Advanced trade liberalization within the framework of the Six was given such a high priority in The Hague that the government eventually decided to push aside its opposition and go along with the association process, albeit always as a difficult partner. Association did not turn out to be a temporary phenomenon, as some in the government had hoped for. When French dependencies in Africa gained independence, preferential treatment and financial aid had to be continued, lest the abolishment of association would be regarded as a form of punishment for accepting independence. Hence, The Hague's acceptance of the Yaoundé treaties. In this respect association resembled an eel-trap: having entered the first compartment of the trap one could still swim, but in a forward direction only, i.e. into the next compartment.

Contrary to its traditional policies, the Dutch government was not prepared to allow the European Commission to play a substantial role on the EC-Africa issue. While generally valuing the Commission's position as an honest broker between the member states, in the Yaoundé process, the Dutch government saw no real advantage in allowing the Commission to play a prominent and independent role. This was primarily caused by negative perceptions of how the Commission's General Directorate for Associated Countries was assembled and operated. The Hague saw DG VIII as basically a French dominated bulwark, directed by the responsible Commissioners Lemaignen and Rochereau, both Frenchmen. Also, the fact that the French *fonctionnaire* Jacques Ferrandi was put in charge of the European investment fund did not contribute to the Dutch trust in the policies and directives coming from Brussels. Ironically, as Dimier and McGeever demonstrate, also the French government took a sceptic view of DG VIII's operations, particularly its attempts to acquire a more independent EC role on the African continent. It was one of the very few issues on which Paris and The Hague easily found agreement.

Throughout the 1960s, The Hague's policy towards EEC and Africa was characterized by three dominant objectives. Firstly, extending the Yaoundé preferences to other, non-French-speaking African countries. Secondly, avoiding or reducing discriminative practices against (former) Dutch overseas territories. And thirdly, reducing the national contribution to EDF and furthering a level playing field for Dutch firms operating in Africa.

As said above, "Yaoundé" was never seen as a popular instrument in The Hague, but at the same time we witness a gradual change of perspective during the period under discussion. At the end of the 1960s and the early 1970s, "Yaoundé" developed from a predominantly French colonial problem into a possible framework for the North to support the countries of the South. In other words, the EC's Africa policy was increasingly regarded as a positive vehicle to further development in the

Third World. In the Netherlands, the change in *Zeitgeist* became visible in the appointment of a Minister for Development Aid at the Ministry of Foreign Affairs, who had his own impact on the framing of government policy. This change of perspective culminated with the installation of a centre-left government coalition in 1973, a coalition which turned development co-operation into one of its key policy issues.

Having said that, "Yaoundé" kept being seen as too limited a framework for development and, therefore, the Netherlands strongly welcomed the inclusion of the Anglophone countries in the association framework, under the Lomé agreement of 1975. This was in line with the government's long-time preference for integration of the entire African continent. However, even the context of "Lomé" was seen as suboptimal. The government placed its hopes in wider – less regional – schemes, preferably such as those offered by organizations like GATT and UNCTAD, to provide more general solutions for global trade problems.

The EEC Treaty and the subsequent association treaties have been of the greatest importance for EEC policies with regard to the developing countries. As Martin Holland words it: "Whilst the Treaty was myopic in its largely francophone definition of the Third World this framework represents the origin of Europe's fragmented and differentiated approach". The consequences were dire, for the developing countries, as well as for EEC itself. Since the dependency of francophone Africa on France for aid and trade, Cosgrove Twitchett argues, "existed independently of the EEC and was in no way consequential to it", the majority of the original member-states were "extremely loath to become involved with former African colonies".[60] The Netherlands was not amongst the latter. Throughout the EEC's formative years Dutch diplomacy sought to overcome the limitations of selective association and to promote a stance in which human need and economic interests rather than historical ties would constitute the driving rationale behind preferential arrangements between Europe and the developing world.

60 Cosgrove Twitchett, *Europe and Africa*, p. 122.

Concluding Observations

Looking back on the Netherlands' role in European integration during the 1950s and 1960s, Joseph Luns, the country's long standing Foreign Minister depicted himself as an exponent of "the Dutch vision". A vision that enabled the country to act as a "leading force" in Europe, thus demonstrating that in specific constellations a middle-sized power can play a role of importance.[1]

What was this "Dutch vision" and was Luns right in ascribing it such importance? In this book we set out to investigate whether, under which conditions and by which means the Netherlands have exerted engineering influence on the economic and institutional architecture of the European Economic Community – as a forerunner of the present-day European Union – during the Community's formative years (1952-1973).

Our analysis demonstrates that the Netherlands have pursued a policy of engineering influence on European cooperation and integration throughout the period under scrutiny. From the late 1940s onwards, successive Dutch governments showed themselves convinced that the economic future of the country lay in Europe and that economic disarmament in the highly protectionist intra-European trade relations was elementary for the country's economic survival and its future prosperity: Loss of empire, the economic collapse of the German *hinterland*, industrialization objectives and the limitations of the country's domestic market – to mention the most important motives – were all conducive to an activist policy aimed at liberalizing intra-European trade. In this respect, Dutch diplomacy during the 1952-1973 period can well be described in Milward's famous characterization as a "European rescue of the nation state".[2]

Conceiving the Common Market

Jan Willem Beyen, on becoming Foreign Minister of the Netherlands in the fall of 1952, brought about a structural change in the country's European policy. He redirected and refocused the Netherlands' European liberalization campaign away from the broad Organization for European Economic Cooperation (OEEC) framework to the more

1 Michel van der Plas, *Luns: "Ik herinner mij...". Vrijmoedige herinneringen van Mr. J.M.A.H. Luns zoals verteld aan Michel van der Plas*, Leiden: Sijthoff, 1972, p. 171.

2 A. S. Milward, *The European Rescue of the Nation-State*, London: Routledge, 1992.

limited grouping of the six members of the European Coal and Steel Community (ECSC), precisely for the reason that in this "little Europe", by means of supranationalism, results could be obtained where OEEC had failed. His 1952 Beyen Plan proposed a supranationally supervised regional economic bloc amongst the six ECSC countries. Beyen, in the course of his ministry, increasingly advocated supranational institutions and supranational decision-making in Europe. He actively pursued these aims, not for federalist reasons, but as a means to an end, to wit, to further and protect the Netherlands' economic and political interests. From the second half of the 1950s onwards the Beyen approach – which we could call "functional supranationalism" – became a leading principle of the Netherlands' policy on Europe. The core of this functional supranationalism was a transfer of national competences to a supranational community endowed with a strong executive.

Originally, Beyen presented his customs union project as a collateral to the projected European Political Community (EPC). The accompanying Dutch stance "No political integration without economic integration" did not go down well with Germany's Federal Chancellor Adenauer, who preferred to hammer through the EPC Treaty without further economic complications. Once timely and efficient Benelux diplomatic cooperation had staved off this threat, French reluctance to engage in economic liberalization had to be overcome. Beyen's tactic, after having successfully obtained the agreement of the other four ECSC countries on the basics of his Plan, was aimed at isolating France. Increasing American pressure on France, he reckoned, would eventually force Paris to accept the proposed liberalization of trade relations amongst the Six. This tactic did not work. The French Parliament's down voting of the European Defence Community Treaty in August 1954 also meant the downfall of the EPC. Beyen's campaign for economic disarmament among the Six came to a grinding halt.

Amidst general scepticism Beyen relaunched his plan in the spring of 1955. The advantages to be expected of a liberal trade regime in Western Europe for the Netherlands, Beyen reasoned, were as formidable as ever. A new government in France from February 1955 onwards meant decidedly improved and propitious circumstances for a relaunch of his plan. Many begged to differ; in various European capitals, in the Dutch government, as well as in Beyen's Foreign Ministry itself. In fact, in the latter, only the Western Cooperation Section showed support for and commitment to the New Beyen Plan. Beyen stuck to his guns. He deprecated the claim that the fate of EDC and EPC had demonstrated that Europe was unfit for new supranational institutions in general: "The ruining of the EDC project has not affected the approach of the Dutch government". Prime Minister Drees was among those who were sceptical about the enterprise, fearing the establishment of yet another expensive international institution whose value for the Netherlands would be far from assured. The federalist minority in Cabinet, led by Agriculture Minister Mansholt, on the other hand, criticized Beyen for once again focusing on the traditional Dutch interest, i.e. the furthering of intra-European trade. Instead, the Dutch initiative should first and foremost be aimed at the establishment of a *political* community. In answering his critics, Beyen stressed the need for a pro-active policy stance: now that plans for European economic cooperation, generally on an intergovernmental footing, were springing up like mushrooms, it would be most unfortunate if the Dutch found themselves in a position in which they could only react to proposals put forward by others.

In spite of all this criticism Beyen miraculously obtained Cabinet permission to prepare for a Benelux initiative on the issue. He contacted Belgian Foreign Minister Spaak, who advocated further sectoral integration in the areas of transport, classical energy and – above all – nuclear energy. In spite of Spaak's initial doubts whether it made sense to initiate a proposal presumably unacceptable to France, he eventually agreed to a combined approach. In their historic hybrid memorandum for the July 1955 Messina conference of the ECSC countries, Benelux proposed the setting up of an intergovernmental conference to negotiate both Spaak's Monnet inspired sectoral integration issues, as well as the question of horizontal integration, i.e. the establishment of a European common market along the lines of the Beyen Plan. By eschewing the notion of "supranationalism" and a further watering down of the Benelux proposals to the status of study objects, the Six at Messina managed to arrive at a compromise based on the Benelux memorandum. The Messina-declaration envisaged an intergovernmental conference on both branches of the Benelux proposal, prepared by an expert's conference under chairmanship of a "political personality".

In the literature the historical importance of "Messina" is sometimes overrated. What basically happened is threefold. Firstly, Messina put European integration back on the negotiation table. Secondly, it was decided that the new talks would be on *economic* integration and thirdly, a certain *method* for these talks was agreed upon.

Thus, Messina created important conditions for successful negotiations. The decisive break through for the Beyen Plan, however, took place *after* this ministerial conference. Between June and September 1955, to the delight of the Dutch delegation at the Brussels experts' conference, the Common Market issue underwent a remarkable upgrading from being an additional topic to the principal objective of the intergovernmental negotiations among the Six. Belgian Foreign Minister Spaak, appointed as the abovementioned political personality presiding the conference, played an important role in this agenda revolution. His personal conversion to the Beyen plan is to be attributed to ECSC representative Pierre Uri's report on the Coal and Steel Community's experiences in regional integration and the lessons to be drawn from the latter for future horizontal integration. Spaak went hook, line and sinker for this brilliant piece of political economy and, from then on, considered the Common Market issue the central issue of the negotiations. An additional benefit for the Dutch accrued from the Uri report in that it argued against overall levelling of wage levels and social securities as advocated by the French and dreaded by the Dutch.

On the institutional issue, however, in the 1957 Rome Treaty, the Dutch did not obtain the 'High Authority' like central role for the projected Executive, Beyen and the Netherlands' government had advocated. The European Commission's own decision-making powers turned out to be of a much more limited nature than the Netherlands deemed desirable for effective implementation of the Common Market and its adherent policies. Neither was the external profile of the new European Economic Community according to the Netherlands' wishes. Overly protectionist in its relations with third countries as it was and, by introducing an unattractive association policy with Belgian and French colonies on top of this, it was looked upon by The Hague with dismay. On agriculture, the single most important export sector for the Dutch, the Treaty did not go beyond formulating a number of general principles.

Realizing the Beyen Plan

All in all, on the one hand the Rome Treaty and its subsequent implementation constituted an important diplomatic victory for the Netherlands in that it committed the Six to the Customs Union and, eventually, the Common Market so highly valued and tenaciously strived for by The Hague. On the other hand the EEC's institutional set-up, policy competences and external economic and political profile ended up a long shot from The Hague's ideals and preferences.

Taking into consideration the situational limitations on the Netherlands' engineerial influence during the negotiations, however, this outcome is not surprising. Dutch policy initiatives and Benelux agenda-setting politics could thrive in a setting in which both France and Germany were internally deeply divided on the European integration issue. In Germany, during most of the 1950s, there was an ongoing debate between economics minister Erhard, who advocated liberalization on a global scale and Federal Chancellor Adenauer, who wanted regional arrangements with – above all – France. In France, the French induced downfall of the French proposed EDC triggered off ever more acrimonious debates on France and Europe. The opposite was the case when in November 1956, Adenauer declared the Brussels negotiations 'Chef-Sache' and travelled to Paris for direct talks with his French counterpart

Guy Mollet. If and when – and this goes for the entire period under scrutiny – French-German bilateral deliberations get under way and turn out to be fruitful it is exceedingly difficult for the three Benelux countries to exert an active, let alone engineerial, influence on the eventual outcome of the negotiations. During the 1955-1957 EEC negotiations, this was *a fortiori* the case, now that the Benelux countries were divided amongst themselves.

Benelux foreign policy cooperation during the 1950s, enabled Luxemburg, Belgium and the Netherlands to streamline their policy positions in a way which greatly enhanced their collective engineering influence, as demonstrated in the above on a number of occasions (rendering innocuous Adenauer's institutionalist EPC programme, manoeuvring the relance-agenda, upgrading the Common Market-issue. And we could relate many more). As such, Benelux foreign policy cooperation provided The Hague with a leverage it could never have had on its own. Such successes may have given rise to a myth: the myth that it was Benelux foreign policy cooperation which enabled the three countries to, if not to dominate the EEC negotiations, at least influence their outcome to an extent well beyond their power station. The primary source material in the Netherlands' archives sends such interpretations to the shredder: The Spaak presidency, so instrumental in bringing about the June-August 1955 agenda revolution, subsequently torpedoed Benelux' chances of setting pressure as a collective. Benelux cooperation remained inoperative because Spaak, eager to arrive at compromises acceptable to France and Germany, explicitly and implicitly discouraged the Belgian delegation at the conference to take sides with the Dutch. Since Luxembourg tended to follow the Belgian point of view, arriving at a common Benelux stance was rendered well nigh impossible.

Be that as it may, Benelux provided its three constituent countries with another source of influence, in that it acted as a test laboratory for regional economic integration. As the first post-Second World War regional experiment in cross border economic disarmament, Benelux provided lessons for regional integration in a wider European framework. Our analysis supports that Benelux demonstrated, firstly, that the benefits of regional economic integration, in terms of economic growth, went well beyond what was generally expected. On this issue, the spectacular development of intra-Benelux trade and the recognition of a Benelux-trade enhancing effect appears to have played an important role in launching Beyen's campaign for establishing a Benelux-like customs union on a broader European base. Beyen's proposal was one amongst many. After all, it did not take a genius to wonder whether the tempestuous development of intra-Benelux trade was convertible to a European scale.

Secondly, Benelux left its empirical mark on the so-called policy harmonisation issue. This issue addresses the question as to which extent regional integration presupposes harmonization of national economic and social policies. The Hague's governing elite distilled from Benelux experiences the lesson that policy harmonization could indeed be the result of, rather than a condition for, market liberalization. In Belgium, due to discontent with unexpected side effects from Benelux, the lesson was the opposite. During the negotiations leading to the Treaties of Rome, Benelux experiences in this respect served as a point of reference, sometimes as an example and sometimes as a spectre.

Thirdly and lastly, Benelux as a regional economic integration experiment demonstrated that the transformation from a national to a larger, encompassing Benelux market took place without dramatic structural changes for the economies involved. Eliminating trade restrictions resulted in increased competition and led in some industries to a loss of capital and jobs. In general, however, such adjustment problems were limited and of a temporary nature. The mild character of the Benelux adjustment process can partly be explained by the fact that sensitive sectors, agriculture above all, were excluded from the Benelux liberalization process. Of comparable importance was the finding that economic specialization resulting from Benelux liberalization manifested itself not so much *between* but rather *within* existing branches of industry, thus leading to more complementary rather than more competing production structures. Benelux also taught that the dynamic effects of regional integration could be relied upon to greatly diminish differences between competitive production structures.

During the EEC negotiations the Netherlands habitually referred to Benelux experiences and lessons as empirical proof and justification for The Hague's policy preferences. More than occasionally, however, the outcomes of the Benelux laboratory for regional integration, effectively pleaded *against* Dutch preferences for solutions amongst the Six. On a number of essential issues – economic and social policy harmonisation, the institutional set-up, the inclusion of agriculture in the Common Market – Benelux was demonstrably not practising what it preached. Such cases of extreme divergence between Benelux practice and the Beyen/Luns programme clearly went to the detriment of Dutch capabilities at exerting engineering influence within the European framework.

Defending the Community

Riding the tide of economic growth and prosperity, the Six completed Beyen's Customs Union by the 1st of July 1968, one and half years before schedule. In spite of the Rome Treaties' vagueness on agriculture, the Six managed to hammer out a Common Agricultural Policy, which increasingly dominated EEC decision-making: when in April

1965 the Cals government came to power "EEC" more or less equalled "agriculture", as 95% of the Community budget, 90% of its regulations and 70% of the time spent on Council meetings was CAP-related. For the Netherlands, as the largest agricultural exporter among the Six, the CAP represented a new life line: Even though CAP was of a dangerously protectionist nature in trade relations with third countries, it provided Dutch farming interests with a long sought for sizeable export market in continental Europe. By and large, and notwithstanding their differences on CAP's protectionist nature, the Netherlands and France saw eye to eye with each other on the issues of agriculture and agricultural policy in Europe. Actually, in most EEC related affairs the two countries cooperated smoothly. Likewise, in (post) colonial affairs mutual understanding and help was the norm. French support for The Hague during the Dutch New Guinea conflict was returned by Dutch support for Paris in the Algerian war.

On European high politics, however, during most of the 1960s, Dutch-French relations were complicated – to put it mildly. In The Hague's analysis the downfall of the French Fourth Republic turned France into the sick man of Western Europe. The democratic intentions and destiny of the new De Gaulle regime were questioned severely. In the eyes of many Dutch policy makers, De Gaulle and his new Republic were an expression of France's problems, rather than part of a hoped for solution. For the latter, De Gaulle's September 1958 letter to MacMillan and Eisenhower, proposing a "triple directorate" for NATO consisting of the USA, the UK and France, seemed the definite proof that in his desire to restore French "grandeur", the new French president was living in a cloud cuckoo land.

In this psychological-political context the French 1959-1962 proposals for a European Political Union came as a most unwelcome visitor. The Hague deprecated a continental foreign policy grouping under French or Franco-German guidance. It did so for Atlanticist reasons, but also because from the Netherlands' perspective, it would never make sense to create an additional *political* division of Western Europe over and above the *economic* one represented by the EEC. In short, De Gaulle's geo-political ambitions should not be allowed to impede future British EEC membership. Due to German unpredictability – it was far from clear how far Chancellor Adenauer would go to gratify De Gaulle – as well as the *maladie de compromis* which The Hague ascribed to its Benelux-partners a positive outcome for the Netherlands was far from certain. In fact, at the February 1961 Paris conference of the Six, the Hague government found itself in a dangerously isolated position. The Netherlands' *préalable anglais*, insisting on British participation as a basic condition for foreign policy cooperation proved effective, in that a number of safeguards for NATO and the Communities could be agreed upon. On the main issue, however, whether the Six should proceed without British participation, no agreement could be reached and in December 1961, Belgian Foreign Minister Spaak broke with the common Benelux front, bowed to the majority and showed himself willing to negotiate on the basis of the French European Political Union propositions. It was De Gaulle who came to the rescue of the Netherlands' negotiators by – arguably intentionally – grossly overplaying his hand in drafting his January 1962 EPU proposal.

De Gaulle's killing of the EPU negotiations, however, did not mean that the Netherlands could lean back and consider its vision on Europe as taken for granted. This vision concentrated on the establishment of a European common market, in which process a supranational executive equipped with far-reaching powers was deemed elementary. Dutch functional or instrumental supranationalism advocated an institutional structure in which decision-making powers in the Community lay with the Executive, that being the European Commission, on all questions related to the establishment and practical functioning of the Common Market. This view on European governance, as devised by Beyen, set the tone for future decades. From the establishment of the Community in 1958 onwards, the Netherlands attempted to defend the powers of the European Commission, advocated their extension, supported the principle of majority voting in EEC decision-making, as well as stressing the sovereign equality of the EC Member States. Once again, it should be pointed out that this stance reflected a functional or instrumental approach towards supranationalism, rather than a federalist creed (hence: functional supranationalism, or "the community method"). In government circles, supranationalism, like European integration as a whole, was considered a means to an end.

The stress on the Commission's position, as the pivot around which the other actors in the decision-making process were to turn, seems attributable to a combination of explanatory factors.

Firstly, an important part was played by the conviction among Dutch policy makers that an intergovernmental organisation would be insufficiently capable of circumventing important national interests where this was necessary, to implement Treaty provisions. This applied in particular to the much sought for Common Agricultural Policy (CAP), crucially important to Dutch exports.

A second reason for placing the European Commission at the fore was constituted by the experience Dutch policy makers had accrued in the Benelux context. The slow, difficult progress in developing Benelux from a customs union towards a full and functioning economic union was, in their view, the fault of its weak institutional structure. It was precisely because Benelux, as an intergovernmental organization, had no supranational agencies with their own powers that it was so difficult to align the policies of the three participatory states and bring about a genuine free market in farm products. If primacy in the decision-making process was not placed with the Commission, Treaty agreements would be surely torpedoed in the Council of Ministers because of lack of unanimity. In short: Benelux was taken as a countermodel for the administrative organization of the EEC.

A third factor was the consideration that the rights and interests of medium and small Member States would best be respected in a supranational context. Precisely this consideration testified to the Dutch fear of being locked into a protectionist block dominated by a Franco-German directorate. Failing British participation in the Communities, The Hague sought guarantees against such domination by the incorporation of Member States on as equal a footing as possible in Community decision-making. In this latter respect particularly, supranationalism embodied the defensive trait, clearly recognisable during the Fouchet negotiations in Dutch policy makers' attacks on intergovernmental decision making structures in which smaller nations, though formally entitled to a veto, *de facto* found themselves forced to follow the lead of the larger ones and the *faits accomplis* with which the latter confronted them.

De Gaulle's political *harakiri* of January 1962 did bring considerable relief which, however, could not last. In the summer of 1965 the French Presidents' "empty chair crisis" hit Europe in its central organs. Once again the Netherlands had to come to the rescue of the European Communities. This time De Gaulle went for an all-out attack, aiming to maim both the European Commission and Qualified Majority Voting in the Council of Ministers. The second half of 1965 witnessed a new constellation in Europe, in that Germany, Italy and the three Benelux countries for the first time managed to uphold a lasting common front against French power politics.

At the outset of the crisis, Dutch diplomacy was, to a large degree, dictated by domestic policy considerations. A well-organized cross-party federalist majority in Parliament saddled the Cals coalition government with an outspoken federalist agenda and coupled its political survival to its record on supporting European institutions. When French unilateralism struck, The Hague's emphasis shifted rapidly from the offensive towards the defensive, prioritising the maintenance of the common front of the Five in order to protect the EEC and its communitarian character.

The 1965-1966 crisis may be characterized as yet another episode in a series of diplomatic disagreements on the future of European integration during the 1960s. As in the past, the French Republic and the Netherlands represented pole positions: The Hague putting up an indefatigable defence of the European Community's supranational character versus determined attempts by Paris to undo the communitarian elements of the Rome Treaty. Due to their common front, the Netherlands, Germany, Italy, Belgium and Luxembourg managed to maintain a united stance against French pressure; these five countries carried the day and The Hague "left the battlefield victorious", as worded by the then State Secretary for European affairs in the Netherlands.

Nevertheless, the outcome of the crisis, known as the "Luxembourg compromise", was discouraging, at least in the short run. The Hague's valiant attempts at creating a more supranational Community had been thwarted. Particularly its efforts to strengthen the controlling and legislative powers of the European Parliament had proven ill fated. Subsequent developments proved, however, that in the longer run, the German-Dutch supported communitarian approach was to prevail over De Gaulle's short-term successes. Today's European Union, in which qualifying majorities and blocking minorities are the order of the day and the co-decision procedure has upgraded the European Parliament to a co-legislative role, *a fortiori* reflects the victory of communitarianism over De Gaulle's confederal ideas.

De Gaulle's resignation as French president in April 1969 opened new avenues, as demonstrated by the December 1969 Hague summit conference. "The Hague" would turn out to be the summit which initiated both the first attempt at Economic and Monetary Union as well as European Political Cooperation. Along with these two fundamental initiatives actual enlargement was also on the agenda, all three to become of the greatest importance in the Communities' development during the 1970s and later decades. In terms of engineering influence, the historical importance of The Hague summit is, by and large, to be attributed to the subsequent implementation and follow-up of the conclusions it reached. Had the subsequent Brussels conference, the Werner and Davignon committees and the enlargement negotiations been unsuccessful, the by now famous triptych "completion, widening and deepening" would have remained null and void. In this respect the "spirit of the Hague" appears to have been of more importance than the actual wording of the compromises arrived at in the *Ridderzaal*.

What was fundamentally new about The Hague summit was the decisive role played by the West-German government, led by Chancellor Brandt. The German contribution went well beyond its advocacy of EMU. For the first time – from The Hague's perspective – widening and deepening the Community, rather than compromising with France, had become the Federal Republic's priority. For Foreign Minister Luns the summit was a definite sign that the Adenauer days of Germany blindly accommodating France were over. As such, for the Netherlands, the German performance heralded a new era in European integration. The

Bundesrepublik at long last freed itself of its historically determined reticence in post-war European affairs and, thus emancipated, was ready and willing to lead the Community towards further integration and against future attempts at dominance. For the Netherlands, German emancipation was all the more important in that, in terms of engineering influence, German-Dutch relations represented an alternative for Benelux foreign policy cooperation. This was attractive, since foreign policy cooperation between Belgium and the Netherlands, in comparison with its impressive 1950s track record, had proved lifeless and ineffective, during most of the 1960s.

Externalizing Europe, reluctantly

As far as the country's Atlantic ties and the Netherlands' geo-political situation were concerned, European integration, in the eyes of The Hague's foreign policy elite, constituted a complication rather than a means to exert engineering influence. On this issue, Europe came at a price.

As a result of this, the government's approach of European Political Co-operation was lukewarm. EPC was seen as potentially dangerous in that it could be used as a Trojan Horse for weakening the Atlantic link, sidelining the Commission and corrupting the community's supranational calling. Nevertheless, EPC foreign policy consultations were to be judged favourably as long as one kept in mind that their intergovernmental set-up seriously limited their scope and that the talks should not be to the detriment of NATO unity. From a communitarian perspective, EPC was considered of little importance: the creation of a foreign-political roof over the Customs Union and later the Common Market was deemed less urgent, especially if this roof lacked a connection with the EC's supranational foundation. This policy line was to remain unaltered, at least until the end of the Cold War in 1990.

At times, however, European policy co-ordination and group diplomacy was not an option, but a dire necessity. Especially the country's isolated geo-political position during the 1973-1974 Middle Eastern crisis and oil boycott was instructive in teaching interdependence the hard way. At this point, it seemed that, for the first time since the Second World War – perhaps with the exception of the de-colonisation of the Dutch Indies and New Guinea – the Atlantic bond failed to give the Netherlands the desired protection and coverage against external threats. Despite the existence of a strong sense of solidarity between the US and the Netherlands, OPEC's oil policy hurt the Netherlands and manoeuvred the country into a vulnerable and diplomatically isolated position. It took the government some time before it realised that going a *Sonderweg* and ignoring EPC harmed the country's national interest. Here Europe came at a price, to wit a humbling experience: for a change, the

Atlantic framework alone did not suffice. Instead, Europe provided the country with an "umbrella" against unilateral vindication by third countries.

Also, the external dimension of the Communities constituted a problem for the Netherlands in the country's relations with the developing world. First of all there was the issue of required associative status with the Common Market for French and Belgian colonies in – above all – Africa. Association did *not* turn out to be a temporary phenomenon, as some in the Dutch government had hoped for. When French dependencies in Africa gained independence, preferential treatment and financial aid had to be continued, lest the abolishment of association would be regarded as a form of punishment for accepting independence. Hence, the Hague's acceptance of the Yaoundé treaties. In this respect, association resembled an eel-trap: having entered the first compartment of the trap one could still swim, but in a forward direction only, i.e. into the next compartment.

Contrary to the main line of its European policies, the Dutch government was *not* prepared to allow the European Commission to play a substantial role on the EC-Africa issue. While generally valuing the Commission's position as an honest broker between the member states, the Dutch government saw no real advantage in allowing the Commission to play a prominent and independent role in the Yaoundé process. This finding emphasizes the functional, or instrumental, rather than federalist nature of Dutch supranationalism at the time. Throughout the 1960s, The Hague's policy towards EEC and Africa was characterized by three dominant objectives. Firstly, extending the Yaoundé preferences to other, non-French-speaking African countries. Secondly, avoiding or reducing discriminative practices against (former) Dutch colonies. And thirdly, reducing the national contribution to EDF and furthering a level playing field for Dutch firms operating in Africa.

Benelux and Small States' Politics

Under specific constellations smaller countries can play a role of amazing relevance. Throughout the 1950s Benelux cooperation provided the Netherlands with a unique framework for furthering the Netherlands' interests in Europe. Admittedly, the policy instruments applied by The Hague at the European negotiation tables were typically of the soft power variety: practical and academic experience with regional economic integration, smart ideas, agenda manipulation and teaming up with the Belgians and Luxembourgians. Again, room for manoeuvre for the Netherlands and its Benelux partners was by and large determined by the ongoing relationship between France and Germany. Konrad Adenauer was the key figure in determining the leeway for the Netherlands and its Benelux partners. If and when the German Chancellor decided to prioritize on a Franco-German understanding – and this was generally the case – Benelux' chances at effectively promoting diverging negotiation outcomes were slender, at least on major issues. Throughout the Adenauer era this state of affairs underlined the importance of Benelux cooperation for The Hague: A united Benelux stance could make the difference. A common Benelux position was considered a potential asset and a proved source of influence. Conversely, a divided Benelux smacked of impotence and a possibly isolated position for the Netherlands amongst the Six.

The German Chancellor's departure from active politics in 1963 constituted an important change: Adenauer's successors in Bonn, by prioritizing a European understanding amongst the Six, considerably broadened The Hague's room for manoeuvre. Likewise, France's president De Gaulle's unilateral policy choices contributed to a new power constellation within the EEC, in which it was France, rather than the Netherlands that painted itself into a corner. Benelux unity in European politics survived as an ideal, but lost out against the new reality in which a basic understanding between Germany, Italy and the Benelux countries (The Five) on the communitarian destiny of the Community and its open character prevailed. Hence we can conclude that in the course of the 1960s European pioneer Benelux was overtaken by the EEC, not just on the issue of regional economic integration but also in terms of foreign policy cooperation. The emancipation of Germany's European policy, effective cooperation between the Five and a new dawn in France collectively triumphed in the Hague summit of December 1969.

For the Netherlands and its Benelux partners the end of the Adenauer era can well be likened to the situation for the smaller countries in Europe at the end of the 19th century. Back then, disagreement amongst the major Powers and a concomitant decline of the Concert of Europe led to a considerable increase in Small Power influence: the Smaller Powers had grown in importance as potential allies for both the *entente cordiale* and the central continental powers.[3] In this respect, the teaming up of the Five for a communitarian Europe is to be seen not only as the outcome of lofty shared ideals but also as a political alliance in the best of Europe's political traditions. All through the 1960s, being part of an effective alliance *cum* sophisticated dynamic enabled the Netherlands to play an essential role in the process of European integration.

3 C.A. Tamse, "Kleine landen als een bijzondere categorie van internationale actoren. Het geval van Nederland en België (1830-1914)", in: C.A. Tamse, *Het huis van Oranje en andere politieke mythes*, Amsterdam: Bakker, 2002, pp. 40-70 (p. 64), previously published in W.F. de Gaay Forman a.o. (eds.), *Achter den tijd. Opstellen aangeboden aan dr. G. Puchinger ter gelegenheid van zijn 65^{e} verjaardag*, Haarlem: Aca-Media, 1986, pp. 183-209.

Hence this study appears to corrobate the principal findings of Small States' Politics, that subdiscipline of International Relations theory discussed in our general Introduction. Since our aim was an historical analysis rather than a political science one – we wanted to tell a story rather than test a theory – this is an issue where modesty and caution are called for. Neveretheless, the case of the Netherlands' role in European affairs during the formative years of the European Union undeniably demonstrates that smaller Powers can play a role of substantial importance in international relations. Our study underlines the relative nature of the dimensions of size and strengh, at least among European states. In our case, the assumed primacy of the Great Powers in European affairs appeared one of a relative nature: For the first time in Western-European history war was categorically ruled out as an acceptable policy instrument for settling interstate problems and conflicts. As a consequence, interstate negotiations resulted in tests of wills and skills, in which "size" had to be dealt with as a variable, rather than a constant. Also, due to internal divisions, France and Germany did not act according to their capabilities. If and when the Benelux countries managed to get their act together they rose to the occasion and exerted considerable, sometimes leading, influence.

Making Europe and the World

The Netherlands pursued a course of engineering influence during the EEC's formative years with a view to furthering the country's national interests. Jan Willem Beyen laid the foundation for a Dutch European policy which was outstanding in that it acknowledged European interdependence and the need for European mutual economic disarmament at a time in which these concepts were far from self-evident.

What goes for Europe, goes for the world. Paraphrasing Mathisen[4] we observe that there are strong indications that, in the longer run and greater scheme of things, the hope of the Smaller Powers rests with the further development of world institutions, for it is the nature of things that Smaller Powers' rights can be better safeguarded by law and order than by the mailed fist.

---

[4] T. Mathisen, *The Functions of Small States in the Strategies of the Great Powers*, Oslo: Universitetsforlaget, 1971, p. 282.

A Note on the Making of the Netherlands' European Policy during the 1950s and 1960s

The Netherlands' policies on Europe have to be understood against the background of the country's political system and the structure and traditions of The Hague's governmental apparatus. In the Dutch system of government, apart from responsibility for their departments, ministers bear *collective responsibility* for government policy in general. At the same time, all ministers have the same constitutional status and enjoy a large measure of autonomy in determining their department's policy.

During the 1952-1973 period covered by this study, European policy was generally considered *foreign* policy. The contemporary constellation, in which European policy making increasingly determines the domestic policy makers' room for manoeuvre, was non-existent. Direct transgovernmental contacts between Dutch ministries and their foreign counterparts, currently a perfectly normal phenomenon, were unheard of at the time. Societal interests groups too were limited in their cross border ambitions and concentrated on domestic issues.

The same went for the *Minister-President*, the Prime Minister, who limited himself to a reticent role in matters of foreign and European policy. The Prime Ministers of the period under scrutiny – Drees, De Quay, Marijnen, Cals, Zijlstra, De Jong and Biesheuvel – were firsts among equals, rather than leaders of government as in Britain, Germany or France. Presiding three to five party coalition governments their first responsibility was to maintain the domestic political balance underlying the ruling coalition. Although both Drees and De Quay attempted to increase their grip on foreign policy making, these attempts remained unsuccessful.

Thus, during the two decades covered by this study, the Dutch Prime Minister acted as chairman of the Cabinet rather than political leader of the government, which helps to understand why Foreign Ministers Stikker, Beyen, Luns and Schmelzer played the main role in both initiating and implementing the Netherlands' foreign policy. They are the hero's of the tale told in this book, rather than the Prime Ministers of the period. Luns, serving the country as Foreign Minister for most of the period under scrutiny (1952-1973), experienced particular freedom of manoeuvre, successfully capitalizing on his experience, popularity and his ministry's information edge in European affairs.

Under these circumstances, good coordination procedures in order to arrive at an unambiguous policy are of the essence.

At ministerial level this coordination took place in the full session of the Council of Ministers or in one of its sub-committees. At official level, it was the responsibility of the ministry directly involved. In both cases, it was a matter of "coordination through consultation", not arbitrating powers in accordance with a "top down" model. The stress on the equality of ministers and departments was still further enhanced by the fact that governments are coalitions. The ministers involved in a single matter were often not from the same political party. For Dutch foreign policy, this situation meant that while primacy for coordinating foreign policy lay with the Ministry of Foreign Affairs, foreign policy was not its exclusive fief. Other departments had a technical and policy contribution of their own to make, and possessed considerable policy instruments in the sphere of foreign policy, going as far as having their own representation abroad.[1] Hence the important role of the ministries of Economic Affairs and Agriculture, as well as the Finance Ministry, in formulating European policy during the decades covered by this book.

The interministerial division of tasks in the sphere of external economic relations went through radical changes in the period from 1945 to 1965. During the first years after the Second World War, this area primarily involved trade policy, specifically the conclusion of bilateral trade and payments agreements. This technical area did not interest the Ministry of Foreign Affairs much[2], nor did it have the requisite in-house economic know-how. On the basis of Cabinet agreements in 1946 and 1950, powers in this area, including those for interdepartmental coordination, were centred in the Directorate-General for External Economic Relations (BEB)[3], falling under the Ministry of Economic Affairs. This went together with a reorganisation of the Ministry of Foreign Affairs, which after 1950 adopted a regional structure in the place of its previous functional one. This created a distinction between foreign policy and external economic policy that was to lead to great problems later on.[4]

1 J.M.M. van den Bos, *Dutch EC Policy Making. A Model-Guided Approach to Coordination and Negotiation*, Amsterdam: Thesis Publishers, 1991, p. 67; J.J.C. Voorhoeve, *Peace, Profits and Principles. A Study of Dutch Foreign Policy*, Leiden: Stenfert Kroese, 1985, pp. 75-76.

2 The attitude at the Foreign Ministry at the time was summarized in the terse formulation of Minister Van Kleffens (1939-1947): "A diplomat does not discuss cheese".

3 BEB stands for: Directoraat-Generaal voor de Buitenlands-Economische Betrekkingen.

4 C.B. Wels, "The Foreign Policy Institutions in the Dutch Republic and the Kingdom of the Netherlands 1579 to 1980", in: Z. Steiner (ed.), *The Times Survey of Foreign Ministries of the World*, London: Times Books, 1982, pp. 363-388.

The BEB grew into a weighty agency. It did not confine itself to bilateral trade questions, but also played the major part in the negotiations on Benelux and the ECSC, and, to a considerable extent, determined Dutch policy towards these organisations. Alongside the BEB, however, a separate government commissioner for the European Recovery Programme was appointed in 1948, charged with Dutch policy in relation to the Marshall Plan. However, this government commissioner, Dr. Hirschfeld, did not fall under any ministry, but took his instructions directly from the *Ministerraad.* He and his office were responsible for determining Dutch policy in the OEEC. Partly in consequence of the great importance of Marshall dollars to the Dutch economy and politics, the Hirschfeld working group secured official control over the most important aspect of external economic policy. When Hirschfeld resigned in 1952, his working-group was taken over as a separate Directorate-General for the Economic and Military Aid Programme (DGEM) in the Ministry of Foreign Affairs. This not only brought a new functional element into the now regional structure of the department; the arrival of DGEM also meant a considerable influx of financial and economic knowledge. Finally, the changeover meant that powers for coordination and the bulk of policy formation on OEEC affairs now lay with the Foreign Ministry and not with the BEB. This last aspect led to a competence dispute between the Economics Ministry (BEB) and Foreign Ministry (DGEM), which was to continue until the 1970s.[5]

DGEM's position was strengthened still further within its own department by Minister Beyen's explicit economic orientation in European integration policy. DGEM supplied the financial and economic expertise to carry through the Beyen Plan. DGEM Director Van der Beugel was, in 1954, also appointed Financial and Economic Advisor to the minister. In interdepartmental relations, DGEM was able to dominate because of the decisive stamp Beyen himself put on Dutch European policy through his initiatives. One consequence of this was that coordinating powers for the Dutch contribution to the EEC negotiations also fell to the Foreign Ministry (DGEM). In the process of these negotiations Beyen successfully sought to confine consultation for coordination purposes in the Cabinet, and thereby the contribution of Prime Minister Drees, to a minimum, interdepartmental consultation at the official level took on great importance. For this, an "Interdepartmental Consultative Committee on European Integration" was set up, chaired by Beyen himself. A score of officials from all the ministries directly or indirectly involved sat on it, and Beyen feared that such a large body could not achieve effective policy formation and would produce an obstructive effect. It

5 E.H. van der Beugel, *Nederland in de Westelijke samenwerking. Enkele aspecten van de Nederlandse beleidsvorming*, Leiden: Brill, 1966, pp. 17-24.

was arguably for these reasons that Drees had urged that it be set up. Beyen coped with this problem by having actual policy coordination carried out in a small informal group of six or seven officials led by Van der Beugel, convoking the big Beyen Committee infrequently and thereby circumventing it with a *fait accompli* policy.[6] This approach succeeded, though it could not prevent interdepartmental discord emerging, sometimes painfully, from the Dutch delegations in Brussels.

The significant and growing influence which the Foreign Ministry and the DGEM thus managed to secure, in the area of European economic integration, was not well perceived by the BEB and the Ministry of Economic Affairs. They had willy-nilly agreed to the Foreign Ministry's coordinating powers for the duration of the negotiations. But as soon as the EEC and Euratom Treaties had come into effect, primacy for both substantive policy implementation and coordination would have to be assigned to the Economics Ministry, as was the case for Benelux and the ECSC.

On the other hand there was not the slightest willingness in the Foreign Ministry to give up the position it had recently secured. In the meantime, in October 1956, the fourth Drees Cabinet had taken office, with Joseph Luns as successor to Beyen at the Ministry of Foreign Affairs, a position he was to retain until 1971. Alongside him, in January 1957, Van der Beugel was appointed Secretary of State responsible for European Integration in the same department. Under his supervision, a new reorganisation was carried out, with the object of improving their own apparatus so as to be able to head off the expected challenge from the Economics Ministry. For this, the DGEM was restructured as a sort of 'super-directorate-general' concentrating all the department's tasks in the area of European Cooperation and Integration: policy towards the OEEC, the EEC, Euratom, the Council of Europe, the policy aspects of Benelux and the ECSC that did not fall to the Economics Ministry, and the talks on the OEEC free-trade area that had just begun. Zijlstra, Minister for Economic Affairs, had already firmly protested against the assigning of policy coordination on the last point to the Foreign Ministry by the Council of Ministers. For him the transformation of the DGEM and its renaming as Directorate-General for European Cooperation (DGES) was impossible to swallow. It prejudiced the future division of tasks between the two ministries most concerned, he argued. Tempers ran high, leading even to an (unusual) vote in the Council of Ministers, which was carried by the Foreign Ministry.

Zijlstra, however, stood firm and insisted that coordination powers for EEC policy should be assigned to the BEB. He was fully supported

6 Ermers and Kragt, "Tussen tradities", pp. 145-147.

by his political backers, the protestant Anti-Revolutionary Party, so that a Cabinet crisis threatened. In July 1958, a difficult compromise was finally reached: policy coordination and the new interdepartmental "Coordinating Committee for European Integration and the Free-Trade Area" (CoCo) were to fall under the Foreign Ministry, but the Chairmanship of the Coordinating Committee was to be held by the Minister for Economic Affairs.[7] As the capstone of this edifice, the Permanent Representation in Brussels that had by now been set up was to act as a connecting link between the Committee and The Hague administration. Former delegation head Linthorst Homan was appointed Dutch Permanent Representative at the EEC and Euratom.

The set-up for decision-making on Dutch EEC policy, structured in this way, did not result in effective policy formation during the period from 1958 to 1965. A first reason for this was the shortage of personnel in the policy-forming bodies and agencies. It is not clear whether the workload on the national administration as a consequence of the Community's beginning operations was underestimated from the outset, or whether, as The Hague documents suggest, it was more a matter of unforeseeable, unbridled expansion in Commission initiatives. In 1959 DGES Director Van Ittersum was already sounding the alarm bell: the most pressing problem presented by the Community was the steadily increasing flow of European policy questions that poured from Brussels on to the desks of the national administrations. The overloading had reached such proportions that intervention was now necessary for physical reasons alone. Blame for this lay, according to Van Ittersum, with the Commission, which "is dragged into this dervish dance by its far too big apparatus of officials". He showed special concern at the signs of physical and mental overstrain at the Permanent Representation in Brussels. The Commission ought to be slowed down by having it draw up, together with the permanent representatives, a scheme of priorities and a timetable.[8] When the matter was discussed in Cabinet, too, the problems were attributed primarily to the Commission; according to Minister Zijlstra, it ought to confine itself to the task laid down in the Treaties of Rome instead of setting about undertaking all sorts of independent activity. The members of the Assembly, too, it was further suggested, should take a stance against the overload, and call for a

---

7 A.M. van der Togt, "Het Ministerie van Buitenlandse Zaken in een veranderende wereld. Organisatorische aspecten van de vorming van het buitenlands beleid 1945-1974" (unpublished thesis, KU Nijmegen 1984), pp. 62-72. After the end of the negotiations on the Free Trade Area, the CoCo was renamed "Coordinating Commission for European Integration and Association Questions". The abbreviation remained the same.

8 Min. BZ, DGES, 1955-1964, 996.0, EEG, algemeen deel I: Van Ittersum to Luns, 16.11.1959.

timetable. Minister Luns did not wish to expand the Permanent Representation's staff, though he did bring the timetabling suggestion up at the Council of Ministers of the Community.[9] The staffing and overload problem was gradually brought under control. Thus, Permanent Representation staff in Brussels grew, despite Luns's intentions, from 11 to 19 policy officers between 1960 and 1964.[10]

Of much greater importance was the failure of the coordination mechanism to work, or work adequately. The first pointer in this direction came in October 1959 from Linthorst Homan. Seriously concerned, he reported to Luns about the lack of communication between the Permanent Representatives and the officials of The Hague ministries taking part in EEC working groups. In only a fraction of cases did it seem that the latter had made prior contact with the Dutch mission before Brussels meetings, and subsequent reporting on the outcome of meetings was insufficient, or reached the Permanent Representation too late. He was thus unable to form an overall picture of what was being discussed, therefore hampering his work. Moreover, it was painful to have to hear from another Permanent Representative or from an official that, say, in Working Group X the Dutch position Y had been worded very differently, or even completely abandoned.[11] DGES Director Van Ittersum also pointed in this connection to the great number of EEC Working Groups made up of national experts and Community officials, which "is becoming so enormously large that there can no longer be any control at all over the instructions the national experts receive and how they carry out these instructions". With such "uncoordination", no solid policy formation could be expected.[12]

The coordination problem proved to be structural in nature. A 1963 study of bottlenecks stressed the fragmented nature of Dutch policy, the inadequate contact between the CoCo and negotiators in Brussels, and the poor functioning of CoCo in general.[13] That the quality of policies being processed suffered from this lack of coordination is obvious. The study mentioned points out that policy fragmentation made it harder to arrive at an overall strategy – when one set of decisions did not completely contradict the other. Thus, again in 1963, after the negotiations

9 NA, MR (410) Notulen Ministerraad, 20.11.1959.

10 Min. BZ, DGES, 1955-1964, 130.1: Luns to Minister van Binnenlandse Zaken, 2.2.1961; *Gids van het Departement van Buitenlandse Zaken en de Buitenlandse Dienst 1960* ('s Gravenhage 1960) p. 235; *Gids van het Departement van Buitenlandse Zaken en de Buitenlandse Dienst 1964*, ('s Gravenhage 1964) p. 316.

11 Min. BZ, DGES, 996.0, EEG, 1955-64, No. 31 Linthorst Homan to Luns, 31.10.1959.

12 Min. BZ, DGES, 996.0, EEG, 1955-1964, algemeen deel I: Van Ittersum to Luns, 16.11.1959.

13 Van der Togt, 'Het Ministerie van Buitenlandse Zaken', p. 76.

in the EEC Council of Ministers on agricultural regulations, it was found by the Cabinet that such small account had been taken from The Hague's standpoint because of the manifest internal division of the Dutch delegation.[14] And Linthorst Homan, looking back in his memoirs at his time in Brussels, points to the tactical consequences of the lack of mutual synchronisation and sifting of the departmental contributions: since a superfluity of subordinate points were brought up, the really important aspects of the Dutch argument were no longer meeting with a hearing from the partner countries.[15]

One important cause of the coordination problem was the continuing competency conflict between the two ministries most concerned, Foreign Affairs and Economic Affairs. The Luns-Zijlstra compromise of July 1958 had not really solved the competency question, because both parties continued to stick to their initial positions. While the Economics Ministry sought to use its CoCo chairmanship to secure a tighter grip for the BEB on coordination, the Foreign Ministry defended its primacy with conviction, seeking in turn to draw to itself Benelux and ECSC matters that fell under Economic Affairs. That practical cooperation in CoCo, and therefore policy coordination, was not best served by this dispute is not hard to guess.

Various solutions to the problem were proposed and tried out. Thus, when the Marijnen government took office in 1963, a special subcommittee of the Council of Ministers, the Council for European Affairs (REZ) was set up in order to consolidate the Council of Ministers' hold over the decision-making process. The Foreign Ministry pressed for the appointment of a new Secretary of State for European Affairs (Van der Beugel's *portfolio* had been abolished after the fall of the Fourth Drees Cabinet in December 1958) to deal chiefly with policy coordination. In 1963 this appointment was made, but the competency conflict between the two ministries was only made the fiercer. The harmful effects of this internecine strife were not confined to the 'unavoidable consequence that the size of Dutch delegations to international talks is only occasionally exceeded by a phalanx of briefcase-toting Italian ambassadors'.[16] What Van der Beugel found still more important was that the policymakers had to spend a disproportionate amount of time solving, or in most cases not solving, competency disputes, thereby making both the unity of policy and the strategic space for the policy suffer. A real solution to the competency question was not found until 1972. The dispute was decided in favour of the Ministry of Foreign Affairs.[17]

14 NA, MR (758) Notulen Ministerraad 22.12.1963.

15 Linthorst Homan, *Wat zijt ghij voor een vent*, p. 241.

16 Van der Beugel, *Nederland in de Westelijke samenwerking*, pp. 23-24.

17 *Ibidem*.

Index

A

B

C

D

E

F

G

H

I

J

K

L

R

S

T

"European Policy"

"European Policy" is an interdisciplinary series devoted to the study of European integration in a broad sense. Although mostly focusing on the European Union, it also encourages the publication of books addressing the wider, pan-European context, as well as comparative work, including other forms of regional integration on the world scene. The core disciplines are politics, economics, law, and history.

While being committed to high academic standards, "European Policy" seeks to be accessible to a wide readership, including policy-makers and practitioners, and to stimulate a debate on European issues. Submissions will normally undergo a thorough peer-review process. The series publishes both in English and in French.

Series Editor: **Pascaline Winand**,
Professor/Director, Monash European and EU Centre
(Monash University, Australia)

Recent Titles

- No.42: *In Pursuit of Influence. The Netherlands' European Policy during the Formative Years of the European Union, 1952-1973*, Anjo G. Harryvan, 2009, 284 p., ISBN 978-90-5201-497-5
- N° 41: *Les États-Unis et l'unification monétaire de l'Europe*, Dimitri Grygowski, 2009, 472 p., ISBN 978-90-5201- 489-0
- N° 40: *Le Traité de Rome. Histoires pluridisciplinaires. L'apport du Traité de Rome instituant la Communauté économique européenne*, Sandrine Devaux, René Leboutte & Philippe Poirier (dir.), 2009, 210 p., ISBN 978-90-5201-500-2
- No.39: *European Integration from Rome to Berlin: 1957-2007. History, Law and Politics*, Julio Baquero Cruz & Carlos Closa Montero (eds.), 2009, 286 p., ISBN 978-90-5201-464-7
- No.38: *European and Turkish Voices in Favour and Against Turkish Accession to the European Union*, Christiane Timmerman, Dirk Rochtus & Sara Mels (eds.), 2008, 149 p., ISBN 978-90-5201-428-9
- N° 37: *Centre et centrisme en Europe aux XIX*[e] *et XX*[e] *siècles. Regards croisés*, Sylvie Guillaume et Jean Garrigues (dir.), 2006, 288 p., ISBN 978-90-5201-317-6

- N° 36: *Vers une Europe fédérale ? Les espoirs et les actions fédéralistes au sortir de la Seconde Guerre mondiale*, Bertrand VAYSSIÈRE, 2006 (2nd printing 2007), 416 p., ISBN 978-90-5201-353-4
- N° 35: *Institutionnaliser l'évaluation des politiques publiques. Étude comparée des dispositifs en Belgique, en France, en Suisse et aux Pays-Bas*, Steve JACOB, 2005, 271 p., ISBN 978-90-5201-078-6
- No.34: *Visions, Votes and Vetoes. The Empty Chair Crisis and the Luxembourg Compromise Forty Years On*, Jean-Marie PALAYRET, Helen WALLACE & Pascaline WINAND (EDS.), 2006, 344 p., ISBN 978-90-5201-031-1
- No.33: *Networks of Empire. The US State Department's Foreign Leader Program in the Netherlands, France, and Britain 1950-70*, Giles SCOTT-SMITH, 2008, 516 p., ISBN 978-90-5201-256-3
- N° 32: *Le droit institutionnel de la sécurité intérieure européenne*, Pierre BERTHELET, 2003, 324 p., ISBN 978-90-5201-193-6
- N° 31 : *La crise autrichienne de la culture politique européenne*, Jacques LE RIDER & Nicolas LEVRAT (dir.), 2004, 241 p., ISBN 978-90-5201-188-2
- N° 30: *Les opinions publiques face à l'Europe communautaire. Entre cultures nationales et horizon européen /Public Opinion and Europe. National Identities and the European Integration Process*, Anne DULPHY & Christine MANIGAND (dir./eds.), 2004, 228 p., ISBN 978-90-5201-186-8
- N° 29: *Droit et souverainetés. Analyse critique du discours européen sur la Yougoslavie*, Barbara DELCOURT, 2003, 487 p., ISBN 978-90-5201-179-0
- N° 28: *L'Europe et ses collectivités territoriales. Réflexions sur l'organisation et l'exercice du pouvoir territorial dans un monde globalisé*, Nicolas LEVRAT, 2005 (2nd printing 2008), 304 p., ISBN 978-90-5201-174-5
- No.27: *The European Union Transformed. Community Method and Institutional Evolution from the Schuman Plan to the Constitution for Europe*, Youri DEVUYST, Revised and updated edition 2006, 205 p., ISBN 978-90-5201-051-9
- No.26: *The Atlantic Alliance for the 21st Century*, Alfred CAHEN, Atlantic Treaty Association, 2001, 139 p., ISBN 978-90-5201-946-8